CW01022535

ISBN 978-1-330-44159-6
PIBN 10062697

FB &c Ltd, Dalton House, 60 Windsor Avenue, London, SW19 2RR.
Company number 08720141. Registered in England and Wales.

THE WESTMINSTER HYMNAL

THE ONLY COLLECTION AUTHORIZED BY
THE HIERARCHY OF ENGLAND AND WALES

THE MUSIC EDITED BY
RICHARD R. TERRY, Mus.Doc. (Dunelm), F.R.C.O.

R. & T. WASHBOURNE, Ltd.
PATERNOSTER ROW, LONDON
AND AT MANCHESTER, BIRMINGHAM, AND GLASGOW
1912

Imprimatur.

EDM. CANONICUS SURMONT,

Vicarius Generalis,

Westmonasterii, die 6th. Maii, 1912.

PREFACE.

BY THE RIGHT REV. THE BISHOP OF NEWPORT,

CHAIRMAN OF THE BISHOPS' COMMITTEE.

THIS Hymnal is issued with the sanction of the Archbishops and Bishops of the Provinces of Westminster, Birmingham and Liverpool. The Hymns that it contains are those which make up the book of Hymns already approved by the Bishops, with seven added to bring up the number to 250. The tunes have been in part selected and in part composed by Mr. R. R. Terry, Mus.D., Organist and Choirmaster of Westminster Cathedral, who has also written and edited the harmonies. This eminent musician has here presented the public with a work of great originality and distinction, for which he is entitled to the thanks of the Catholic Church in English-speaking countries. The Hymns are what we have been accustomed to, but the musical setting is, on the whole, far more scientific and satisfying than anything that has hitherto appeared. There can be no doubt that it will conduce very much to the devotion and decorum of extra-liturgical worship and popular services to have one common manual of Hymns, which at once offers a suitable variety and prevents the undesirable introduction of amateur efforts and unedifying novelties. It often happens, moreover, that a hymn or a setting, in the course of use, has undergone slight variations in different localities, and it is useful to have an authentic version both of text and music. The book has been printed and got up with great care and in good form. The Hymnal may be strongly recommended to the clergy and to all concerned. The hymns are arranged and numbered in the order prescribed by the Bishops' Committee.

PREFACE.

Thanks have already been expressed to the owners of copyright, and the various hymn-writers and translators for the use of the Hymns to which their names are attached; among the rest, Archbishop Bagshawe, Bishop Casartelli, Mgr. L. Hall, the Fathers Provincial of the Dominicans and the Redemptorists, the Revv. Dom Bede Camm, O.S.B., F. Stanfield, Matthew Russell, S.J., E. Gaynor, C.M., and Messrs. Burns & Oates, Browne & Nolan, Watson & Co. and H. Thomson.

✠ JOHN CUTHBERT, O.S.B., Bishop of Newport.

Feast of St. George, 1912.

MUSICAL EDITOR'S PREFACE.

THIS collection contains a large number of entirely new tunes and a considerable quantity of older ones in use amongst Catholics on the Continent, which, after the test of centuries, are still popular to-day. Many other Catholic tunes have only been known in this country through their presence in Protestant hymnals. They are here restored to the worship of the Catholic Church in this country. The collection also includes all the popular tunes in common use amongst English-speaking Catholics. Some of these tunes are good, some are indifferent, and some bad. But it has been felt that since those of the last-named class have been—for one generation at least—bound up with the pious associations of so many holy lives, this is hardly the occasion for their suppression. They have therefore been retained, although this retention cannot be justified on musical or other artistic grounds. Alternative tunes have been provided to most of them, so that they need not be used by those to whom they are distasteful.

NEED FOR UNIFORMITY.

It has been felt that the chief defect in Catholic hymn-singing to-day, is the lack of uniformity in the melodies of even the most popular hymns. Each congregation is a law unto itself, and the variants of almost every popular tune are so numerous, that chaos is the result when (at any great Catholic gathering, for instance) different congregations unite in singing, each their own version of the same tune. To take a few familiar examples:—

AUTHENTIC VERSION.

MUSICAL EDITOR'S PREFACE.

But as often as not we hear :—

And as very few congregations indeed observe the minim in bar 2, the result is generally :—

Or again :—

AUTHENTIC VERSION.

But the following is quite common :—

The last two lines of this hymn suffer even more :—

AUTHENTIC VERSION.

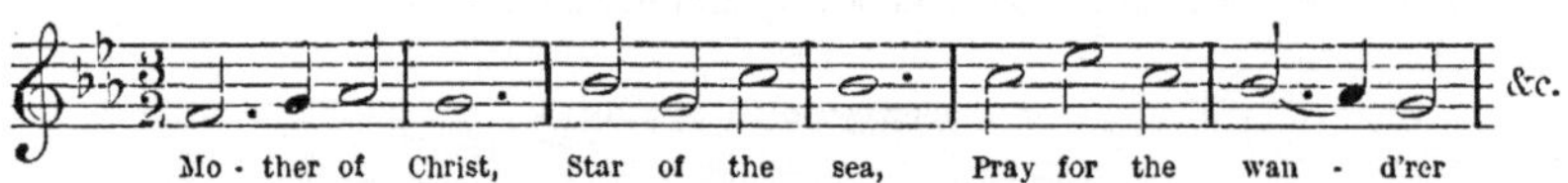

which is varied by many congregations thus :—

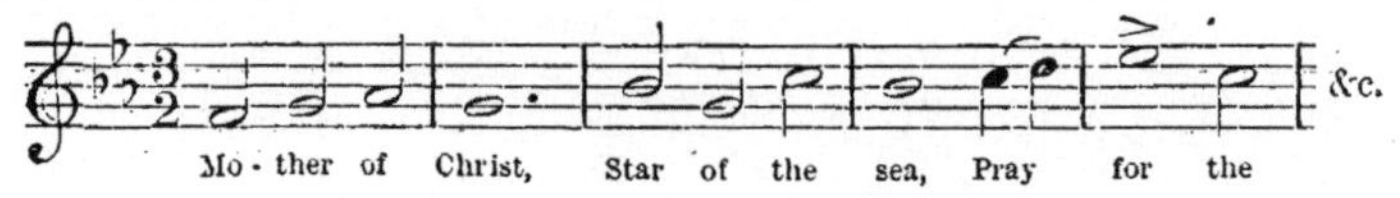

MUSICAL EDITOR'S PREFACE.

Richardson's beautiful tune to "Look down, O Mother Mary," has fortunately escaped mutilation, but who has not heard the following version of "Sing, sing, ye Angel Bands," as frequently as the correct one?

"Mother of Mercy" has been only slightly varied, but as the different versions occur in the first bar, confusion results from the beginning. Again, take "God bless our Pope." The chorus of this hymn was written by the composer in simple common time:—

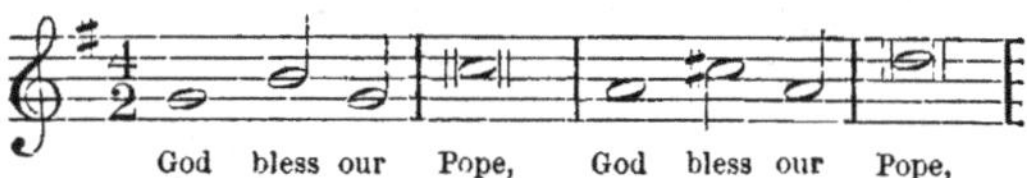

But five congregations out of every ten, turn it into compound triple time thus:—

Or again, take "To Jesus' Heart all burning," we hear both—

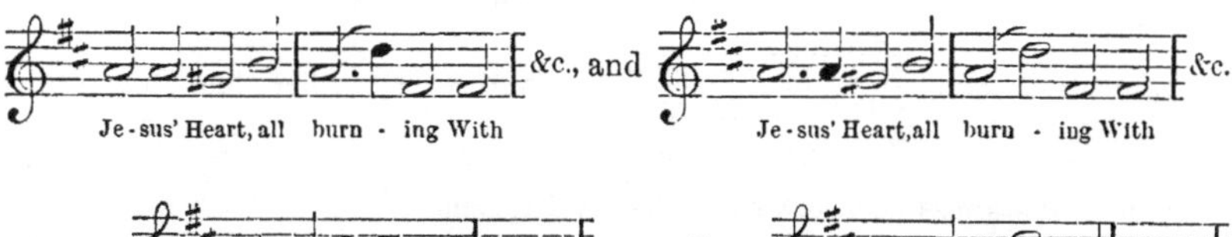

Also: raise the joy - ful strain. as well as raise the joy - ful strain.

MUSICAL EDITOR'S PREFACE.

Or take the third line of hymn 16:—

we have the penultimate bar frequently sung  and sometimes . Or again, in "Jesus, my Lord, behold at length the time," some congregations sing the last four lines straight through. Others make a repeat after "I will never more offend Thee."

In Haydn's tune (to Hymn 197) we often hear the last line begin thus:—

In Webbe's "O Salutaris" the composer wrote 

, but one commonly hears 

. In fact, the endings of each line of the music are varied by congregations at will. In his "Tantum ergo" the same kind of variations appear at the end of each line. In his equally widely used "Veni Sancte Spiritus," he wrote , but quite half our congregations sing 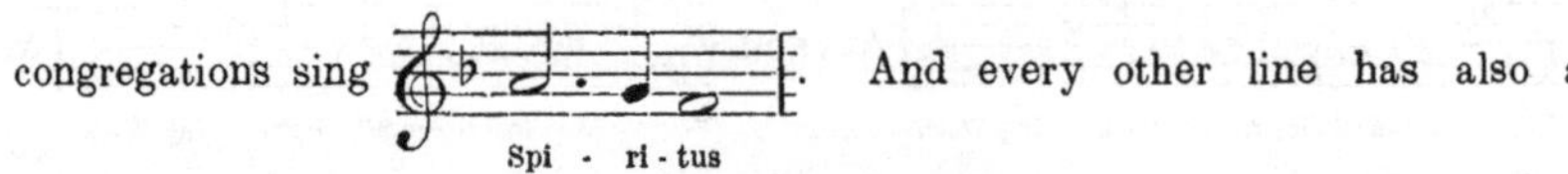

. And every other line has also a variant. Instances need not be further multiplied.

MUSICAL EDITOR'S PREFACE.

In this book, the variations have been reduced to uniformity by giving the tune as the composer originally wrote it, or where this was not ascertainable, by reverting to the earliest form of the melody. It is too much to expect that adult members of congregations accustomed to mutilated or transformed melodies, will at once assimilate the correct form of them. But if one standard version is carefully and consistently taught in the schools, the next generation will see English Catholics in all parts of the country singing, at any rate, the same form of the same tune to any given hymn.

CHARACTER OF THE TUNES.

Since vernacular hymns are essentially intended for the congregation rather than the choir, the first requisite is a strong and well-defined melody which lends itself easily to unison singing. Experience has shown that the difficult tunes for a congregation are those in which the melody lies at a high pitch throughout, and not those which contain an occasional high note. Ewing's well known tune to "Jerusalem the golden" is a case in point. It takes the congregation to F sharp (top treble line), yet it is invariably sung with lusty vigour, and remains one of the most popular tunes in English-speaking countries. The keys chosen for the tunes of this book have been those which secured the requisite brightness, while placing the tune as a whole within the range of the average singer, to whom it would not cause strain or fatigue.

SOURCES OF THE MELODIES.

It has been deemed advisable that the tunes, like the hymns, should be by Catholic authors, or from Catholic sources. In the case of Continental tunes the authorship is sometimes difficult to fix, since many are sung by Catholics and Protestants alike. The presence of such tunes in Catholic Chorale books and their constant use amongst Catholic congregations has been deemed sufficient warrant for their inclusion here. In the case of old English tunes, whose actual authors are unknown, many were no doubt the product of the Reformation, while others bear every trace of "folk-tunes," which were the common property of the people. One or two anonymous tunes of the latter class have been here included. In the case of old tunes, the form of which has varied in the course of time, or in different localities, the object has been to give the best version, not necessarily the earliest. In some cases a particular version is already familiar in England (Webbe's arrangement of "*O Filii et Filiae,*" for example), and has therefore been included on that ground alone. In other cases the original tune is unfamiliar in England, but adaptations of it have become well known and stereotyped (*e.g.* Monk's adaptation of "*Ave hierarchia*": Hymn 261, second tune). In such cases it has been deemed advisable to adhere to the English form of the tune. On artistic and archæological grounds this may be regrettable, but the Editor realises that vernacular hymn-singing amongst English Catholics is in its early stages: this book is intended for immediate practical use; and while a reversion to the original form of ancient tunes is possible in a country with an unbroken Catholic tradition, it is *at present* in England (with the shadow of the Penal Times barely lifted) rather a counsel of perfection than a practicable idea.

THE PLAINSONG MELODIES.

The Plainsong melodies in this book have been taken from the Vatican Graduale, or (when not contained in the Graduale) from the Solesmes Antiphoner. On the vexed question of accompaniment the Editor has kept in view four points:—simplicity, directness, due regard to the accentuation of the words, and strict adherence to the Mode in which the melody is written. Point III, however, cannot always be strictly observed in the case of metrical hymns containing a number of verses, since it would have involved the great expense of printing each separate verse in full. For example, in Hymn 55 the tonic accents at the beginning of the first two lines in verses 1 and 2 respectively, are:—

(1) Véni Creator Spiritus,
(2) Qui díceris Paraclitus,

MUSICAL EDITOR'S PREFACE.

The "counsel of perfection" would be to bring out these tonic accents by different harmonies, *e.g.*:—

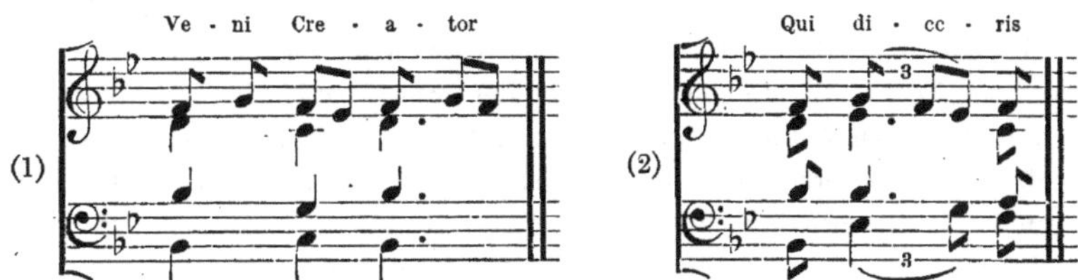

But for practical purposes, the accompaniments (as they stand in the book) in such cases, can produce the desired effect at the hands of any competent organist.

Any suggestion of heaviness in the accompaniments cannot be too strongly deprecated. Nothing contributes more to this effect than the monotonous booming of the pedals throughout. Occasional verses or phrases on the manuals alone will give the necessary relief.

ACKNOWLEDGMENTS.

The Editor's original intention was to make the book an anthology of tunes by English composers. This was frustrated by the refusal of two proprietors of large collections of tunes to use their copyrights. No such difficulty, however, has been experienced with individual composers; permission to use their copyright tunes having invariably been willingly given. Their names appear in the index opposite their respective contributions, and the Editor's grateful thanks are here tendered. Special thanks are due to Mr. W. Tozer, for his kindness in allowing the Editor to make a selection from the copyrights of his brother, the late Dr. A. E. Tozer; to the Very Rev. Anselm Burge, O.S.B., for placing a collection of tunes unreservedly at the disposal of the Editor; to the Rev. Sebastian Bowden, for the use of tunes 92 and 160, formerly the copyright of the late Rev. C. Bowden; to the Rev. C. Raymond-Barker, S.J., for his original tunes, his harmonies to Hymn 112, and for many valuable suggestions;

to Mr. W. Sewell, for his original tunes (129, 175, 187, 234), and for his harmonies to tunes 3, 11, 30, 44, 100 (second tune), 101 (first tune), 106, 113, 115, 118, 138 (first tune), 139 (first tune), 144, 147, 149, 158, 164, 179, 198, 203, 211, 215, 225, 231, 239, 242; to Mrs. Swinnerton Hughes, for permission to use tunes 77 and 91, the composition of her father, the late R. L. de Pearsall; to Dr. R. Vaughan-Williams, for permission to use his harmonies to tune 244 in so far as the different form of the melody permitted; to Miss A. D. Scott, for generously undertaking tunes to difficult metres for which there was great difficulty in securing composers; to the families of the late Geo. Herbert and F. Westlake, for their tunes Nos. 26 (second tune), 225 and 108; to the Rt. Rev. Abbot Ford, O.S.B., Chairman of the Musical Committee; the Rev. Sebastian Gates, O.P.; the Rev. Anthony Pollen, C.O.; Mr. Edward d'Evry; and the other members of the Musical Committee already named, for their valuable advice and useful suggestions. But the Editor's chiefest thanks are due to Mr. F. A. Keene, Mus.B., F.R.C.O., L.R.A.M., for his invaluable assistance in the laborious work of proof correcting, as well as for his sound advice and healthy criticism throughout.

No pains have been spared to discover the owners of copyright tunes. If any infringement of copyright has unwittingly been committed, the Editor begs to offer his sincere apologies, and will remedy the error in future editions. He also wishes to thank all those who have kindly submitted tunes which he has been unable to include.

R. R. TERRY.

ADVENT.

1

En clara vox redarguit.

LAUDS.

HARK ! an awful voice is sounding ;
  " Christ is nigh ! " it seems to say ;
" Cast away the dreams of darkness,
  O ye children of the day ! "

Startled at the solemn warning,
  Let the earth-bound soul arise ;
Christ her Sun, all sloth dispelling,
  Shines upon the morning skies.

Lo ! the Lamb so long expected,
  Comes with pardon down from Heaven ;
Let us haste, with tears of sorrow,
  One and all to be forgiven.

So when next He comes with glory,
  Wrapping all the earth in fear,
May He then as our Defender
  On the clouds of Heav'n appear.

Honour, glory, virtue, merit,
  To the Father and the Son,
With the co-eternal Spirit
  While eternal ages run.

[TR. REV. E. CASWALL]

ADVENT.

2

Creator alme siderum.

VESPERS.

DEAR Maker of the starry skies!
  Light of believers evermore!
Jesu, Redeemer of mankind!
  Be near us who Thine aid implore.

When man was sunk in sin and death,
  Lost in the depth of Satan's snare,
Love brought Thee down to cure our ills,
  By taking of those ills a share.

Thou for the sake of guilty men
  Permitting Thy pure blood to flow,
Didst issue from Thy Virgin shrine
  And to the Cross a Victim go.

So great the glory of Thy might,
  If we but chance Thy name to sound,
At once all Heaven and Hell unite
  In bending low with awe profound.

Great Judge of all! in that last day,
  When friends shall fail, and foes combine,
Be present then with us, we pray,
  To guard us with Thy arm divine.

To God the Father with the Son,
  And Holy Spirit, One and Three,
Be honour, glory, blessing, praise,
  All through the long eternity.

[TR. REV. E. CASWALL]

ADVENT.

3

Our Lady's Expectation.

LIKE the dawning of the morning,
  On the mountain's golden heights,
Like the breaking of the moonbeams
  On the gloom of cloudy nights,
Like a secret told by angels,
  Getting known upon the earth,
Is the Mother's Expectation
  Of Messias' speedy birth !

Thou wert happy, blessèd Mother !
  With the very bliss of Heaven,
Since the angel's salutation
  In thy raptured ear was given ;
Since the Ave of that midnight,
  When thou wert anointed Queen,
Like a river overflowing
  Hath the grace within thee been.

Thou hast waited, child of David !
  And thy waiting now is o'er !
Thou hast seen Him, blessèd Mother !
  And wilt see Him evermore !
Oh, His Human Face and Features !
  They were passing sweet to see :
Thou beholdest them this moment !
  Mother, show them now to me.

[REV. F. W. FABER]

ADVENT.

4

Verbum supernum prodiens.

MATINS.

O THOU, who Thine own Father's breast
Forsaking, Word sublime!
Didst come to aid a world distress'd
In Thy appointed time:

Our hearts enlighten with Thy ray,
And kindle with Thy love;
That, dead to earthly things, we may
Live but to things above.

So when before the Judgment-seat
The sinner hears his doom,
And when a voice divinely sweet
Shall call the righteous home;

Safe from the black and fiery flood
That sweeps the dread abyss,
May we behold the face of God
In everlasting bliss.

To God the Father, with the Son,
And Spirit evermore,
Be glory while the ages run,
As in all time before.

[TR. REV. E. CASWALL]

CHRISTMAS.

5

Adeste fideles.

COME, all ye faithful,
Joyful and triumphant,
O hasten, O hasten to Bethlehem ;
See in a manger
The Monarch of angels.
O come and let us worship
Christ the Lord.

God of God eternal,
Light from light proceeding,
He deigns in the Virgin's womb to lie ;
Very God of very God,
Begotten, not created.
O come, &c.

Sing alleluia,
All ye choirs of angels ;
Sing, all ye citizens of heaven above,
Glory to God
In the highest.
O come, &c.

Yea, Lord, we greet Thee,
Born this happy morning ;
To Thee, O Jesus, be glory given ;
True Word of the Father,
In our flesh appearing.
O come, &c.

[TR. CANON OAKELEY]

CHRISTMAS.

6

CHRISTMAS.

SEE, amid the winter's snow,
Born for us on earth below,
See, the tender Lamb appears,
Promised from eternal years!
Hail, thou ever-blessed morn!
Hail, Redemption's happy dawn!
Sing through all Jerusalem,
Christ is born in Bethlehem!

Lo, within a manger lies
He who built the starry skies;
He, who throned in heights sublime
Sits amid the Cherubim!
Hail, &c.

Say, ye holy Shepherds, say,
What your joyful news to-day;
Wherefore have ye left your sheep
On the lonely mountain steep?
Hail, &c.

"As we watch'd at dead of night,
Lo, we saw a wondrous light;
Angels singing peace on earth,
Told us of the Saviour's birth."
Hail, &c.

Sacred Infant all divine,
What a tender love was Thine;
Thus to come from highest bliss,
Down to such a world as this!
Hail, &c.

Teach, O teach us, holy Child,
By Thy face so meek and mild,
Teach us to resemble Thee,
In Thy sweet humility!
Hail, &c.

Virgin Mother, Mary blest,
By the joys that fill thy breast,
Pray for us, that we may prove
Worthy of the Saviour's love.
Hail, &c. [REV. E. CASWALL]

CHRISTMAS.

7

CHRISTMAS.

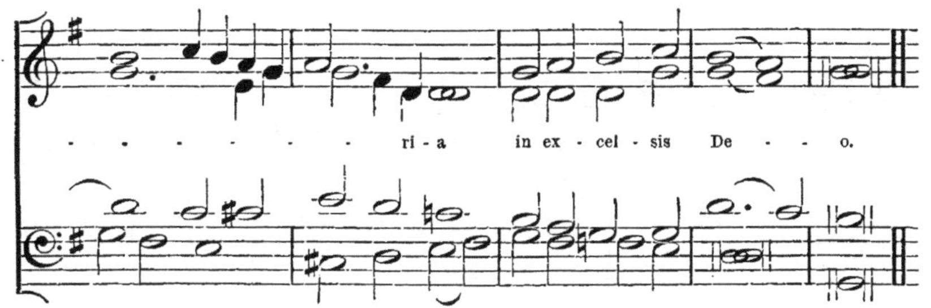

ANGELS we have heard on high,
Sweetly singing o'er our plains,
And the mountains in reply,
Echoing their joyous strains.
Gloria in excelsis Deo.

Shepherds, why this Jubilee?
Why your rapturous strain prolong?
What may the gladsome tidings be,
Which inspire your heavenly song?
Gloria in excelsis Deo.

Come to Bethlehem, and see
Him whose birth the angels sing:
Come, adore on bended knee,
Christ the Lord, the new-born King.
Gloria in excelsis Deo.

See Him in a manger laid
Whom the choirs of angels praise!
Mary, Joseph, lend your aid
While our hearts in love we raise.
Gloria in excelsis Deo.

[BISHOP CHADWICK]

CHRISTMAS.

8

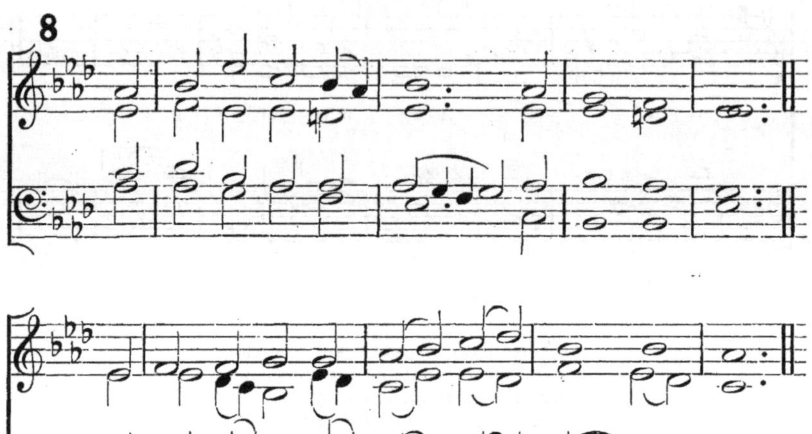

THE snow lay on the ground,
  The stars shone bright,
When Christ our Lord was born
  On Christmas night.

'Twas Mary, daughter pure
  Of Holy Anne,
That brought into this world
  The God made man.

She laid Him in a stall
  At Bethlehem,
The ass and oxen shared
  The roof with them.

St. Joseph, too, was by
  To tend the Child,
To guard Him and protect
  His Mother mild.

The angels hovered round
  And sang this song :
Venite adoremus
  Dominum.

And then that manger poor
  Became a throne ;
For He whom Mary bore
  Was God the Son.

O come, then let us join
  The heavenly host,
To praise the Father, Son,
  And Holy Ghost.

[OLD ENGLISH CAROL]

CHRISTMAS.

9

LEAD me to Thy peaceful manger,
Wond'rous Babe of Bethlehem ;
Shepherds hail Thee, yet a stranger ;
Let me worship Thee with them.
I am vile, but Thou art holy ;
Oh, unite my heart to Thee ;
Make me contrite, keep me lowly,
Pure as Thou wouldst have me be.

Let me listen to the story,
Full of all-surpassing love,
How the Lord of grace and glory
Left for us His throne above:

Touch'd with sympathy so tender,
Man adores while seraphs gaze,
And with gladness we surrender
Soul and body to Thy praise.

Blessèd Jesus, holy Saviour,
Offspring of the royal Maid,
By Thy meek and pure behaviour
In her folding arms display'd ;
By the tears of earliest anguish,
On Thine infant brow impearl'd,
By the love that could not languish
Thou hast saved a ruin'd world !

[M. BRIDGES]

CHRISTMAS.

10

SLEEP, Holy Babe,
Upon Thy Mother's breast!
Great Lord of earth and sea and sky,
How sweet it is to see Thee lie
In such a place of rest!

Sleep, Holy Babe!
Thine Angels watch around;
All bending low, with folded wings,
Before th' Incarnate King of kings,
In reverent awe profound!

Sleep, Holy Babe!
While I with Mary gaze
In joy upon that face awhile,
Upon the loving infant smile,
Which there divinely plays.

Sleep, Holy Babe!
Ah, take Thy brief repose;
Too quickly will Thy slumbers break
And Thou to lengthen'd pains awake,
That death alone shall close.

Then must those hands,
Which now so fair I see;
Those little pearly feet of Thine,
So soft, so delicately fine,
Be pierced and rent for me!

Then must that brow
Its thorny crown receive;
That cheek more lovely than the rose,
Be drench'd with blood, and marr'd with [blows,
That I thereby may live.

O Lady blest!
Sweet Virgin, hear my cry!
Forgive the wrong that I have done
To thee, in causing thy dear Son
Upon the Cross to die!

[REV. E. CASWALL]

CHRISTMAS.

11

STARS of glory, shine more brightly;
Purer be the moonlight's beam;
Glide, ye hours and moments, lightly,
Swiftly down Time's deep'ning stream.
Bring the hour that banish'd sadness,
Brought Redemption down to earth;
When the shepherds heard with gladness
Tidings of a Saviour's birth.

Lo, a beauteous angel soaring
In the bright celestial blaze;
On the shepherds low adoring
Rest his mild effulgent rays:
"Fear not!" cries the heavenly stranger;
"Him whom ancient Jews foretold,
Weeping in a lowly manger,
Shepherds, haste ye to behold."

See the shepherds quickly rising,
Hast'ning to the humble stall,
And the new-born INFANT prizing
As the mighty Lord of all.
Lowly now they bend before Him
In His helpless infant state;
Firmly faithful, they adore Him,
And His greatness celebrate.

Hark! the swell of heavenly voices
Peals along the vaulted sky;
Angels sing, while earth rejoices,
Glory to our God on high:
Glory in the highest Heaven,
Peace to humble men on earth;
Joy to these and bliss is given
In the great Redeemer's birth.

[CANON HUSENBETH]

CHRISTMAS.

12

St. Luke ii. 7–16.

ALL in a stable cold and bare
  A lovely Infant lay;
The night was dark, but round that Babe
  Was bright as summer day.
A lowly maiden watched beside
  To soothe His plaintive cry,
While angel voices filled the air
  With sweetest lullaby.

The wond'ring shepherds heard the strain,
  As by their flocks they staid;
The light of heav'n around them shone,
  And they were sore afraid.
But—"Fear ye not,"—an angel said,
  "Good news to you I bring:
This night is born in Bethlehem
  Your Saviour and your King.

"Yet, not in kingly state He lies,
  In royal robes arrayed:
But meanly wrapped in swathing bands,
  And in a manger laid."
Then carolled forth a heavenly throng
  Beyond all human ken:—
"To God be glory in the height,
  And peace on earth to men!"

Then said the shepherds one and all:
  "To Bethlehem let us go,
And see this wonder come to pass,
  Which God hath let us know."
And soon they found the heav'nly Babe,
  And bowed them down before:
Oh! children, let us join with them,
  And our sweet Lord adore.

[TR. REV. E. GAYNER]

CHRISTMAS.

13

A solis ortus cardine.

LAUDS.

FROM where the rising sun ascends,
To where his daily pathway ends,
Through every region let us sing,
The Maiden's offspring, Christ, our King.

The great Creator deigns assume
Our servile form from Mary's womb,
That clothed in flesh He might reclaim
The fallen flesh Himself did frame.

By Heaven o'ershadowed, filled with grace,
A spotless maid of David's race,
Surpassing nature's law, contains
The fruit without the mother's pains.

O dwelling ever pure and bright!
The fane where dwells the God of might,
To which descends at Heaven's behest,
The Word conceived in Mary's breast.

The angel's voice the deed foretells,
And Christ within her bosom dwells,
And John, unborn, exults to find
The Lord made flesh to save mankind.

In manger laid your Lord behold!
The hay His bed in winter's cold;
Behold Him fed on infant fare,
Who feeds the feathered fowls of air.

And, hark! the choir angelic raise
To God the joyful song of praise,
And bid the lowly shepherds know
The Shepherd-Lord of all below.

To God the Father, God the Son
Of Mary born, be homage done!
The like to God the Spirit be,
Eternal Godhead, One in Three.

[TR. REV. FR. TRAPPES]

CHRISTMAS.

14

Salvete flores martyrum.

THE HOLY INNOCENTS.

FLOWERS of martyrdom all hail!
Smitten by the tyrant foe
On life's threshold,—as the gale
Strews the roses ere they blow.

First to bleed for Christ, sweet lambs!
What a simple death ye died!
Sporting with your wreaths and palms,
At the very altar side!

Honour, glory, virtue, merit,
Be to thee, O Virgin's Son!
With the Father, and the Spirit,
While eternal ages run.

[TR. REV. E. CASWALL]

15

Jesu, Redemptor omnium.

VESPERS.

JESU, Redeemer of the world!
Before the earliest dawn of light
From everlasting ages born,
Immense in glory as in might;

Immortal Hope of all mankind!
In whom the Father's face we see;
Hear Thou the prayers Thy people pour
This day throughout the world to Thee.

Remember, O Creator Lord!
That in the Virgin's sacred womb
Thou wast conceived, and of her flesh
Didst our mortality assume.

This ever-blest recurring day
Its witness bears, that all alone,
From Thy own Father's bosom forth,
To save the world Thou camest down.

O day! to which the seas and sky,
And earth and Heav'n, glad welcome sing;
O day! which heal'd our misery,
And brought on earth salvation's King!

We too, O Lord, who have been cleansed
In Thy own fount of blood divine,
Offer the tribute of sweet song,
On this dear natal day of Thine.

O Jesu! born of Virgin bright,
Immortal glory be to Thee;
Praise to the Father infinite,
And Holy Ghost eternally.

[TR. REV. E. CASWALL]

OLD YEAR AND NEW YEAR.

16

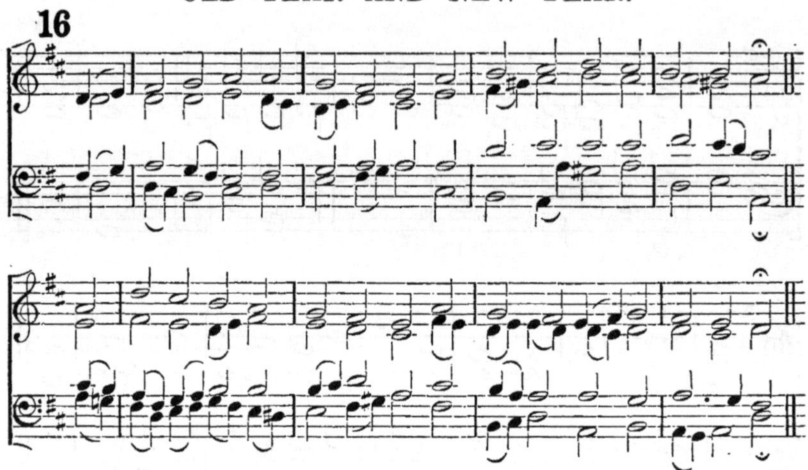

Lapsus est annus.

A YEAR is dead, a year is born ;
 Thus time flies by on silent wing :
Thou, Lord, alone canst guide our course
 And safe to heaven Thy people bring.

For all past gifts we render thanks ;
 For graces new we humbly pray.
Oh, grant that we and those we love
 May ne'er from Faith and duty stray.

O Lord, our daily wants supply ;
 Protect from sickness and disease ;
And deign to give, O God of Love,
 The blessing of unbroken peace.

Oh, blot out all our ancient sins
 And give us strength to fall no more ;
When fight is o'er and victory won,
 Then crown us on the eternal shore.

For all the old year's sins we grieve ;
 Our hearts we consecrate to Thee.
Grant us, when all our years are sped,
 Our Heavenly Father's face to see.

[TR. MGR. CANON HALL]

OLD YEAR AND NEW YEAR.

(First Tune.) **17**

Crudelis Herodes Deum.

Epiphany, Vespers.

O CRUEL Herod! why thus fear
  Thy King and God, who comes below?
No earthly crown comes He to take,
  Who heavenly kingdoms doth bestow.

The wiser Magi see the star,
  And follow as it leads before;
By its pure ray they seek the Light,
  And with their gifts that Light adore.

Behold at length the heavenly Lamb
  Baptized in Jordan's sacred flood;
There consecrating by His touch
  Water to cleanse us in His blood.

But Cana saw her glorious Lord
  Begin His miracles divine;
When water, reddening at His word,
  Flow'd forth obedient in wine.

To Thee, O Jesu, who Thyself
  Hast to the Gentile world display'd,
Praise, with the Father evermore,
  And with the Holy Ghost, be paid.

[TR. REV. E. CASWALL]

OLD YEAR AND NEW YEAR.

17 (Second Tune.)

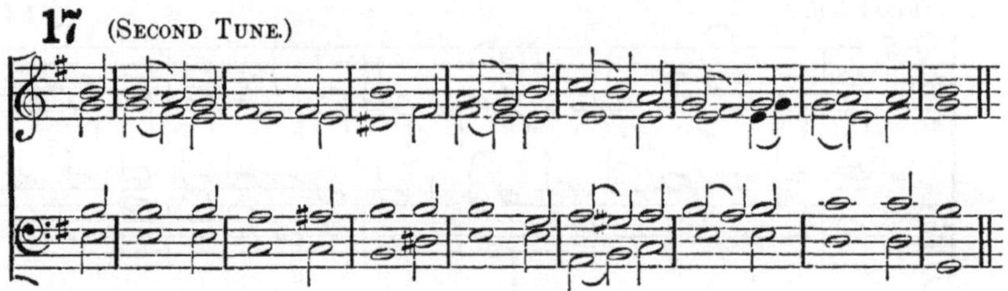

Crudelis Herodes Deum.

Epiphany, Vespers.

O CRUEL Herod! why thus fear
  Thy King and God, who comes below?
No earthly crown comes He to take,
  Who heavenly kingdoms doth bestow.

The wiser Magi see the star,
  And follow as it leads before;
By its pure ray they seek the Light,
  And with their gifts that Light adore.

Behold at length the heavenly Lamb
  Baptized in Jordan's sacred flood;
There consecrating by His touch
  Water to cleanse us in His blood.

But Cana saw her glorious Lord
  Begin His miracles divine;
When water, reddening at His word,
  Flow'd forth obedient in wine.

To Thee, O Jesu, who Thyself
  Hast to the Gentile world display'd,
Praise, with the Father evermore,
  And with the Holy Ghost, be paid.

[TR. REV. E. CASWALL]

OLD YEAR AND NEW YEAR.

18

O sola magnarum urbium.

EPIPHANY, LAUDS.

BETHLEHEM ! of noblest cities
None can once with thee compare ;
Thou alone the Lord from Heaven
Didst for us Incarnate bear.

Fairer than the sun at morning
Was the star that told His birth ;
To the lands their God announcing,
Hid beneath a form of earth.

By its lambent beauty guided,
See, the Eastern kings appear ;
See them bend, their gifts to offer,—
Gifts of incense, gold, and myrrh.

Solemn things of mystic meaning !—
Incense doth the God disclose ;
Gold a royal child proclaimeth ;
Myrrh a future tomb foreshews.

Holy Jesu ! in Thy brightness
To the Gentile world display'd !
With the Father, and the Spirit,
Praise eterne to Thee be paid.

[TR. REV. E. CASWALL]

THE MOST HOLY NAME.

19

N.B.—*Tune 24 is usually sung to this hymn.*

Jesu dulcis memoria.

VESPERS.

JESU ! the very thought of Thee
  With sweetness fills my breast ;
But sweeter far Thy face to see,
  And in Thy presence rest.

Nor voice can sing, nor heart can frame,
  Nor can the memory find,
A sweeter sound than Thy blest name,
  O Saviour of mankind !

O hope of every contrite heart,
  O joy of all the meek,
To those who fall, how kind Thou art !
  How good to those who seek !

But what to those who find ? ah ! this
  Nor tongue nor pen can show :
The love of Jesus, what it is,
  None but His lovers know.

Jesu ! our only joy be Thou,
  As Thou our prize wilt be ;
Jesu ! be Thou our glory now
  And through eternity.

[TR. REV. E. CASWALL]

20

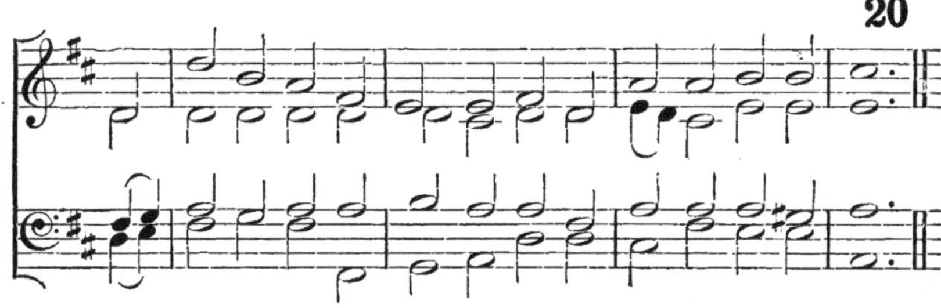

Jesu Rex admirabilis.

MATINS.

O JESU ! King most wonderful !
  Thou Conqueror renown'd !
Thou Sweetness most ineffable !
  In whom all joys are found !

When once Thou visitest the heart,
  Then truth begins to shine ;
Then earthly vanities depart ;
  Then kindles love divine.

O Jesu ! Light of all below !
  Thou Fount of life and fire !
Surpassing all the joys we know.
  And all we can desire.

May every heart confess Thy name,
  And ever Thee adore ;
And seeking Thee, itself inflame
  To seek Thee more and more.

Thee may our tongues for ever bless ;
  Thee may we love alone ;
And ever in our lives express
  The image of Thine own.

[TR. REV. E. CASWALL]

THE MOST HOLY NAME.

21

Jesu decus angelicum.

LAUDS.

O JESU ! Thou the beauty art
  Of angel worlds above ;
Thy Name is music to the heart,
  Enchanting it with love.

Celestial sweetness unalloy'd !
  Who eat Thee hunger still ;
Who drink of Thee still feel a void,
  Which nought but Thou can fill.

O my sweet Jesu ! hear the sighs
  Which unto Thee I send ;
To Thee mine inmost spirit cries,
  My being's hope and end !

Stay with us, Lord, and with Thy light
  Illume the soul's abyss ;
Scatter the darkness of our night,
  And fill the world with bliss.

O Jesu ! spotless Virgin flower !
  Our life and joy ! to Thee
Be praise, beatitude, and power,
  Through all eternity.

[TR. REV. E. CASWALL]

22

NOW are the days of humblest prayer,
When consciences to God lie bare,
And mercy most delights to spare.
Oh, hearken when we cry,
Chastise us with Thy fear;
Yet, Father! in the multitude
Of Thy compassions, hear!

Now is the season, wisely long,
Of sadder thought and graver song,
When ailing souls grow well and strong.
Oh, hearken, &c.

The feast of penance! Oh so bright,
With true conversion's heavenly light,
Like sunrise after stormy night!
Oh, hearken, &c.

Oh, happy time of blessèd tears,
Of surer hopes, of chastening fears
Undoing all our evil years.
Oh, hearken, &c.

We, who have loved the world, must learn,
Upon that world our backs to turn,
And with the love of God to burn.
Oh, hearken, &c.

Vile creatures of such little worth!—
Than we, there can be none on earth
More fallen from their Christian birth.
Oh, hearken, &c.

Full long in sin's dark ways we went,
Yet now our steps are heavenward bent,
And grace is plentiful in Lent.
Oh, hearken, &c.

All glory to redeeming grace,
Disdaining not our evil case,
But showing us our Saviour's face!
Oh, hearken, &c.

[REV. F. W. FABER]

LENT.

23

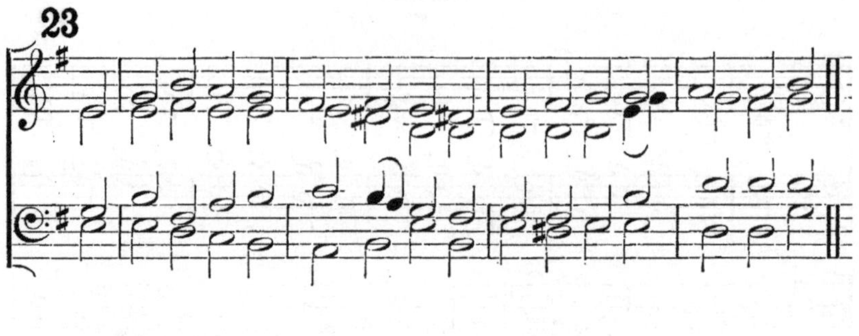

Audi benigne Conditor.

VESPERS.

THOU loving Maker of mankind,
  Before Thy throne we pray and weep;
Oh, strengthen us with grace divine,
  Duly this sacred Lent to keep.

Searcher of hearts! Thou dost discern
  Our ills, and all our weakness know:
Again to Thee with tears we turn;
  Again to us Thy mercy show.

Much have we sinn'd; but we confess
  Our guilt, and all our faults deplore:
Oh, for the praise of Thy great Name,
  Our fainting souls to health restore!

And grant us, while by fasts we strive
  This mortal body to control,
To fast from all the food of sin,
  And so to purify the soul.

Hear us, O Trinity thrice blest!
  Sole Unity! to Thee we cry:
Vouchsafe us from these fasts below
  To reap immortal fruit on high.

[TR. REV. E. CASWALL]

24

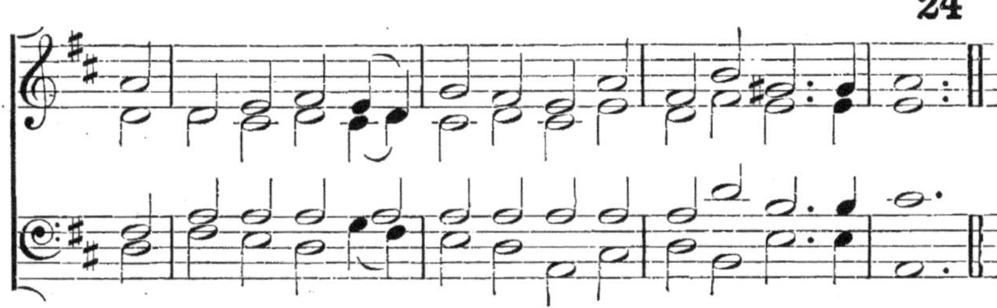

Quicunque certum quæritis.

OLD OFFICE OF THE SACRED HEART.

ALL ye who seek a comfort sure
  In trouble and distress,
Whatever sorrow vex the mind,
  Or guilt the soul oppress:

Jesus, who gave Himself for you
  Upon the cross to die,
Opens to you His sacred Heart,—
  Oh, to that Heart draw nigh!

Ye hear how kindly He invites;
  Ye hear His words so blest;—
"All ye that labour, come to Me,
  And I will give you rest."

What meeker than the Saviour's Heart?—
  As on the Cross He lay,
It did His murderers forgive,
  And for their pardon pray.

O Heart! thou joy of Saints on high!
  Thou Hope of sinners here!
Attracted by those loving words,
  To Thee I lift my prayer.

Wash Thou my wounds in that dear Blood
  Which forth from Thee doth flow;
New grace, new hope inspire; a new
  And better heart bestow.

[TR. REV. E. CASWALL]

PASSIONTIDE.

25

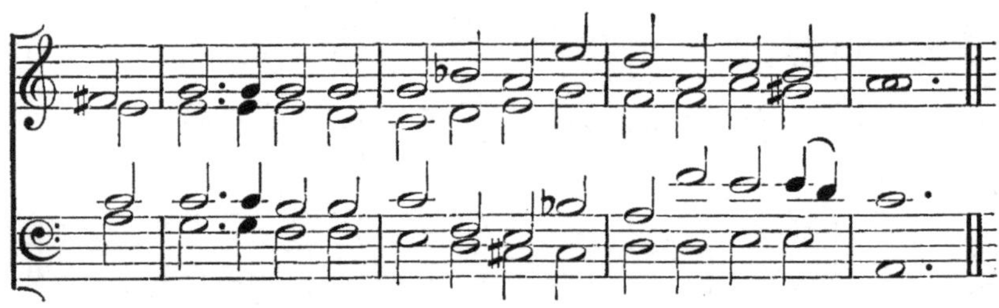

Sævo dolorum turbine.

O'ERWHELM'D in depths of woe,
Upon the Tree of scorn
Hangs the Redeemer of mankind,
With racking anguish torn.

See! how the nails those hands
And feet so tender rend;
See! down His face, and neck, and breast,
His sacred Blood descend.

Hark! with what awful cry
His Spirit takes its flight;
That cry, it smote His Mother's heart
And wrapt her soul in night.

Earth hears, and to its base
Rocks wildly to and fro;
Tombs burst; seas, rivers, mountains quake;
The veil is rent in two.

The sun withdraws his light;
The midday heavens grow pale;
The moon, the stars, the universe,
Their Maker's death bewail.

Shall man alone be mute?
Come, youth! and hoary hairs!
Come, rich and poor! come, all mankind!
And bathe those feet in tears.

Come! fall before His Cross,
Who shed for us His blood;
Who died the victim of pure love,
To make us sons of God.

Jesu! all praise to Thee,
Our joy and endless rest!
Be Thou our Guide while pilgrims here,
Our crown amid the blest.

[TR. REV. E. CASWALL]

(First Tune.) **26**

Gesù mio, con dure funi.

My Jesus! say, what wretch has dared
Thy sacred hands to bind?
And who has dared to buffet so
Thy face so meek and kind?
'Tis I have thus ungrateful been,
Yet, Jesus, pity take!
Oh spare and pardon me, my Lord,
For Thy sweet mercy's sake.

My Jesus! who with spittle vile
Profaned Thy sacred brow?
And whose unpitying scourge has made
Thy precious blood to flow?
'Tis I have thus ungrateful been, &c.

My Jesus! whose the hands that wove
That cruel thorny crown?
Who made that hard and heavy cross
Which weighs Thy shoulders down?
'Tis I have thus ungrateful been, &c.

My Jesus! who has mocked Thy thirst
With vinegar and gall;
Who held the nails that pierced Thy hands,
And made the hammer fall?
'Tis I have thus ungrateful been, &c.

My Jesus! say, who dared to nail
Those tender feet of Thine;
And whose the arm that raised the lance
To pierce that Heart divine?
'Tis I have thus ungrateful been, &c.

And, Mary! who has murdered thus
Thy lov'd and only One?
Canst thou forgive the blood-stained hand
That robbed thee of thy Son?
'Tis I have thus ungrateful been
To Jesus and to thee;
Forgive me for thy Jesus' sake,
And pray to Him for me.

[St. Alphonsus. Tr. Rev. E. Vaughan, C.SS.R.]

PASSIONTIDE.

26 (Second Tune.)

Gesù mio, con dure funi.

MY Jesus ! say, what wretch has dared
  Thy sacred hands to bind ?
And who has dared to buffet so
  Thy face so meek and kind ?
    'Tis I have thus ungrateful been,
      Yet, Jesus, pity take !
    Oh spare and pardon me, my Lord,
      For Thy sweet mercy's sake.

My Jesus ! who with spittle vile
  Profaned Thy sacred brow ?
And whose unpitying scourge has made
  Thy precious blood to flow ?
    'Tis I have thus ungrateful been, &c.

My Jesus ! whose the hands that wove
  That cruel thorny crown ?
Who made that hard and heavy cross
  Which weighs Thy shoulders down ?
    'Tis I have thus ungrateful been, &c.

My Jesus ! who has mocked Thy thirst
  With vinegar and gall ;
Who held the nails that pierced Thy hands,
  And made the hammer fall !
    'Tis I have thus ungrateful been, &c.

My Jesus ! say, who dared to nail
  Those tender feet of Thine ;
And whose the arm that raised the lance
  To pierce that Heart divine ?
    'Tis I have thus ungrateful been, &c.

And, Mary ! who has murdered thus
  Thy lov'd and only One ?
Canst thou forgive the blood-stained hand
  That robbed thee of thy Son ?
    'Tis I have thus ungrateful been
      To Jesus and to thee ;
    Forgive me for thy Jesus' sake,
      And pray to Him for me.

[St. Alphonsus. Tr. Rev. E. Vaughan, C.SS.R.]

PASSIONTIDE.

(First Tune.) **27**

Oh come and mourn with me awhile!
  See, Mary calls us to her side;
Oh come and let us mourn with her;
  Jesus, our Love, is crucified!

Have we no tears to shed for Him,
  While soldiers scoff and Jews deride?
Ah! look how patiently He hangs;
  Jesus, our Love, is crucified!

Seven times He spoke, seven words of love,
  And all three hours His silence cried
For mercy on the souls of men;
  Jesus, our Love, is crucified!

Come, take thy stand beneath the Cross,
  And let the Blood from out that Side
Fall gently on thee drop by drop;
  Jesus, our Love, is crucified!

A broken heart, a fount of tears
  Ask, and they will not be denied;
A broken heart, Love's cradle is;
  Jesus, our Love, is crucified!

O Love of God! O sin of man!
  In this dread act your strength is tried;
And victory remains with Love;
  For He, our Love, is crucified!

[REV. F. W. FABER]

PASSIONTIDE.

27 (Second Tune.)

Oh come and mourn with me awhile!
  See, Mary calls us to her side;
Oh come and let us mourn with her;
  Jesus, our Love, is crucified!

Have we no tears to shed for Him,
  While soldiers scoff and Jews deride?
Ah! look how patiently He hangs;
  Jesus, our Love, is crucified!

Seven times He spoke, seven words of love,
  And all three hours His silence cried
For mercy on the souls of men;
  Jesus, our Love, is crucified!

Come, take thy stand beneath the Cross,
  And let the Blood from out that Side
Fall gently on thee drop by drop;
  Jesus, our Love, is crucified!

A broken heart, a fount of tears
  Ask, and they will not be denied;
A broken heart, Love's cradle is;
  Jesus, our Love, is crucified!

O Love of God! O sin of man!
  In this dread act your strength is tried;
And victory remains with Love;
  For He, our Love, is crucified!

[REV. F. W. FABER]

28

Stabat Mater dolorosa.

SEQUENCE OF THE SEVEN DOLOURS.

AT the Cross her station keeping
Stood the mournful Mother weeping,
Close to Jesus to the last:
Through her heart, His sorrow sharing,
All His bitter anguish bearing,
Now at length the sword had pass'd.

Oh, how sad and sore distress'd
Was that Mother highly blest
Of the sole-begotten One!
Christ above in torment hangs;
She beneath beholds the pangs
Of her dying glorious Son.

Is there one who would not weep,
Whelm'd in miseries so deep
Christ's dear Mother to behold?
Can the human heart refrain
From partaking in her pain,
In that Mother's pain untold?

Bruised, derided, cursed, defiled,
She beheld her tender Child
All with bloody scourges rent;
For the sins of His own nation,
Saw Him hang in desolation,
Till His Spirit forth He sent.

O thou Mother! fount of love!
Touch my spirit from above,
Make my heart with thine accord:
Make me feel as thou hast felt;
Make my soul to glow and melt
With the love of Christ my Lord.

Holy Mother! pierce me through;
In my heart each wound renew
Of my Saviour crucified:
Let me share with thee His pain,
Who for all my sins was slain,
Who for me in torments died.

Let me mingle tears with thee,
Mourning Him who mourn'd for me,
All the days that I may live:
By the Cross with thee to stay;
There with thee to weep and pray;
Is all I ask of thee to give.

Virgin of all virgins best!
Listen to my fond request:
Let me share thy grief divine:
Let me, to my latest breath,
In my body bear the death
Of that dying Son of thine.

Wounded with His every wound,
Steep my soul till it hath swoon'd
In His very blood away;
Be to me, O Virgin, nigh,
Lest in flames I burn and die,
In His awful Judgment day.

Christ, when Thou shalt call me hence,
Be Thy Mother my defence,
Be Thy Cross my victory;
While my body here decays,
May my soul Thy goodness praise,
Safe in Paradise with Thee.

[TR. REV. E. CASWALL]

D.

PASSIONTIDE.

29

PASSIONTIDE.

SAY, oh ! say, My people,
  Why thus ungrateful prove ?
Why repay with coldness
  The ardour of My love ?
If I am He who died to save,
Who life-redeeming ransom gave,
    Must I complain,
    That all this love was vain ?

When for child did father bear,
  What I for you have borne ;
When did child to father give,
  Like you, such cause to mourn ?
And yet this heart, though outraged so,
Can nought but fond forgiveness show :
    Then come,—return,
    Nor all its mercy spurn.

Think not that My heart demands
  A sacrifice too great ;
It asks of guilty man but love,
  And man returns but hate,—
Heedful of every passion's word,
But deaf to Me, his God and Lord,
    The more I press,
    He heeds My voice the less.

Yes, we come, sweet Jesus,
  We hearken to Thy call,
And yield Thee willing tribute
  Of love,—life,—freedom,—all ;
No more the world's deceitful charms
Shall wrest Thy children from Thy arms ;
    Nor Satan win
    Our hearts from Thee to sin. Amen.

D

30

Vexilla Regis prodeunt.

Vespers of Passion Sunday.

FORTH comes the Standard of the King:
  All hail, thou Mystery adored!
Hail, Cross! on which the Life Himself
  Died, and by death our life restored.

On which the Saviour's holy side,
  Rent open with a cruel spear,
Its stream of blood and water pour'd,
  To wash us from defilement clear.

O sacred Wood! fulfill'd in thee
  Was holy David's truthful lay;
Which told the world, that from a Tree
  The Lord should all the nations sway.

Most royally empurpled o'er,
  How beauteously thy stem doth shine!
How glorious was its lot to touch
  Those limbs so holy and divine!

Thrice blest, upon whose arms outstretch'd
  The Saviour of the world reclined;
Balance sublime! upon whose beam
  Was weigh'd the ransom of mankind.

Hail, Cross! thou only hope of man,
  Hail on this holy Passion day!
To saints increase the grace they have;
  From sinners purge their guilt away.

Salvation's Fount, blest Trinity,
  Be praise to Thee through earth and skies:
Thou through the Cross the victory
  Dost give; Oh give us too the prize!

[TR. REV. E. CASWALL]

31

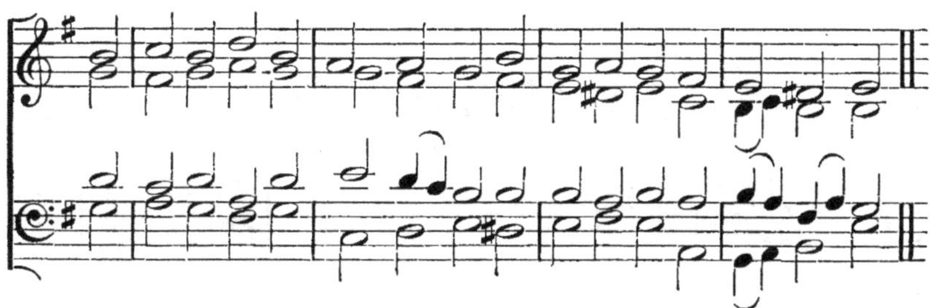

O SOUL of Jesus, sick to death !
Thy Blood and prayer together plead;
My sins have bowed Thee to the ground,
As the storm bows the feeble reed.

Deep waters have come in, O Lord !
All darkly on Thy Human Soul ;
And clouds of supernatural gloom
Around Thee are allowed to roll.

My God ! My God ! and can it be
That I should sin so lightly now,
And think no more of evil thoughts
Than of the wind that waves the bough?

Shall it be always thus, O Lord?
Wilt Thou not work this hour in me
The grace Thy Passion merited,
Hatred of self and love of Thee?

Oh, by the pains of Thy pure love
Grant me the gift of holy fear ;
And give me of Thy Bloody Sweat
To wash my guilty conscience clear !

Ever, when tempted, make me see,
Beneath the olive's moon-pierced shade,
My God, alone, outstretched, and bruised,
And bleeding, on the earth He made

[REV. F. W. FABER]

PASSIONTIDE.

32

Slowly.

Jesu, nostros ob reatus.

JESUS ! all hail, who for my sin
Didst die, and by that death didst win
Eternal life for me ;
Send me Thy grace, good Lord ! that I
Unto the world and flesh may die,
And hide my life with Thee.

Jesus ! from out Thine open Side
Thou hast the thirsty world supplied
With endless streams of love ;
Come ye who would your sickness quell,
Draw freely from that sacred well,
Its heavenly virtues prove.

Jesus ! Who at this very hour
At God's Right Hand in pomp and power
Our nature still doth wear,
Oh let Thy Wounds still intercede,
And by their simple silence plead
Thy countless merits there.

Jesus ! Who shalt in glory come
With angels to the final doom,
Men's works and wills to weigh,
Since from that pomp I cannot flee,
Be pitiful, great Lord ! to me
In that tremendous day.

[TR. REV. F. W. FABER]

33

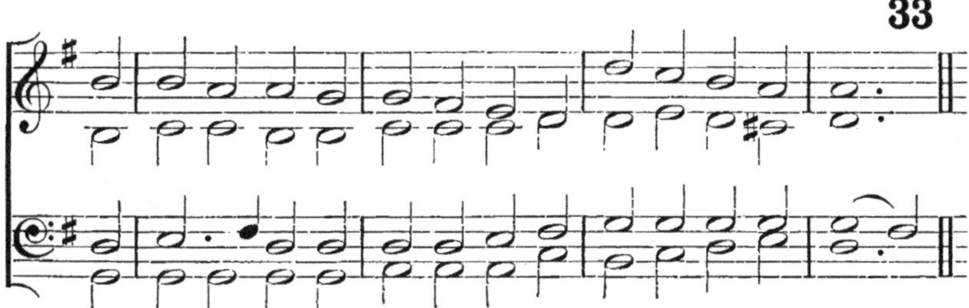

O Deus, ego amo Te.

MY God, I love Thee, not because
  I hope for Heav'n thereby:
Nor because they, who love Thee not,
  Must burn eternally.

Thou, O my Jesus, Thou didst me
  Upon the Cross embrace;
For me didst bear the nails and spear,
  And manifold disgrace;

And griefs and torments numberless,
  And sweat of Agony;
E'en death itself—and all for one
  Who was Thine enemy.

Then why, O blessèd Jesu Christ!
  Should I not love Thee well;
Not for the sake of winning Heaven,
  Or of escaping Hell:

Not with the hope of gaining ought;
  Not seeking a reward;
But, as Thyself hast lovèd me,
  O ever-loving Lord?

E'en so I love Thee, and will love,
  And in Thy praise will sing;
Solely because Thou art my God,
  And my eternal King.

[ST. FRANCIS XAVIER. TR. REV. E. CASWALL]

PASSIONTIDE.

34

Jesu dulcis amor meus.

THE HOLY WINDING SHEET.

JESU! as though Thyself wert here,
I draw in trembling sorrow near;
And, hanging o'er Thy Form Divine,
Kneel down to kiss these wounds of Thine.

Hail, awful brow! hail, thorny wreath!
Hail, countenance now pale in death!
Whose glance but late so brightly blazed,
That Angels trembled as they gazed.

And hail to thee, my Saviour's side;
And hail to thee, thou wound so wide
Thou wound more ruddy than the rose,
True antidote of all our woes!

Oh, by those sacred hands and feet
For me so mangled! I entreat,
My Jesu, turn me not away,
But let me here for ever stay.

[FR. REV. E. CASWALL]

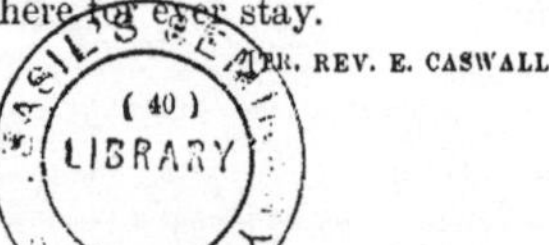

35

Ira justa Conditoris.

FEAST OF THE PRECIOUS BLOOD.

HE Who once, in righteous vengeance,
Whelm'd the world beneath the flood,
Once again in mercy cleansed it
With the stream of His own Blood,
Coming from His throne on high
On the painful Cross to die.

Blest with this all-saving shower,
Earth her beauty straight resumed;
In the place of thorns and briers,
Myrtles sprang, and roses bloom'd:
Bitter wormwood of the waste
Into honey changed its taste.

Scorpions ceased; the slimy serpent
Laid his deadly poison by;
Savage beasts of cruel instinct
Lost their wild ferocity;
Welcoming the gentle reign
Of the Lamb for sinners slain.

Oh, the wisdom of th' Eternal!
Oh, its depth, and height divine!
Oh, the sweetness of that mercy
Which in Jesus Christ doth shine!
Slaves we were condemned to die!
Our King pays the penalty!

When before the Judge we tremble,
Conscious of His broken laws,
May this Blood, in that dread hour,
Cry aloud, and plead our cause:
Bid our guilty terrors cease,
Be our pardon and our peace.

Prince and Author of Salvation!
Lord of majesty supreme!
Jesu! praise to Thee be given
By the world Thou didst redeem;
Who with the Father and the Spirit,
Reignest in eternal merit.

[TR. REV. E. CASWALL]

PASSIONTIDE.

36

I SEE my Jesus crucified,
His wounded hands and feet and side,
His sacred flesh all rent and torn,
His bloody crown of sharpest thorn.

Those cruel nails I drove them in,
Each time I pierced Him with my sin;
That crown of thorns 'twas I who wove,
When I despised His gracious love.

Then to those feet I'll venture near,
And wash them with a contrite tear,
And every bleeding wound I see,
I'll think He bore them all for me.

Deep graven on my sinful heart,
Oh, never may that form depart,
That with me always may abide
The thought of Jesus crucified.

37

MAN of Sorrows, wrapt in grief,
Bow Thine ear to our relief:
Thou for us the path hast trod
Of the dreadful wrath of God;
Thou the cup of fire hast drained
Till its light alone remained.
Lamb of Love! we look to Thee:
Hear our mournful litany.

By the garden, fraught with woe,
Whither Thou full oft wouldst go;
By Thine agony of prayer
In the desolation there;
By the dire and deep distress
Of that mystery fathomless—
Lord, our tears in mercy see:
Hearken to our litany.

By the chalice brimming o'er
With disgrace and torment sore;
By those lips which fain would pray
That it might but pass away;
By the heart which drank it dry,
Lest a rebel race should die—
Be Thy pity, Lord, our plea:
Hear our solemn litany.

Man of Sorrows! let Thy grief
Purchase for us our relief:
Lord of mercy! bow Thine ear,
Slow to anger, swift to hear:
By the Cross's royal road
Lead us to the throne of God,
There for aye to sing to Thee
Heaven's triumphant litany.

[M. BRIDGES]

EASTERTIDE.

38 (First Tune.)

Victimæ Paschali laudes.

CHRIST the Lord is risen to-day:
Christians, haste your vows to pay;
Offer ye your praises meet
At the Paschal Victim's feet;
For the sheep the Lamb hath bled,
Sinless in the sinner's stead.
Christ the Lord is ris'n on high;
Now He lives, no more to die.

Christ, the Victim undefil'd,
Man to God hath reconcil'd;
When in strange and awful strife
Met together death and life;
Christians, on this happy day
Haste with joy your vows to pay.
Christ the Lord is ris'n on high:
Now He lives, no more to die.

Say, O wond'ring Mary, say,
What thou sawest on thy way.
"I beheld, where Christ had lain,
Empty tomb and angels twain;
I beheld the glory bright
Of the rising Lord of light:
Christ my hope is ris'n again;
Now He lives, and lives to reign."

Christ, Who once for sinners bled,
Now the first-born from the dead,
Thron'd in endless might and power,
Lives and reigns for evermore.
Hail, eternal hope on high!
Hail, Thou King of victory!
Hail, Thou Prince of life ador'd!
Help and save us, gracious Lord.

[TR. MISS LEESON]

(SECOND TUNE.) **38**

Victimæ Paschali laudes.

CHRIST the Lord is risen to-day :
Christians, haste your vows to pay ;
Offer ye your praises meet
At the Paschal Victim's feet ;
For the sheep the Lamb hath bled,
Sinless in the sinner's stead.
Christ the Lord is ris'n on high ;
Now He lives, no more to die.

Christ, the Victim undefil'd,
Man to God hath reconcil'd ;
When in strange and awful strife
Met together death and life ;
Christians, on this happy day
Haste with joy your vows to pay.
Christ the Lord is ris'n on high :
Now He lives, no more to die.

Say, O wond'ring Mary, say,
What thou sawest on thy way.
" I beheld, where Christ had lain,
Empty tomb and angels twain ;
I beheld the glory bright
Of the rising Lord of light :
Christ my hope is ris'n again ;
Now He lives, and lives to reign."

Christ, Who once for sinners bled,
Now the first-born from the dead,
Thron'd in endless might and power,
Lives and reigns for evermore.
Hail, eternal hope on high !
Hail, Thou King of victory !
Hail, Thou Prince of life ador'd !
Help and save us, gracious Lord.

[TR. MISS LEESON]

EASTERTIDE.

39 *To be sung in unison.*

EASTERTIDE.

O filii et filiæ.

ALLELUIA ! ALLELUIA ! ALLELUIA !

YE sons and daughters of the Lord !
The King of glory, King adored,
This day Himself from death restored.
Alleluia !

All in the early morning grey
Went holy women on their way,
To see the tomb where Jesus lay.
Alleluia !

Of spices pure a precious store
In their pure hands those women bore,
To anoint the sacred Body o'er.
Alleluia !

Then straightway one in white they see,
Who saith, "Ye seek the Lord ; but He
Is risen, and gone to Galilee."
Alleluia !

This told they Peter, told they John ;
Who forthwith to the tomb are gone,
But Peter is by John outrun.
Alleluia !

That self-same night, while out of fear
The doors were shut, their Lord most dear
To His Apostles did appear.
Alleluia !

But Thomas, when of this he heard,
Was doubtful of his brethren's word ;
Wherefore again there comes the Lord.
Alleluia !

"Thomas, behold My side," saith He ;
"My hands, My feet, My body see,
And doubt not, but believe in Me."
Alleluia !

When Thomas saw that wounded side,
The truth no longer he denied ;
"Thou art my Lord and God !" he cried.
Alleluia !

Oh, blest are they who have not seen
Their Lord, and yet believe in Him !
Eternal life awaiteth them.
Alleluia !

Now let us praise the Lord most high,
And strive His name to magnify
On this great day, through earth and sky :
Alleluia !

Whose mercy ever runneth o'er ;
Whom men and Angel Hosts adore ;
To Him be glory evermore.
Alleluia !

[TR. REV. E. CASWALL]

EASTERTIDE.

40

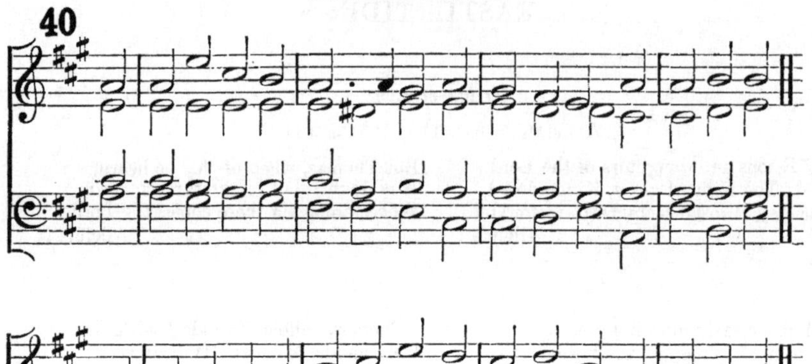

ALL hail! dear Conqueror! all hail!
  Oh what a victory is Thine!
How beautiful Thy strength appears,
  Thy crimson wounds, how bright they shine!

Thou camest at the dawn of day;
  Armies of souls around Thee were,
Blest spirits thronging to adore
  Thy flesh, so marvellous, so fair.

Ye Heavens, how sang they in your courts,
  How sang the angelic choirs that day,
When from His tomb the imprisoned God,
  Like the strong sunrise, broke away?

Down, down, all lofty things on earth,
  And worship Him with joyous dread!
O Sin! thou art outdone by Love!
  O Death! thou art discomfited!

[REV. F. W. FABER]

41

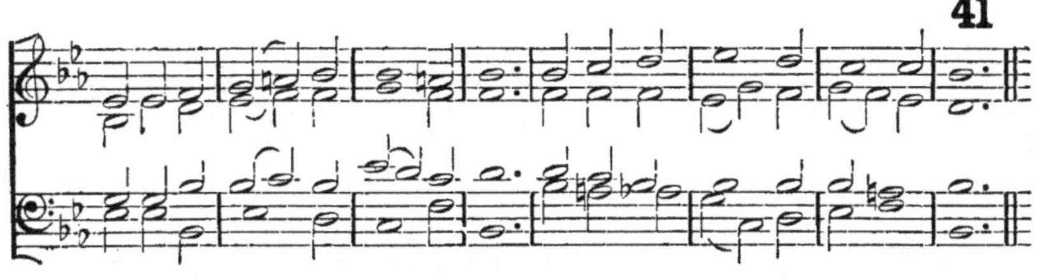

Ad regias Agni dapes.

NOW at the Lamb's high royal feast,
In robes of saintly white, we sing,
Through the Red Sea in safety brought
By Jesus our immortal King.

O depth of love! for us He drains
The chalice of His agony;
For us a Victim on the Cross
He meekly lays Him down to die.

And as the avenging Angel pass'd
Of old the blood-besprinkled door;
As the cleft sea a passage gave,
Then closed to whelm th' Egyptians o'er;

So Christ, our Paschal Sacrifice,
Has brought us safe all perils through;
While for unleaven'd bread He asks
But heart sincere and purpose true.

Hail, purest Victim Heav'n could find
The powers of Hell to overthrow!
Who didst the bonds of Death unbind;
Who dost the prize of Life bestow.

Hail, victor Christ! hail, risen King!
To Thee alone belongs the crown;
Who hast the heavenly gates unbarr'd,
And cast the Prince of darkness down.

O Jesu! from the death of sin
Keep us, we pray; so shalt Thou be
The everlasting Paschal joy
Of all the souls new-born in Thee.

To God the Father, with the Son
Who from the grave immortal rose,
And Thee, O Paraclete, be praise,
While age on endless ages flows.

[TR. REV. E. CASWALL]

ASCENSION.

42

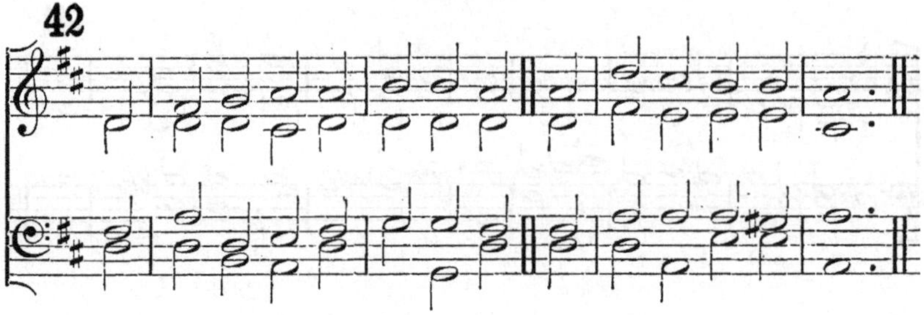

Æterne Rex altissime.

O THOU eternal King most high!
Who didst the world redeem;
And conquering Death and Hell, receive
A dignity supreme.

Thou, through the starry orbs, this day,
Didst to Thy throne ascend;
Thenceforth to reign in sovereign power,
And glory without end.

There, seated in Thy majesty,
To Thee submissive bow
The Heav'n of Heav'ns, the earth beneath,
The realms of Hell below.

With trembling there the angels see
The changed estate of men;
The flesh which sinn'd by Flesh redeem'd;
Man in the Godhead reign.

There, waiting for Thy faithful souls,
Be Thou to us, O Lord!
Our joy of joys while here we stay,
In Heav'n our great reward.

Renew our strength; our sins forgive;
Our miseries efface;
And lift our souls aloft to Thee,
By Thy celestial grace.

So, when Thou shinest on the clouds,
With Thy angelic train,
May we be saved from deadly doom
And our lost crowns regain.

To Christ returning gloriously
With victory to Heaven,
Praise with the Father evermore
And Holy Ghost be given.

[TR. REV. E. CASWALL]

ASCENSION.

RISE, glorious Victor, rise
Into Thy native skies,—
Assume Thy right;
And where in many a fold
The clouds are backward roll'd,
Pass through those gates of gold,
And reign in light.

Enter, Incarnate God;
No feet but Thine have trod
The serpent down;
The full-voiced trumpets blow,
Wider the portals throw;
Saviour, triumphant go
And take Thy crown.

O Lord, ascend Thy throne;
For Thou shalt rule alone,
Beside Thy Sire
And blessèd Paraclete,
The Three in One complete,
Before whose awful feet
All foes expire.

[M. BRIDGES]

ASCENSION.

44

Salutis humanæ Sator.

LAUDS.

O THOU pure light of souls that love,
True joy of every human breast,
Sower of life's immortal seed,
Our Maker, and Redeemer blest!

What wondrous pity Thee o'ercame
To make our guilty load Thine own,
And sinless suffer death and shame,
For our transgressions to atone!

Thou, bursting Hades open wide,
Didst all the captive souls unchain;
And thence to Thy dread Father's side
With glorious pomp ascend again.

O still may pity Thee compel
To heal the wounds of which we die;
And take us in Thy Light to dwell,
Who for Thy blissful Presence sigh.

Be Thou our guide, be Thou our goal;
Be Thou our pathway to the skies;
Our joy when sorrow fills the soul;
In death our everlasting prize.

[TR. REV. E. CASWALL]

ASCENSION.

45

Jesu dulcis memoria.

PART OF HYMN TO THE HOLY NAME.

O THOU, in whom my love doth find
  Its rest and perfect end ;
O Jesu, Saviour of mankind !
  And their eternal friend !

Return, return, pure Light of Light,
  To Thy dread throne again ;
Go forth victorious from the fight,
  And in Thy glory reign.

Lead where Thou wilt, I follow Thee,
  And will not stay behind ;
For Thou hast torn my heart from me,
  O Glory of our kind !

Ye Heav'ns, your gates eternal raise,
  Come forth to meet your King ;
Come forth with joy, and sing His praise,
  His praise eternal sing !

O King of glory ! King of might !
  From whom all graces come ;
O beauty, honour, infinite,
  Of our celestial home !

O Fount of mercy ! Light of Heaven !
  Our darkness cast away ;
And grant us all, through Thee forgiven,
  To see the perfect day.

Hark ! how the Heav'ns with praise o'erflow ;
  O priceless gift of blood !
Jesus makes glad the world below,
  And gains us peace with God.

In peace He reigns—that peace divine,
  For mortal sense too high ;
That peace for which my soul doth pine,
  To which it longs to fly.

Christ to His Father is return'd,
  And sits upon His throne ;
For Him my panting heart hath yearn'd,
  And after Him is gone.

To Him praise, glory, without end,
  And adoration be ;
O Jesu, grant us to ascend,
  And reign in Heav'n with Thee !

[TR. REV. E. CASWALL]

ASCENSION.

46

* *Verse 3 ends here.*

ASCENSION.

Psalm xxiii.

LIFT up, ye princes of the sky—
Lift up your portals, lift them high ;
And you, ye everlasting gates,
Back on your golden hinges fly :
For lo, the King of glory waits
To enter in victoriously.
Who is this King of glory ? Tell,
O ye who sing His praise so well.

The Lord of strength and matchless might,
The Lord all-conquering in the fight ;
Lift, lift your portals, lift them high,
Ye princes of the conquered sky ;
And you, ye everlasting gates,
Back on your golden hinges fly :
For lo, the King of glory waits,
The Lord of hosts, the Lord most high.

Who is this King of glory ? Tell,
O ye who sing His praise so well.
The Lord of hosts, the Lord most high,
Almighty King o' the conquered sky.

[TR. REV. J. D. AYLWARD, O.P.]

PENTECOST.

47

Veni Creator Spiritus.

VESPERS.

COME, Holy Ghost, Creator, come
  From Thy bright heav'nly throne,
Come, take possession of our souls,
  And make them all Thy own.

Thou who art called the Paraclete,
  Best gift of God above,
The living spring, the living fire,
  Sweet unction and true love.

Thou who art sev'nfold in Thy grace,
  Finger of God's right hand;
His promise teaching little ones
  To speak and understand;

O, guide our minds with Thy bless'd light
  With love our hearts inflame;
And with Thy strength, which ne'er decays,
  Confirm our mortal frame.

Far from us drive our deadly foe;
  True peace unto us bring;
And through all perils lead us safe
  Beneath Thy sacred wing.

Through Thee may we the Father know,
  Through Thee th' eternal Son,
And Thee, the Spirit of them both,
  Thrice-blessèd Three in One.

All glory to the Father be,
  With His co-equal Son;
The same to Thee, great Paraclete,
  While endless ages run.

[TR. J. DRYDEN]

48

Veni Sancte Spiritus.

SEQUENCE.

COME, Holy Ghost, send down those beams
Which sweetly flow in silent streams
From Thy bright throne above;
O come, Thou Father of the poor;
O come, Thou source of all our store;
Come, fill our hearts with love.

O Thou, of comforters the best;
O Thou, the soul's delightful guest,
The pilgrim's sweet relief;
Thou art true rest in toil and sweat,
Refreshment in th' excess of heat,
And solace in our grief.

Thrice-blessèd light, shoot home Thy darts,
And pierce the centres of those hearts
Whose faith aspires to Thee;

Without Thy Godhead nothing can
Have any price or worth in man,
Nothing can harmless be.

Lord, wash our sinful stains away,
Refresh from heaven our barren clay,
Our wounds and bruises heal;
To Thy sweet yoke our stiff necks bow,
Warm with Thy fire our hearts of snow,
Our wand'ring feet repeal.

Grant to Thy faithful, dearest Lord,
Whose only hope is Thy sure word,
The seven gifts of Thy Spirit;
Grant us in life Thy helping grace,
Grant us in death to see Thy face,
And endless joy inherit.

[TR. J. AUSTIN]

PENTECOST.

48ᴬ

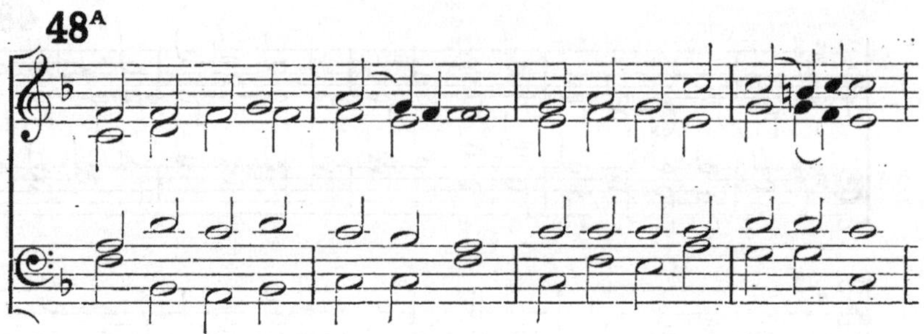

PENTECOST.

Veni Sancte Spiritus.

HOLY Spirit, Lord of light,
From the clear celestial height,
Thy pure beaming radiance give.
Come, Thou Father of the poor,
Come with treasures which endure;
Come, Thou Light of all that live!

Thou, of all consolers best,
Thou, the soul's delightsome guest,
Dost refreshing peace bestow:
Thou in toil art comfort sweet;
Pleasant coolness in the heat;
Solace in the midst of woe.

Light immortal, Light divine,
Visit Thou these hearts of Thine,
And our inmost being fill:
If Thou take Thy grace away,
Nothing pure in man will stay;
All his good is turned to ill.

Heal our wounds, our strength renew;
On our dryness pour Thy dew;
Wash the stains of guilt away:
Bend the stubborn heart and will;
Melt the frozen, warm the chill;
Guide the steps that go astray.

Thou, on those who evermore
Thee confess and Thee adore,
In Thy sevenfold gifts descend:
Give them comfort when they die;
Give them life with Thee on high;
Give them joys that never end.

[TR. REV. E. CASWALL]

PENTECOST.

49

PENTECOST.

Qui procedis ab utroque.

SPIRIT of grace and union!
Who from the Father and the Son
Dost equally proceed,
Inflame our hearts with holy fire,
Our lips with eloquence inspire,
And strengthen us in need.

The Father and the Son through Thee
Are linked in perfect unity,
And everlasting love;
Ineffably Thou dost pervade
All nature; and Thyself unsway'd
The whole creation move.

O inexhaustive Fount of light!
How doth Thy radiance put to flight
The darkness of the mind!
The pure are only pure through Thee;
Thou only dost the guilty free,
And cheer with light the blind.

Thou to the lowly dost display
The beautiful and perfect way
Of justice and of peace:
Shunning the proud and stubborn heart,
Thou to the simple dost impart
True wisdom's rich increase.

Thou teaching, nought remains obscure;
Thou present, every thought impure
Is banish'd from the breast;
And full of cheerfulness serene,
The conscience sanctified and clean
Enjoys a perfect rest.

Each elemental change is Thine;
The Sacraments their force divine
From Thee alone obtain;
Thou only dost temptation quell,
And breaking every snare of Hell,
The rage of Satan chain.

Dear Soother of the troubled heart!
At Thy approach all cares depart,
And melancholy grief;
More balmy than the summer breeze,
Thy presence lulls all agonies,
And lends a sweet relief.

The grace eternal truth instils;
The ignorant with knowledge fills;
Awakens those who sleep;
Inspires the tongue; informs the eye;
Expands the heart with charity;
And comforts all who weep.

O Thou the weary pilgrim's rest!
Solace of all that are oppress'd!
Befriender of the poor!
O Thou in whom the wretched find
A sweet Consoler ever kind,
A refuge ever sure!

Teach us to aim at Heav'n's high prize,
And for its glory to despise
The world and all below;
Cleanse us from sin; direct us right;
Illuminate us with Thy light;
Thy peace on us bestow:

And as Thou didst in days of old
On the first Shepherds of the Fold
In tongues of flame descend,
Now also on its Pastors shine,
And fill with fire of grace divine
The world from end to end!

So unto Thee, who with the Son
And Father art for ever One,
In nature as in name!
Of Both alike the Spirit blest!
Different in Person, but confess'd
In Deity the same!

Lord of all sanctity and might!
Immense, immortal, infinite!
The life of earth and Heaven!
Be, through eternal length of days,
All honour, glory, blessing, praise,
And adoration given!

[ADAM OF ST. VICTOR. TR. REV. E. CASWALL]

PENTECOST.

50

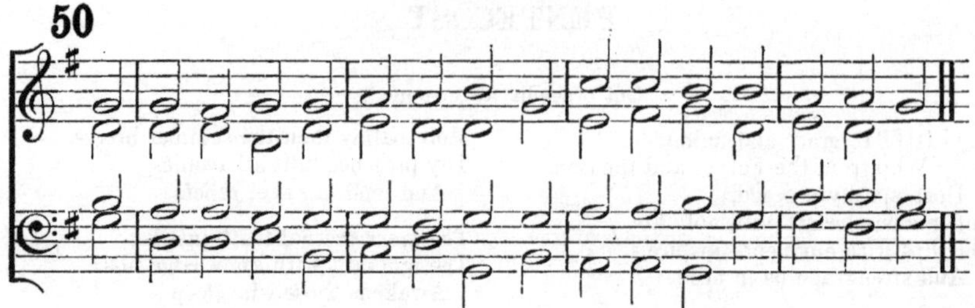

THE Eternal Father's Intellect,
The Godhead's Source, His Word conceives.
Their Love breathes forth the Holy Ghost,
Who Deity from them receives.

O Holy Ghost, Thou dost proceed
From God the Father and the Son;
A Person equal and Divine,
Dwelling in them, in Godhead one.

Eternal Spirit of God's Love,
Sweet Impulse of His tenderness,
To Father and to Son alike
Their mutual love Thou dost express.

O Fire of All-Holy Love!
O inmost Bond of Love Divine!
Loved by the Father and the Son,
Infinite blessedness is Thine.

Man is to God's own image made,
Like God by nature and by grace;
Thou, Spirit of God's Love, didst breathe
The breath of life into his face.

And in his heart Thou dost diffuse
The fire of holy charity;
The love and grace of God, whereby
God's son and heir he is made to be.

Thou art the Guide of God's own Church,
And to the Church all truth doth teach,
Her members Thou dost sanctify,
Thou dwellest in the soul of each.

O then, sweet Holy Paraclete,
Guide Thou our minds in Thine own way;
Fill with the love of God our souls,
And teach us how we ought to pray.

[ARCHBISHOP BAGSHAWE]

51

SIGNED with the Cross that Jesus bore,
We kneel, and tremblingly adore
Our King upon His throne.
The lights upon the altar shine
Around His Majesty divine,
Our God and Mary's Son.

Now, in that Presence dread and sweet,
His own dear Spirit we entreat,
Who sevenfold gifts hath shed
On us, who fall before Him now,
Bearing the Cross upon our brow
On which our Master bled.

Spirit of Wisdom ! turn our eyes
From earth and earthly vanities
To heavenly truth and love.
Spirit of understanding true !
Our souls with heavenly light endue
To seek the things above.

Spirit of Counsel ! be our guide,
Teach us, by earthly struggles tried,
Our heavenly crown to win.
Spirit of Fortitude ! Thy power
Be with us in temptation's hour,
To keep us pure from sin.

Spirit of Knowledge ! lead our feet
In Thine own paths so safe and sweet,
By angel footsteps trod ;
Where Thou our Guardian true shalt be,
Spirit of gentle piety,
To keep us close to God.

But most of all, be ever near,
Spirit of God's most holy fear !
Within our inmost shrine :
Our souls with awful reverence fill,
To worship His most holy Will,
All-righteous and divine.

So, dearest Lord, through peace or strife,
Lead us to everlasting life,
Where only rest may be,
And grant, where'er our lot is cast,
We may in peace be brought at last
To Mary and to Thee !

[REV. H. A. RAWES]

CONFIRMATION.

52

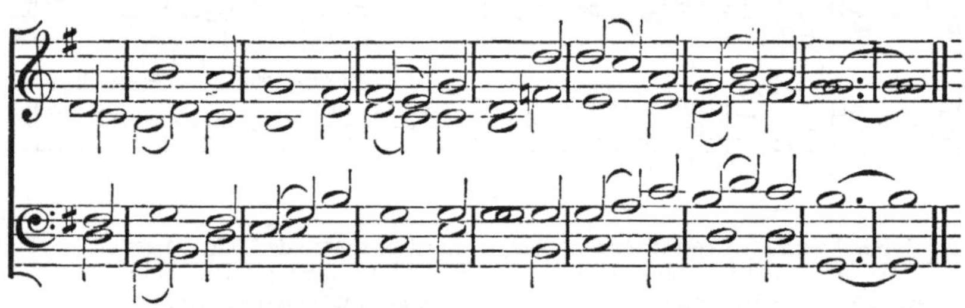

MY God, accept my heart this day,
  And make it always Thine—
That I from Thee no more may stray,
  No more from Thee decline.

Before the Cross of Him who died,
  Behold I prostrate fall:
Let every sin be crucified—
  Let Christ be all in all.

Anoint me with Thy heavenly grace,
  Adopt me for Thine own—
That I may see Thy glorious face
  And worship at Thy throne.

May the dear blood, once shed for me,
  My blest atonement prove—
That I from first to last may be
  The purchase of Thy love!

Let every thought, and work, and word
  To Thee be ever given—
Then life shall be Thy service, Lord,
  And death the gate of heaven!

[M. BRIDGES]

THE HOLY TRINITY.

53

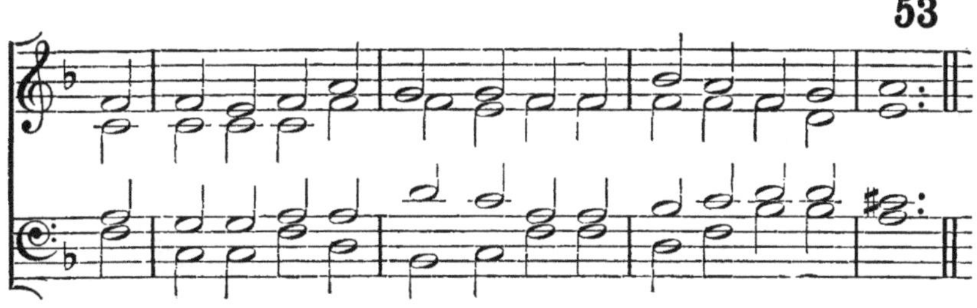

HAVE mercy on us, God Most High!
Who lift our hearts to Thee;
Have mercy on us worms of earth,
Most holy Trinity!

When heaven and earth were yet unmade,
When time was yet unknown,
Thou in Thy bliss and majesty
Didst live and love alone!

Most ancient of all mysteries!
Before Thy throne we lie;
Have mercy now, most merciful,
Most holy Trinity!

Thou wert not born; there was no fount
From which Thy Being flowed;
There is no end which Thou canst reach:
But Thou art simply God.

How wonderful creation is,
The work that Thou didst bless;
And, oh! what then must Thou be like,
Eternal Loveliness?

[REV. F. W. FABER]

THE HOLY TRINITY.

THE HOLY TRINITY.

Æterna lux, Divinitas.

O THOU immortal Light divine!
Dread Trinity in Unity!
Almighty One! Almighty Trine!
Give ear to Thy creation's cry.

Father! in Majesty enthron'd!
Thee we confess with Thy dear Son;
Thee, Holy Ghost! eternal Bond
Of love, uniting Both in One.

As from the Father increate,
His Son and Word eternal came;
So, too, from Each the Paraclete
Proceeds, in Deity the same;

Three Persons!—among whom is none
Greater in majesty or less;
In substance, essence, nature, One;
Equal in might and holiness.

Three Persons!—One Immensity
Encircling utmost space and time!
One Greatness, Glory, Sanctity,
One everlasting Truth sublime!

O Lord, most holy, wise, and just!
Author of nature! God of grace!
Grant that as now in Thee we trust,
So we may see Thee face to face.

Thou art the Fount of all that is;
Thou art our origin and end;
On Thee alone our future bliss
And perpetuity depend.

Thou solely didst the worlds create,
Subsisting still by Thy decree;
Thou art the light, the glory great,
And prize of all who hope in Thee!

To Father, Son, and Holy Ghost,
Triunal Lord of earth and Heaven!
From earth and from the heavenly host
Be sempiternal glory given!

[TR. REV. E. CASWALL]

F 2

THE HOLY TRINITY.

55

FULL of glory, full of wonders,
  Majesty Divine!
'Mid Thine everlasting thunders
  How Thy lightnings shine!
Shoreless Ocean! who shall sound Thee?
Thine own eternity is round Thee,
  Majesty Divine!

Timeless, spaceless, single, lonely,
  Yet sublimely Three,
Thou art grandly, always, only
  God in Unity!
Lone in grandeur, lone in glory,
Who shall tell Thy wondrous story,
  Awful Trinity?

Speechlessly, without beginning,
  Sun that never rose!
Vast, adorable, and winning,
  Day that hath no close!
Bliss from Thine own glory tasting,
Everliving, everlasting,
  Life that never grows!

Splendours upon splendours beaming
  Change and intertwine;
Glories over glories streaming
  All translucent shine!
Blessings, praises, adorations
Greet Thee from the trembling nations!
  Majesty Divine!

[REV. F. W. FABER]

THE HOLY TRINITY.

56

PRAISE to the Holiest in the height,
  And in the depth be praise:
In all His words most wonderful;
  Most sure in all His ways.

O loving wisdom of our God!
  When all was sin and shame,
A second Adam to the fight
  And to the rescue came.

O wisest love! that flesh and blood
  Which did in Adam fail,
Should strive afresh against the foe,
  Should strive and should prevail;

And that a higher gift than grace
  Should flesh and blood refine,
God's Presence and His very Self,
  And Essence all-divine.

O generous love! That He who smote
  In man for man the foe,
The double agony in man
  For man should undergo;

And in the garden secretly,
  And on the cross on high,
Should teach His brethren and inspire
  To suffer and to die.

[CARDINAL NEWMAN'S "THE DREAM OF GERONTIUS"]

THE HOLY TRINITY.

57

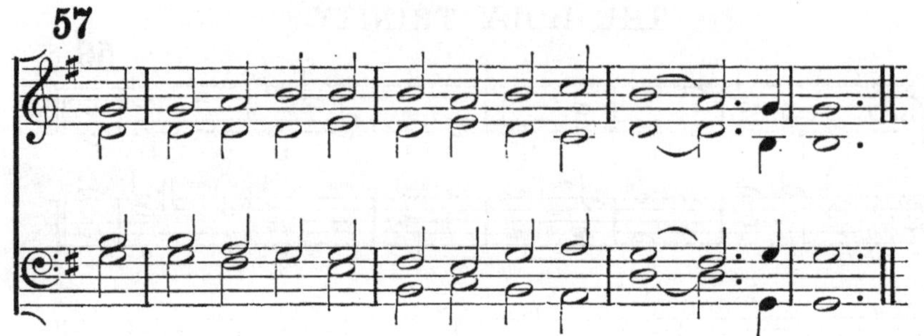

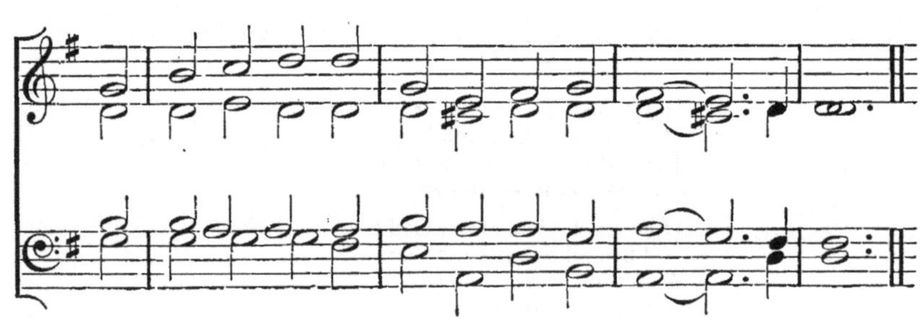

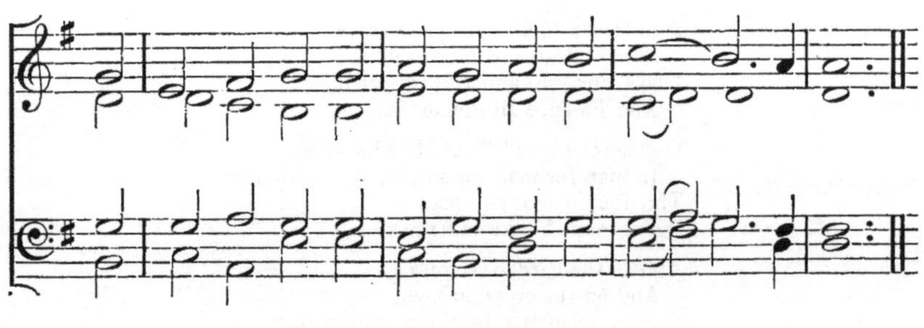

THE HOLY TRINITY.

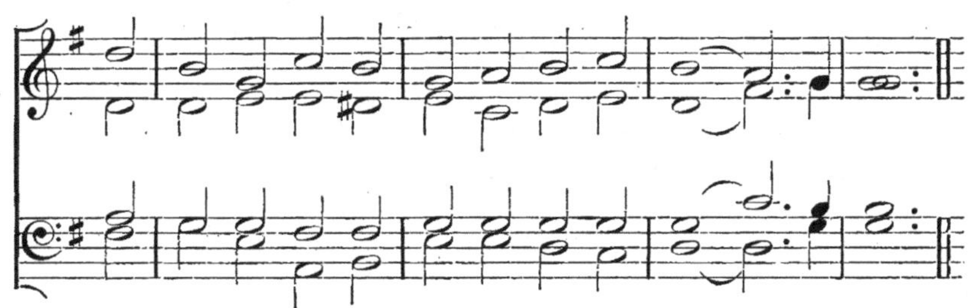

O bello Dio, Signor del Paradiso.

O GOD of loveliness,
  O Lord of Heaven above,
How worthy to possess
  My heart's devoted love!
So sweet Thy countenance,
  So gracious to behold,
That one, one only glance
  To me were bliss untold.

Thou art blest Three in One,
  Yet undivided still;
Thou art that One alone
  Whose love my heart can fill.
The heavens, the earth below,
  Were fashioned by Thy Word;
How amiable art Thou,
  My ever-dearest Lord!

To think Thou art my God,—
  O thought for ever blest!
My heart has overflowed
  With joy within my breast.
My soul so full of bliss
  Is plunged as in a sea,
Deep in the sweet abyss
  Of holy charity.

No object here below
  Awakens my desire;
No suffering nor woe
  Can grief or pain inspire.
The world I could despise,
  Though it were all of gold;
Thee only do I prize,
  O mine of wealth untold.

Were hearts as countless mine
  As sands upon the shore,
All should in choir combine
  To love Thee evermore.
And every heart should yearn
  With tenderest desire,
And in my bosom burn
  With flames of holiest fire.

O Loveliness supreme,
  And Beauty infinite;
O ever-flowing Stream,
  And Ocean of Delight;
O Life by which I live,
  My truest life above,
To Thee alone I give
  My undivided love.

[ST. ALPHONSUS. TR. REV. E. VAUGHAN C.SS.R.]

OUR BLESSED LORD.

58

OUR BLESSED LORD.

JESUS is God! The solid earth,
  The ocean broad and bright,
The countless stars, like golden dust,
  That strew the skies at night,
The wheeling storm, the dreadful fire,
  The pleasant, wholesome air,
The summer's sun, the winter's frost,
  His own creations were.

Jesus is God! The glorious bands
  Of golden angels sing
Songs of adoring praise to Him,
  Their Maker and their King.
He was true God in Bethlehem's crib,
  On Calvary's cross true God,
He who in Heaven eternal reigned
  In time on earth abode.

Jesus is God! Let sorrow come,
  And pain, and every ill;
All are worth while, for all are means
  His glory to fulfil;
Worth while a thousand years of life
  To speak one little word,
If by our Credo we might own
  The Godhead of our Lord!

Jesus is God! Oh could I now
  But compass land and sea,
To teach and tell this single truth,
  How happy should I be!
Oh had I but an angel's voice
  I would proclaim so loud,—
Jesus, the good, the beautiful,
  Is everlasting God!

Jesus is God! If on the earth
  This blessèd faith decays,
More tender must our love become,
  More plentiful our praise.
We are not angels, but we may
  Down in earth's corners kneel,
And multiply sweet acts of love,
  And murmur what we feel.

[REV. F. W. FABER]

OUR BLESSED LORD.

59

OUR BLESSED LORD.

Gelobt sey Jesus Christ!

WHEN morning gilds the skies,
My heart awaking cries:
May Jesus Christ be praised.
Alike at work and prayer,
To Jesus I repair:
May Jesus Christ be praised.

The sacred minster bell,
It peals o'er hill and dell:
May Jesus Christ be praised.
Oh! hark to what it sings,
As joyously it rings:
May Jesus Christ be praised.

To Thee, my God above,
I cry with glowing love:
May Jesus Christ be praised.
The fairest graces spring
In hearts that ever sing:
May Jesus Christ be praised.

My tongue shall never tire
Of chanting in the choir:
May Jesus Christ be praised.
This song of sacred joy,
It never seems to cloy:
May Jesus Christ be praised.

When sleep her balm denies,
My silent spirit sighs:
May Jesus Christ be praised.
When evil thoughts molest,
With this I shield my breast:
May Jesus Christ be praised.

Does sadness fill my mind?
A solace here I find:
May Jesus Christ be praised.
Or fades my earthly bliss?
My comfort still is this:
May Jesus Christ be praised.

Though break my heart in twain,
Still this shall be my strain:
May Jesus Christ be praised.
When you begin the day,
Oh! never fail to say:
May Jesus Christ be praised.

And at your work rejoice,
To sing with heart and voice:
May Jesus Christ be praised.
Be this at meals your grace,
In every time and place:
May Jesus Christ be praised.

Be this, when day is past;
Of all your thoughts the last:
May Jesus Christ be praised.
In want and bitter pain,
None ever said in vain:
May Jesus Christ be praised.

Should guilt your spirit wring,
Remember Christ your King:
May Jesus Christ be praised.
The night becomes as day,
When from the heart we say.
May Jesus Christ be praised.

In Heav'n's eternal bliss,
The loveliest strain is this:
May Jesus Christ be praised.
The powers of darkness fear,
When this sweet chant they hear:
May Jesus Christ be praised.

To God the Word on high,
The host of angels cry:
May Jesus Christ be praised.
Let mortals, too, upraise,
Their voice in hymns of praise:
May Jesus Christ be praised.

Let earth's wide circle round
In joyful notes resound:
May Jesus Christ be praised.
Let air, and sea, and sky,
From depth to height reply:
May Jesus Christ be praised.

Be this, while life is mine,
My canticle divine:
May Jesus Christ be praised.
Be this th' eternal song,
Through all the ages on:
May Jesus Christ be praised.

[TR. REV. E. CASWALL]

OUR BLESSED LORD.

60

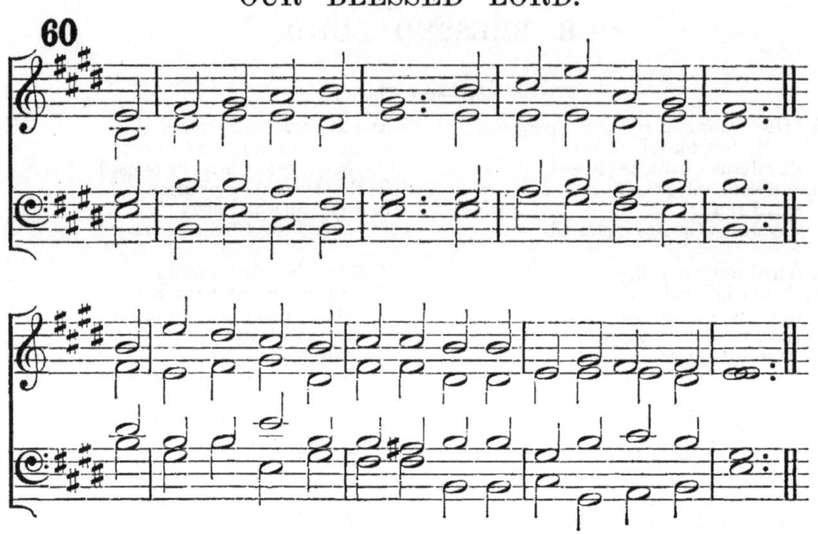

Lux alma, Jesu, mentium.

TRANSFIGURATION.

LIGHT of the anxious heart,
  Jesus, Thou dost appear,
To bid the gloom of guilt depart,
  And shed Thy sweetness here.

Joyous is he, with whom,
  God's Word, Thou dost abide;
Sweet Light of our eternal home,
  To fleshly sense denied.

Brightness of God above!
  Unfathomable grace!
Thy Presence be a fount of love
  Within Thy chosen place.

To Thee, whom children see,
  The Father ever blest,
The Holy Spirit, One and Three,
  Be endless praise addrest. Amen.

[TR. CARDINAL NEWMAN]

OUR BLESSED LORD.

61

O JESUS, Jesus! dearest Lord!
Forgive me if I say
For very love Thy Sacred Name
A thousand times a day.

I love Thee so, I know not how
My transports to control;
Thy love is like a burning fire
Within my very soul.

O wonderful! that Thou shouldst let
So vile a heart as mine
Love Thee with such a love as this,
And make so free with Thine.

For Thou to me art all in all,
My honour and my wealth,
My heart's desire, my body's strength,
My soul's eternal health.

What limit is there to thee, love?
Thy flight where wilt thou stay?
On! on! our Lord is sweeter far
To-day than yesterday.

Oh love of Jesus! Blessèd love!
So will it ever be;
Time cannot hold thy wondrous growth,
No, nor eternity!

[REV. F. W. FABER]

OUR BLESSED LORD.

62

"*A Light that shineth in a dark place until the day dawns, and the day-star arise in your hearts.*"—2 Peter i. 19.

WHEN evening's last faint beams are gone
And cheerless night comes stealing on,
The gentle moon grows kindly bright,
And brightest shines in deepest night.

And thus when worldly hope departs,
When sadness shades our lonely hearts,
Thy love, dear Lord, begins to shine,
And cheers those hearts with joy divine!

O Lord, my God, my Light, my Life,
My Peace in toil, my Strength in strife,
Continue Thou my Joy to be
Till dawns a bright eternity!

[CANON SCANNELL]

63

I MET the good Shepherd,
  But now on the plain,
As homeward He carried
  His lost one again.
I marvell'd how gently
  His burden He bore ;
And, as He pass'd by me,
  I knelt to adore.

" O Shepherd, good Shepherd,
  Thy wounds they are deep ;
The wolves have sore hurt Thee,
  In saving Thy sheep ;
Thy raiment all over
  With crimson is dyed ;
And what is this rent
  They have made in Thy side ?

Ah, me ! how the thorns
  Have entangled Thy hair,
And cruelly riven
  That forehead so fair !
How feebly Thou drawest
  Thy faltering breath !
And lo on Thy face
  Is the shadow of death !

O Shepherd, good Shepherd !
  And is it for me
This grievous affliction
  Has fallen on Thee ?
Ah, then let me strive,
  For the love Thou hast borne,
To give Thee no longer
  Occasion to mourn ! "

[REV. E. CASWALL]

OUR BLESSED LORD.

64

OUR BLESSED LORD.

CROWN Him with many crowns,
  The Lamb upon His throne ;
Hark, how the heavenly anthem drowns
  All music but its own :
Awake, my soul, and sing
  Of Him who died for thee ;
And hail Him as thy matchless King
  Through all eternity.

Crown Him the Virgin's Son,
  The God Incarnate born ;
Whose arm those crimson trophies won
  Which now His Brow adorn !
Fruit of the Mystic Rose,
  As of that Rose the Stem ;
The Root, whence Mercy ever flows,
  The Babe of Bethlehem.

Crown Him the Lord of love :
  Behold His Hands and Side,
Rich wounds, yet visible above
  In beauty glorified :
No angel in the sky
  Can fully bear that sight,
But downward bends his burning eye
  At mysteries so bright.

Crown Him the Lord of peace :
  Whose power a sceptre sways
From pole to pole, that wars may cease
  Absorbed in prayer and praise :
His reign shall know no end,
  And round His piercèd feet
Fair flowers of Paradise extend
  Their fragrance ever sweet.

Crown Him the Lord of years,
  The Potentate of time,
Creator of the rolling spheres,
  Ineffably sublime :
Glazed in a sea of light,
  Whose everlasting waves
Reflect His form, the Infinite,
  Who lives, and loves, and saves.

Crown Him the Lord of heaven,
  One with the Father known,
And the blest Spirit through Him given
  From yonder triune throne :
All hail, Redeemer, hail,
  For Thou hast died for me ;
Thy praise shall never, never fail
  Throughout eternity.

[M. BRIDGES]

OUR BLESSED LORD.

65

Mondo più per me non sei.

JESUS, Lord, be Thou my own;
Thee I long for, Thee alone;
All myself I give to Thee;
Do whate'er Thou wilt with me.

Life without Thy love would be
Death, O Sovereign Good, to me;
Bound and held by Thy dear chains
Captive now my heart remains.

Thou, O God, my heart inflame,
Give that love which Thou dost claim;
Payment I will ask for none;
Love demands but love alone.

God of beauty, Lord of light,
Thy good will is my delight;
Now henceforth Thy will divine
Ever shall in all be mine.

[ST. ALPHONSUS. TR. REV. E. VAUGHAN, C.SS.R.]

66

O BRIGHTNESS of eternal light,
  I worship at Thy feet ;
Though all unworthy in Thy sight,
  Thy mercies I repeat.
To save our souls from sin and strife
  Is still Thy work divine ;
The gates of everlasting life,
  O gracious Lord, are Thine.

I love to praise Thee when the sun
  Pours forth his early light,
And when the bright stars one by one
  Come twinkling out at night.
If I am free from care and loss,
  I love to praise Thy name,
If I am call'd to bear Thy cross,
  I bless Thee all the same.

If roses on my path I meet,
  I feel the gift is Thine ;
If thorns spring up to pierce my feet,
  I still will not repine.
The blessings sent to win my love,
  O Lord, I freely take ;
The trials sent my faith to prove,
  I bear for Thy dear sake.

Then let me on my journey go,
  And fear not for the end ;
It matters not who is my foe,
  If Jesus be my friend.
In Thee, sweet Lord, I put my trust ;
  Oh, guard me while I live ;
And when this dust returns to dust,
  My soul in Heaven receive.

[ANON. "HYMNS FOR THE YEAR," 1867]

OUR BLESSED LORD.

67

OUR BLESSED LORD.

Jesu dulcis memoria.

JESU, the only thought of Thee
With sweetness fills my breast;
But sweeter still it is to see
And on Thy beauty feast.
No theme so soft, nor sound so gay
Can art of music frame;
No words, nor even thought, can say
Thy most mellifluous name.

Sole hope, when we our sins repent,
So bounteous of Thy grace;
If thus Thou'rt good while we lament,
Oh, what when face to face?
Jesus, that name inspires my mind
With springs of life and light;
More than I ask in Thee I find,
And lavish in delight.

No eloquence nor art can reach
The joys of those above;
The blest can only know, not reach,
What they in Jesus prove.
Thee, then, I'll seek, retired apart,
From world and business free;
When noise invades I'll shut my heart,
And keep it all for Thee.

An early pilgrim thus I'll come,
With Magdalen, to find
In sighs and tears my Saviour's tomb,
And there refresh my mind.
My tears upon His grave shall flow,
My sighs the garden fill;
Then at His feet myself I'll throw,
And there I'll seek His will.

Jesus, in Thy blest steps I'll tread,
And haunt Thee through Thy ways;
I'll mourn, and never cease to plead
Till I'm restored to grace.
Great Conqueror of death, Thy fire
Does such sweet flames excite,
That first it raises the desire,
Then fills it with delight.

Thy quickening presence shines so clear
Through every sense and way,
That souls, who once have seen Thee near,
See all things else decay.
Come, then, dear Lord, possess my heart,
And chase the shades of night;
Come, pierce it with Thy flaming dart,
And ever-shining light.

Then, I'll for ever Jesus sing,
And with the blest rejoice;
Then all the vaulted towers shall ring,
And echoing hearts and voices sing,
And still repeat, "Rejoice."

[TR. J. DRYDEN]

N.B.—If the last verse of this hymn is sung, the above must be interpolated between the asterisks. The last bar on line 1 of the music will in that case be omitted, and the verse will end with line 2 of the music.

OUR BLESSED LORD.

68

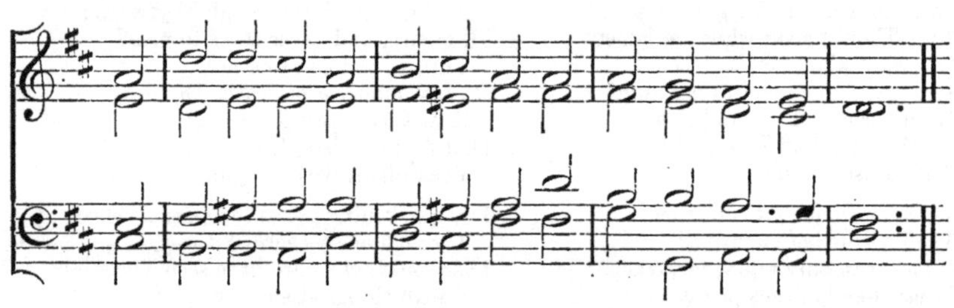

I NEED Thee, precious Jesus,
I need a friend like Thee ;
A friend to soothe and sympathise,
A friend to care for me.

I need Thy Heart, sweet Jesus,
To feel each anxious care ;
I long to tell my every want,
And all my sorrows share.

I need Thy Blood, sweet Jesus,
To wash each sinful stain :
To cleanse this sinful soul of mine,
And make it pure again.

I need Thy Wounds, sweet Jesus,
To fly from perils near,
To shelter in these hallowed clefts,
From every doubt and fear.

I need Thee, sweetest Jesus,
In Thy Sacrament of Love ;
To nourish this poor soul of mine,
With the treasures of Thy love.

I'll need Thee, sweetest Jesus,
When death's dread hour draws nigh,
To hide me in Thy Sacred Heart,
Till wafted safe on high.

[ANON. "HYMNS FOR THE YEAR," 1867]

69

Cœli Deus sanctissime.

Vespers of Wednesday.

LORD of eternal purity!
  Who dost the world with light adorn,
And paint the fields of azure sky
  With lovely hues of eve and morn:

Who didst command the sun to light
  His fiery wheel's effulgent blaze;
Didst set the moon her circuit bright;
  The stars their ever-winding maze:

That, each within its order'd sphere,
  They might divide the night from day;
And of the seasons, through the year,
  The well-remember'd signs display:

Scatter our night, eternal God,
  And kindle Thy pure beam within;
Free us from guilt's oppressive load,
  And break the deadly bonds of sin.

Father of mercies! hear our cry;
  Hear us, O sole-begotten Son!
Who, with the Holy Ghost most high,
  Reignest while endless ages run.

[TR. REV. E. CASWALL]

THE BLESSED SACRAMENT.

70

Ave, verum corpus natum.

HAIL to Thee! true Body, sprung
From the Virgin Mary's womb!
The same that on the Cross was hung,
And bore for man the bitter doom!

Thou, whose side was pierced, and flow'd
Both with water and with blood;
Suffer us to taste of Thee,
In our life's last agony.

Son of Mary, Jesu blest!
Sweetest, gentlest, holiest!

[TR. REV. E. CASWALL]

THE BLESSED SACRAMENT.

71

Pange lingua gloriosi.

CORPUS CHRISTI VESPERS.

SING, my tongue, the Saviour's glory,
  Of His Flesh the mystery sing;
Of the Blood, all price exceeding,
  Shed by our immortal King,
Destined, for the world's redemption,
  From a noble womb to spring.

Of a pure and spotless Virgin
  Born for us on earth below,
He, as Man with man conversing,
  Stay'd, the seeds of truth to sow;
Then He closed in solemn order
  Wondrously His life of woe.

On the night of that Last Supper,
  Seated with His chosen band,
He the Paschal victim eating,
  First fulfils the Law's command;
Then, as Food to His Apostles
  Gives Himself with His own hand.

Word made Flesh, the bread of nature
  By His word to Flesh He turns;
Wine into His Blood He changes :—
  What though sense no change discerns?
Only be the heart in earnest,
  Faith her lesson quickly learns.

Tantum ergo sacramentum.

Down in adoration falling,
  Lo! the sacred Host we hail;
Lo! o'er ancient forms departing,
  Newer rites of grace prevail;
Faith, for all defects supplying,
  Where the feeble senses fail.

To the Everlasting Father,
  And the Son who reigns on high,
With the Holy Ghost proceeding
  Forth from Each eternally,
Be salvation, honour, blessing,
  Might, and endless majesty.

[TR. REV. E CASWALL]

THE BLESSED SACRAMENT.

72 (Part I.)

THE BLESSED SACRAMENT.

JESUS! my Lord, my God, my all!
How can I love Thee as I ought?
And how revere this wondrous gift,
So far surpassing hope or thought?
Sweet Sacrament! we Thee adore!
Oh, make us love Thee more and more!

Had I but Mary's sinless heart
To love Thee with, my dearest King,
Oh, with what bursts of fervent praise
Thy goodness, Jesus, would I sing!
Sweet Sacrament! we Thee adore!
Oh, make us love Thee more and more!

Ah, see! within a creature's hand
The vast Creator deigns to be,
Reposing, infant-like, as though
On Joseph's arm, or Mary's knee.
Sweet Sacrament! we Thee adore!
Oh, make us love Thee more and more!

Thy Body, Soul, and Godhead, all!
O mystery of love divine!
I cannot compass all I have,
For all Thou hast and art are mine!
Sweet Sacrament! we Thee adore!
Oh, make us love Thee more and more!

Sound, sound His praises higher still,
And come, ye angels, to our aid,
'Tis God! 'tis God! the very God,
Whose power both man and angels made!
Sweet Sacrament! we Thee adore!
Oh, make us love Thee more and more!

PART II.—FOR PROCESSIONS.

Ring joyously, ye solemn bells!
And wave, oh wave, ye censers bright!
'Tis Jesus cometh, Mary's Son,
And God of God, and Light of Light!
Sweet Sacrament! we Thee adore!
Oh, make us love Thee more and more!

O earth! grow flowers beneath His feet,
And Thou, O sun, shine bright this day!
He comes! He comes! O Heaven on earth!
Our Jesus comes upon His way!
Sweet Sacrament! we Thee adore!
Oh, make us love Thee more and more!

He comes! He comes! the Lord of Hosts,
Borne on His Throne triumphantly!
We see Thee, and we know Thee, Lord;
And yearn to shed our blood for Thee.
Sweet Sacrament! we Thee adore!
Oh, make us love Thee more and more!

Our hearts leap up; our trembling song
Grows fainter still; we can no more;
Silence! and let us weep—and die
Of very love, while we adore.
Great Sacrament of love divine!
All, all we have or are be Thine!

[REV. F. W. FABER]

THE BLESSED SACRAMENT.

73 (First Tune.)

Partendo dal mondo.

When the loving Shepherd,
  Ere He left the earth,
Shed, to pay our ransom,
  Blood of priceless worth,
These His lambs so cherish'd,
  Purchas'd for His own,
He would not abandon
  In the world alone.

Ere He makes us partners
  Of His realm on high,
Happy and immortal
  With Him in the sky,—
Love immense, stupendous,
  Makes Him here below
Partner of our exile
  In this world of woe.

Jesus, food of angels,
  Monarch of the heart;
Oh, that I could never
  From Thy face depart!
Yes, Thou ever dwellest
  Here for love of me,
Hidden Thou remainest,
  God of Majesty.

Soon I hope to see Thee,
  And enjoy Thy love,
Face to face, sweet Jesus,
  In Thy Heaven above.
But on earth an exile,
  My delight shall be
Ever to be near Thee,
  Veiled for love of me.

[St. Alphonsus. Tr. Rev. E. Vaughan, C.SS.R.]

(SECOND TUNE.) **73**

Partendo dal mondo.

WHEN the loving Shepherd,
  Ere He left the earth,
Shed, to pay our ransom,
  Blood of priceless worth,
These His lambs so cherish'd,
  Purchas'd for His own,
He would not abandon
  In the world alone.

Ere He makes us partners
  Of His realm on high,
Happy and immortal
  With Him in the sky,—
Love immense, stupendous,
  Makes Him here below
Partner of our exile
  In this world of woe.

Jesus, food of angels,
  Monarch of the heart;
Oh, that I could never
  From Thy face depart!
Yes, Thou ever dwellest
  Here for love of me,
Hidden Thou remainest,
  God of Majesty.

Soon I hope to see Thee,
  And enjoy Thy love,
Face to face, sweet Jesus,
  In Thy Heaven above.
But on earth an exile,
  My delight shall be
Ever to be near Thee,
  Veiled for love of me.

[ST. ALPHONSUS. TR. REV. E. VAUGHAN, C.SS.R.]

THE BLESSED SACRAMENT.

74

Anima Christi.

SOUL of my Saviour, sanctify my breast!
Body of Christ, be Thou my saving guest!
Blood of my Saviour, bathe me in Thy tide!
Wash me, ye waters, gushing from His side!

Strength and protection may His passion be;
O blessèd Jesus, hear and answer me!
Deep in Thy wounds, Lord, hide and shelter me;
So shall I never, never part from Thee.

Guard and defend me from the foe malign;
In death's drear moments make me only Thine;
Call me, and bid me come to Thee on high,
When I may praise Thee with Thy saints for aye.

75

Verbum supernum prodiens.

CORPUS CHRISTI, LAUDS.

THE Word, descending from above,
  Though with the Father still on high,
Went forth upon His work of love,
  And soon to life's last eve drew nigh.

He shortly to a death accursed
  By a disciple shall be given ;
But, to His twelve disciples, first
  He gives Himself, the Bread from Heaven.

Himself in either kind He gave ;
  He gave His Flesh, He gave His Blood ;
Of flesh and blood all men are made ;
  And He of man would be the Food.

At birth our brother He became ;
  At meat Himself as food He gives ;
To ransom us He died in shame ;
  As our reward, in bliss He lives.

O salutaris Hostia.

O saving Victim ! open wide
  The gate of Heav'n to man below !
Sore press our foes from every side ;
  Thine aid supply, Thy strength bestow.

To Thy great Name be endless praise,
  Immortal Godhead, One in Three !
Oh, grant us endless length of days,
  In our true native land, with Thee !

[TR. REV. E. CASWALL]

THE BLESSED SACRAMENT.

THE BLESSED SACRAMENT.

Adoro Te devote, latens Deitas.

O GODHEAD hid, devoutly I adore Thee,
Who truly art within the forms before me;
To Thee my heart I bow with bended knee,
As failing quite in contemplating Thee.

Sight, touch, and taste in Thee are each deceived;
The ear alone most safely is believed:
I believe all the Son of God has spoken,
Than Truth's own word there is no truer token.

God only on the Cross lay hid from view;
But here lies hid at once the Manhood too:
And I, in both professing my belief,
Make the same prayer as the repentant thief.

Thy wounds, as Thomas saw, I do not see;
Yet Thee confess my Lord and God to be:
Make me believe Thee ever more and more;
In Thee my hope, in Thee my love to store.

O thou Memorial of our Lord's own dying!
O Bread that Living art and vivifying!
Make ever Thou my soul on thee to live;
Ever a taste of Heavenly sweetness give.

O loving Pelican! O Jesu, Lord!
Unclean I am, but cleanse me in Thy blood;
Of which a single drop, for sinners spilt,
Is ransom for a world's entire guilt.

Jesu! whom for the present veil'd I see,
What I so thirst for, oh, vouchsafe to me:
That I may see Thy countenance unfolding,
And may be blest Thy glory in beholding.

O Shepherd of the Faithful, O Jesu, gracious be;
Increase the faith of all who put their faith in Thee.

[ST. THOMAS AQUINAS. TR. REV. E. CASWALL]

THE BLESSED SACRAMENT.

77

O JESUS Christ, remember,
  When Thou shalt come again,
Upon the clouds of Heaven,
  With all Thy shining train;—
When every eye shall see Thee
  In Deity reveal'd,
Who now upon this altar
  In silence art conceal'd;—

Remember then, O Saviour,
  I supplicate of Thee,
That here I bow'd before Thee
  Upon my bended knee;
That here I own'd thy Presence,
  And did not Thee deny;
And glorified Thy greatness
  Though hid from human eye.

Accept, Divine Redeemer,
  The homage of my praise;
Be Thou the light and honour
  And glory of my days.
Be Thou my consolation
  When death is drawing nigh;
Be Thou my only treasure
  Through all eternity.

[REV. E. CASWALL]

THE BLESSED SACRAMENT.

78

SWEET Sacrament divine!
  Hid in Thine earthly home,
Lo! round Thy lowly shrine,
  With suppliant hearts we come.
Jesus, to Thee our voice we raise,
In songs of love and heartfelt praise,
  Sweet Sacrament divine!

Sweet Sacrament of Peace!
  Dear home for every heart,
Where restless yearnings cease,
  And sorrows all depart.
There in Thine ear, all trustfully
We tell our tale of misery,
  Sweet Sacrament of Peace!

Sweet Sacrament of Rest!
  Ark from the ocean's roar,
Within Thy shelter blest
  Soon may we reach the shore.
Save us, for still the tempest raves;
Save, lest we sink beneath the waves;
  Sweet Sacrament of Rest!

Sweet Sacrament divine!
  Earth's Light and Jubilee,
In Thy far depths doth shine
  Thy Godhead's Majesty.
Sweet Light, so shine on us, we pray,
That earthly joys may fade away,
  Sweet Sacrament divine!

[REV. F. STANFIELD]

Repeat last line of each verse.

THE BLESSED SACRAMENT.

79

I COME to Thee once more, my God!
  No longer will I roam;
For I have sought the wide world through,
  And never found a home.

Though bright and many are the spots
  Where I have built a nest,
Yet in the brightest still I pined
  For more abiding rest.

Riches could bring me joy and power,
  And they were fair to see;
Yet gold was but a sorry god
  To serve instead of Thee.

Then honour and the world's good word
  Appeared a nobler faith;
Yet could I rest on bliss that hung
  And trembled on a breath?

The pleasure of the passing hour
  My spirit next could wile;
But soon, full soon, my heart fell sick
  Of pleasure's weary smile.

More selfish grown, I worshipped health,
  The flush of manhood's power;
But then it came and went so quick,
  It was but for an hour.

And thus a not unkindly world
  Hath done its best for me;
Yet I have found, O God! no rest,
  No harbour short of Thee.

For Thou hast made this wondrous soul
  All for Thyself alone;
Ah! send Thy sweet transforming grace
  To make it more Thine own.

[REV. F. W. FABER]

THE BLESSED SACRAMENT.

Lauda Sion Salvatorem.

Corpus Christi Sequence.

SION, lift thy voice, and sing;
Praise thy Saviour and thy King;
Praise with hymns thy Shepherd true:
Dare thy most to praise Him well;
For He doth all praise excel;
None can ever reach His due.

Special theme of praise is thine,
That true living Bread divine,
That life-giving Flesh adored,
Which the brethren twelve received,
As most faithfully believed,
At the Supper of the Lord.

Let the chant be loud and high;
Sweet and tranquil be the joy
Felt to-day in every breast;
On this Festival divine
Which recounts the origin
Of the glorious Eucharist.

At this Table of the King,
Our new Paschal offering
Brings to end the olden rite;
Here, for empty shadows fled,
Is Reality instead;
Here, instead of darkness, Light.

THE BLESSED SACRAMENT.

80 (Part II.)

His own act, at supper seated,
Christ ordain'd to be repeated,
  In His Memory Divine ;
Wherefore now, with adoration,
We the Host of our salvation
  Consecrate from bread and wine.

Hear what holy Church maintaineth,
That the bread its substance changeth
  Into Flesh, the wine to Blood.
Doth it pass thy comprehending ?
Faith, the law of sight transcending,
  Leaps to things not understood.

Here, in outward signs are hidden
Priceless things, to sense forbidden ;
  Signs, not things, are all we see ;—
Flesh from bread, and Blood from wine ;
Yet is Christ, in either sign,
  All entire, confess'd to be.

THE BLESSED SACRAMENT.

(Part III.) **80**

They, too, who of Him partake,
Sever not, nor rend, nor break,
But entire, their Lord receive.
Whether one or thousands eat,
All receive the self-same meat,
Nor the less for others leave.

Both the wicked and the good
Eat of this celestial Food;
But with ends how opposite!
Here 'tis life; and there 'tis death;
The same, yet issuing to each
In a difference infinite.

THE BLESSED SACRAMENT.

80 (Part IV.)

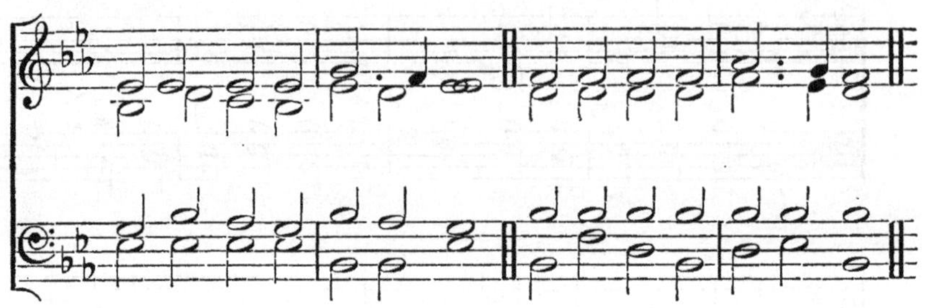

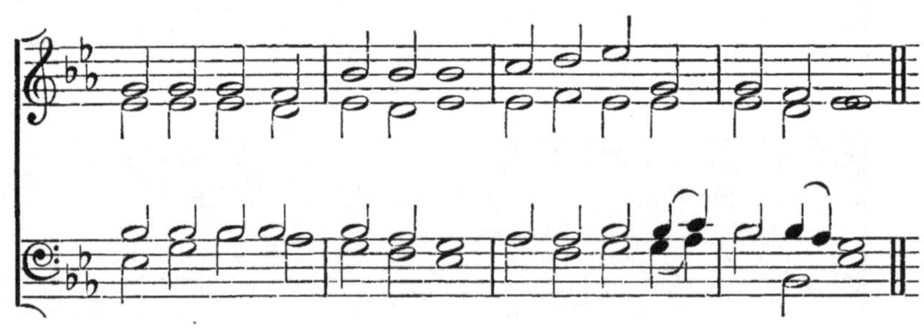

THE BLESSED SACRAMENT.

Nor a single doubt retain,
When they break the Host in twain,
But that in each part remains
  What was in the whole before;
Since the simple sign alone
Suffers change in state or form,
The Signified remaining One
  And the Same for evermore.

Ecce panis angelorum.

Lo! upon the Altar lies,
Hidden deep from human eyes,
Angels' Bread from Paradise,
  Made the food of mortal man:
Children's meat to dogs denied;
In old types foresignified;
In the manna from the skies,
  In Isaac, and the Paschal Lamb.

Jesu, Shepherd of the sheep!
Thy true flock in safety keep.
Living Bread! Thy life supply;
Strengthen us or else we die;
  Fill us with celestial grace;
Thou, who feedest us below!
Source of all we have or know!
Grant that with Thy Saints above,
*Sitting at the feast of love,
  We may see Thee face to face.

[TR. REV. E. CASWALL]

* *For last two lines of this verse, repeat music from* ✱.

THE BLESSED SACRAMENT.

81

THE BLESSED SACRAMENT.

Adoro Te devote, latens Deitas.

THEE prostrate I adore, the Deity that lies
Beneath these humble veils concealed from human eyes;
My heart doth wholly yield, subjected to Thy sway,
For contemplating Thee it wholly faints away.
Hail, Jesus, hail; do Thou, good Shepherd of the sheep,
Increase in all true hearts the faith they fondly keep.

The sight, the touch, the taste, in Thee are here deceived;
But by the ear alone this truth is safe believed;
I hold whate'er the Son of God hath said to me;
Than this blest word of truth no word can truer be.
Hail, Jesus, hail, &c.

Upon the cross Thy Godhead only was concealed;
But here Thy manhood too doth lie as deeply veiled;
And yet, in both these truths confessing my belief,
I pray as prayed to Thee the poor repentant thief.
Hail, Jesus, hail, &c.

I see not with mine eyes Thy wounds, as Thomas saw;
Yet own Thee for my God with equal love and awe;
Oh grant me, that my faith may ever firmer be,
That all my hope and love may still repose in Thee.
Hail, Jesus, hail, &c.

Memorial sweet, that shows the death of my dear Lord;
Thou living bread, that life dost unto man afford;
O grant, that this my soul may ever live on Thee,
That Thou mayst evermore its only sweetness be.
Hail, Jesus, hail, &c.

O mystic pelican, Jesu, my loving Lord,
Cleanse me of my defilements in Thy blood adored,
Whereof one only drop, in Thy sweet mercy spilt,
Would have the power to cleanse the world of all its guilt.
Hail, Jesus, hail, &c.

O Jesu, lying here concealed before mine eye,
I pray Thou grant me that for which I ceaseless sigh,
To see the vision clear of Thine unveilèd face,
Blest with the glories bright that fill Thy dwelling-place.
Hail, Jesus, hail; do Thou, good Shepherd of the sheep,
Increase in all true hearts the faith they fondly keep.

[ST. THOMAS AQUINAS. TR. REV. J. D. AYLWARD, O.P.]

THE BLESSED SACRAMENT.

82

JESUS, gentlest Saviour!
God of might and power!
Thou Thyself art dwelling
In us at this hour.

Nature cannot hold Thee,
Heaven is all too strait
For Thine endless glory
And Thy royal state.

Out beyond the shining
Of the furthest star,
Thou art ever stretching
Infinitely far.

Yet the hearts of children
Hold what worlds cannot,
And the God of wonders
Loves the lowly spot.

As men to their gardens
Go to seek sweet flowers,
In our hearts dear Jesus
Seeks them at all hours.

Jesus, gentlest Saviour!
Thou art in us now;
Fill us full of goodness
Till our hearts o'erflow.

Pray the prayer within us
That to heaven shall rise;
Sing the song that angels
Sing above the skies.

Multiply our graces,
Chiefly love and fear,
Ah, dear Lord! the chiefest—
Grace to persevere.

Oh, how can we thank Thee
For a gift like this—
Gift that truly maketh
Heaven's eternal bliss!

Ah! when wilt Thou always
Make our hearts Thy home?
We must wait for Heaven—
Then the day will come.

Now at least we'll keep Thee
All the time we may—
But Thy grace and blessing
We will keep alway.

When our hearts Thou leavest,
Worthless though they be,
Give them to Thy Mother
To be kept for Thee.

[REV. F. W. FABER]

THE SACRED HEART.

83

Summi Parentis filio.

OLD OFFICE OF THE SACRED HEART.

TO Christ, the Prince of Peace,
And Son of God most high,
The Father of the world to come,
Sing we with holy joy.

Deep in His Heart for us
The wound of love He bore;
That love wherewith He still inflames
The hearts that Him adore.

O Jesu! Victim blest!
What else but love divine,
Could Thee constrain to open thus
That sacred Heart of Thine?

O Fount of endless life!
O Spring of water clear!
O Flame celestial, cleansing all
Who unto Thee draw near!

Hide me in Thy dear Heart,
For thither do I fly;
There seek Thy grace through life, in death
Thine immortality.

Praise to the Father be,
And sole-begotten Son;
Praise, Holy Paraclete, to Thee,
While endless ages run.

[TR. REV. E. CASWALL]

THE SACRED HEART.

84 (First Tune.)

THE SACRED HEART.

Dem Herzen Jesu singe.

TO Jesus' Heart, all burning
With fervent love for men,
My heart with fondest yearning
Shall raise its joyful strain.
While ages course along,
Blest be with loudest song
The Sacred Heart of Jesus
By every heart and tongue!

O Heart, for me on fire
With love no man can speak,
My yet untold desire
God gives me for Thy sake.
While ages course along, &c.

Too true I have forsaken
Thy love by wilful sin;
Yet now let me be taken
Back by Thy grace again.
While ages course along, &c.

As Thou art meek and lowly,
And ever pure of heart,
So may my heart be wholly
Of Thine the counterpart.
While ages course along, &c.

O that to me were given
The pinions of a dove,
I'd speed aloft to Heaven,
My Jesus' love to prove.
While ages course along, &c.

When life away is flying,
And earth's false glare is done;
Still, Sacred Heart, in dying
I'll say I'm all Thine own.
While ages course along, &c.

[ALOYS SCHLOR. TR. REV. A. J. CHRISTIE, S.J.]

THE SACRED HEART.

84 (Second Tune.)

THE SACRED HEART.

Dem Herzen Jesu singe.

TO Jesus' Heart, all burning
  With fervent love for men,
My heart with fondest yearning
  Shall raise its joyful strain.
    While ages course along,
      Blest be with loudest song
    The Sacred Heart of Jesus
      By every heart and tongue!

O Heart, for me on fire
  With love no man can speak,
My yet untold desire
  God gives me for Thy sake.
    While ages course along, &c.

Too true I have forsaken
  Thy love by wilful sin;
Yet now let me be taken
  Back by Thy grace again.
    While ages course along, &c.

As Thou art meek and lowly,
  And ever pure of heart,
So may my heart be wholly
  Of Thine the counterpart.
    While ages course along, &c.

O that to me were given
  The pinions of a dove,
I'd speed aloft to Heaven,
  My Jesus' love to prove.
    While ages course along, &c.

When life away is flying,
  And earth's false glare is done;
Still, Sacred Heart, in dying
  I'll say I'm all Thine own.
    While ages course along, &c.

[ALOYS SCHLÖR. TR. REV. A. J. CHRISTIE, S.J.]

THE SACRED HEART.

85

Auctor beate sæculi.

THE SACRED HEART, VESPERS.

JESU, Creator of the world!
Of all mankind Redeemer blest!
True God of God! in whom we see
The Father's Image clear express'd!

Thee, Saviour, love alone constrain'd
To make our mortal flesh Thine own;
And as a second Adam come,
For the first Adam to atone.

That selfsame love, which made the sky,
Which made the sea, and stars, and earth,
Took pity on our misery,
And broke the bondage of our birth.

O Jesu! in Thy Heart divine
May that same love for ever glow;
For ever mercy to mankind
From that exhaustless fountain flow.

For this, Thy Sacred Heart was pierced,
And both with blood and water ran;
To cleanse us from the stains of guilt,
And be the hope and strength of man.

To God the Father, and the Son,
All praise, and power, and glory be;
With Thee, O Spirit Paraclete,
All through the long eternity.

[TR. REV. E. CASWALL]

THE SACRED HEART.

86

O SACRED Heart!
Our home lies deep in Thee.
On earth Thou art an exile's rest,
In heaven the glory of the blest,
O Sacred Heart!

O Sacred Heart!
Thou fount of contrite tears,
Wherc'er those living waters flow,
New life to sinners they bestow,
O Sacred Heart!

O Sacred Heart!
Bless our dear native land.
May England's sons to truth e'er stand,
With faith's bright banner still in hand,
O Sacred Heart!

O Sacred Heart!
Our trust is all in Thee;
For though earth's night be dark and drear,
Thou breathest rest where Thou art near,
O Sacred Heart!

O Sacred Heart!
When shades of death shall fall,
Receive us 'neath Thy gentle care,
And save us from the tempter's snare:
O Sacred Heart!

O Sacred Heart!
Lead exiled children home,
Where we may ever rest near Thee,
In peace and joy eternally,
O Sacred Heart!

[REV. F. STANFIELD]

THE SACRED HEART.

87

THE SACRED HEART.

O SACRED Heart! all blissful light of Heaven,
  Rapture of Angels, beaming ever bright,—
Ravishing joys, in rich and radiant splendour,
  Flow from Thy glory in torrents of delight.

O Sacred Heart! O hope of sinner's sorrow,
  Rest of the weary, careworn, and depressed;
Sweetly lead home earth's lone estrangèd exiles,
  Where 'neath Thy love we may lie down and rest.

O Sacred Heart! Thy light is softly rising
  O'er the dark night of England's cheerless gloom;
Bright dawns the day of Faith's undying glory,
  Sweetly Thou seekest a loved but long-lost home.

O Sacred Heart! as strain of softest rapture,
  Sweet falls the music of that voice so blest:
"Come unto Me, all ye who mourn and labour,
  Come heavy laden, and I will give you rest."

O Sacred Heart! when shades of death are falling,
  Gather Thy children 'neath the wings of love;
Hush us to rest in Thine own gentle mercy,
  Bear troubled spirits to brighter realms above.

O Sacred Heart! what bliss, what thrilling rapture
  E'er to rest near Thee on Thine own bright shore;
Ever to gaze upon Thy beaming splendour,
  Never to part—to weep, to mourn no more.

[REV. F. STANFIELD]

THE SACRED HEART.

88

Cor Jesu, Cor purissimum.

O HEART of Jesus, purest Heart,
Altar of holiness Thou art,
Cleanse Thou my heart, so sordid, cold,
And stained by sins so manifold.

Take from me, Lord, this tepid will,
Which doth Thy Heart with loathing fill;
And then infuse a spirit new—
A fervent spirit, deep and true.

Most humble Heart of all that beat,
Heart full of goodness, meek and sweet,
Give me a heart more like to Thine,
And light the flame of love in mine.

But, ah, were e'en my heart on fire
With all the seraphim's desire,
Till love a conflagration proved,
Not yet would'st Thou enough be loved.

That therefore Thou may'st worthily
Be loved, O loving Lord, by me,
That love which in Thy Heart doth burn
Give me to love Thee in return.

May this Thy love's most fiery dart
Strike deep and set on fire my heart,
And in that burning may it be
Dissolved and all-consumed in Thee.

Death to be sought with yearnings high,
Thus from love's violence to die;
Ah, may my heart love's victim prove
For the Redeemer's Heart of love.

So let me die for love of Thee,
O Heart, all full of love for me,
That with a new heart's virgin-hoard
I may begin to love Thee, Lord.

[TR. REV. M. RUSSELL, S.J.]

THE SACRED HEART.

89

O HEART of Jesus, Heart of God,
  O source of boundless love,
By angels praised, by saints adored,
  From their bright thrones above.

The poorest, saddest heart on earth,
  May claim Thee for its own ;
O burning, throbbing Heart of Christ,
  Too late, too little known.

The very sound of those sweet words,
  "The Sacred Heart," can give,
To the most lone and burthened soul,
  Strength to endure and live.

A mother may forget her child,
  A father prove untrue ;
A brother or a sister turn
  Unkind and thankless too.

The hearts of men are often hard
  And full of selfish care ;
But in the Sacred Heart we find
  A refuge from despair.

To Thee, my Jesus, then I come,
  A poor and helpless child ;
And on Thine own words, "Come to Me,"
  My only hope I build.

The world is cold, and life is sad,
  I crave the blessèd rest
Of those who lay their weary heads
  Upon Thy sacred breast.

For love is stronger far than death,
  And who can love like Thee,
My Saviour, whose appealing Heart
  Broke on the cross for me ?

The purest, deepest, earthly love,
  What is it, Lord, to Thine ?
A single drop from a great fount,
  Eternal and divine.

[LADY G. FULLERTON]

THE SACRED HEART.

90

Sto prigione entro quel Core.

I DWELL a captive in this Heart,
  Inflamed with love divine;
'Tis here I live alone in peace,
  And constant joy is mine.

It is the Heart of God's own Son
  In His humanity,
Who, all enamour'd of my soul,
  Here burns with love of me.

Here like the dove within the ark
  Securely I repose;
Since now the Lord is my defence,
  I fear no earthly foes.

What though I suffer, still in love
  I ever true will be;
My love of God shall deeper grow
  When crosses fall on me.

From every bond of earth, O Lord,
  Thy grace hath set me free;
My soul, deliver'd from the snare,
  Enjoys true liberty.

Nought more can I desire than this,
  To see Thy face in Heaven;
And this I hope since He on earth
  His Heart in pledge hath given.

[ST. ALPHONSUS. TR. REV. E. VAUGHAN, C.SS.R.]

THE SACRED HEART.

91

A MESSAGE from the Sacred Heart :
  What may its message be ?
"My child, My child, give Me thy heart—
  My Heart has bled for thee."
This is the message Jesus sends
  To my poor heart to-day,
And eager from His throne He bends
  To hear what I shall say.

A message to the Sacred Heart ;
  Oh, bear it back with speed :
"Come, Jesus, reign within my heart—
  Thy Heart is all I need."
Thus, Lord, I'll pray until I share
  That home whose joy Thou art :
No message, dearest Jesus, there—
  For heart will speak to heart.

[REV. M. RUSSELL, S.J.]

THE SACRED HEART.

92

HEART of Jesus! golden chalice
  Brimming with the ruddy Wine,
Trodden in the press of fury,
  Purest juice of truest vine,
From the Vineyards of Engeddi,
  Quench this thirsty heart of mine!

Heart of Jesus! Rose of Sharon
  Glistening with the dew of tears,
All among the thorny prickles
  Lo! Thy blood-stained Head appears!
Spread Thy fragrance all around us,
  Sweetly lulling all our fears!

Heart of Jesus! Comb of honey
  From the cleft of Calvary's rock,
Sweetness coming from the Strong One,
  Dripping from the greenwood stock;
Famishing of death is on us;
  Feed, oh, feed Thy hungry flock!

Heart of Jesus! broken Vial
  Full of precious spikenard!
Alabaster vase of ointment!
  See, our souls are sore and hard:
Let Thy healing virtue touch them,
  And from sin's corruption guard!

[BISHOP CASARTELLI]

THE SACRED HEART.

93

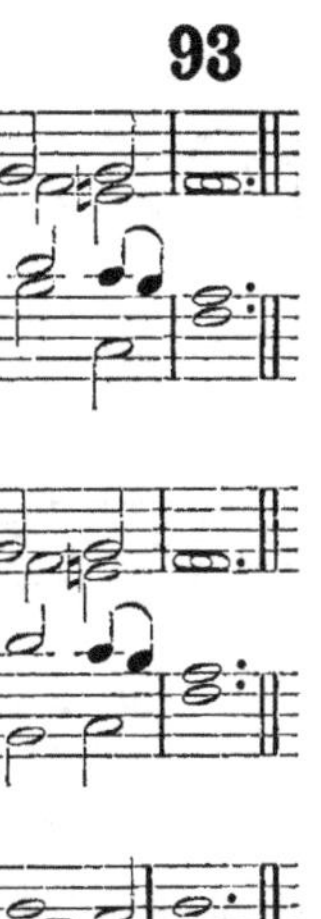

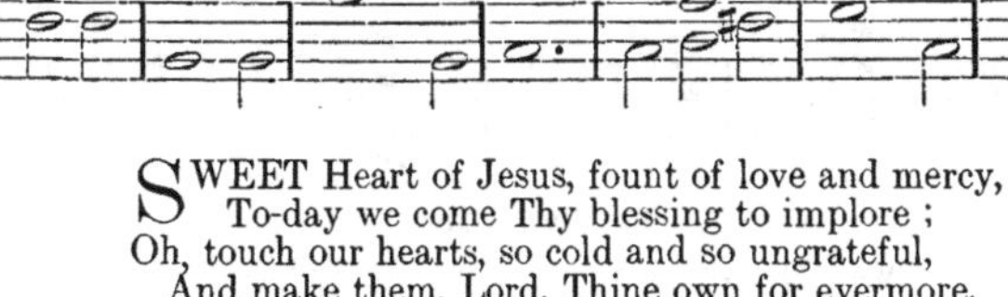

SWEET Heart of Jesus, fount of love and mercy,
To-day we come Thy blessing to implore ;
Oh, touch our hearts, so cold and so ungrateful,
And make them, Lord, Thine own for evermore.
Sweet Heart of Jesus ! we implore,
Oh, make us love Thee more and more.

Sweet Heart of Jesus ! make us know and love Thee,
Unfold to us the treasures of Thy grace,
That so our hearts, from things of earth uplifted,
May long alone to gaze upon Thy Face.
Sweet Heart of Jesus, &c.

Sweet Heart of Jesus ! make us pure and gentle,
And teach us how to do Thy blessèd will ;
To follow close the print of Thy dear footsteps,
And when we fall—Sweet Heart, oh, love us still.
Sweet Heart of Jesus, &c.

Sweet Heart of Jesus ! bless all hearts that love Thee,
And may Thine own Heart ever blessèd be,
Bless us, dear Lord, and bless the friends we cherish,
And keep us true to Mary and to Thee.
Sweet Heart of Jesus, &c.

THE PRECIOUS BLOOD.

94

Viva! Viva! Gesù.

HAIL, Jesus, hail! who for my sake
Sweet blood from Mary's veins didst [take
And shed it all for me;
Oh, blessèd be my Saviour's Blood,
My light, my life, my only good,
To all eternity.

To endless ages let us praise
The Precious Blood, whose price could raise
The world from wrath and sin;
Whose streams our inward thirst appease
And heal the sinner's worst disease,
If he but bathe therein.

Oh, sweetest Blood, that can implore
Pardon of God, and Heaven restore,
The Heaven which sin had lost;
While Abel's blood for vengeance pleads,
What Jesus shed still intercedes
For those who wrong Him most.

Oh, to be sprinkled from the wells
Of Christ's own sacred Blood, excels
Earth's best and highest bliss;
The ministers of wrath divine
Hurt not the happy hearts that shine
With those red drops of His!

Ah! there is joy amid the saints,
And hell's despairing courage faints
When this sweet song we raise:
Oh, louder then, and louder still,
Earth with one mighty chorus fill,
The Precious Blood to praise!

[TR. REV. F. W. FABER]

N.B.—Repeat third and last lines of each verse.

THE PRECIOUS BLOOD.

95

Viva! Viva! Gesù.

GLORY be to Jesus,
  Who in bitter pains
Pour'd for me the life-blood
  From His sacred veins!

Grace and life eternal
  In that Blood I find;
Blest be His compassion,
  Infinitely kind!

Blest through endless ages
  Be the precious stream,
Which from endless torment
  Doth the world redeem!

There the fainting spirit
  Drinks of life her fill;
There as in a fountain
  Leaves herself at will.

Oh, the Blood of Christ!
  It soothes the Father's ire;
Opes the gate of Heaven;
  Quells eternal fire.

Abel's blood for vengeance
  Pleaded to the skies;
But the Blood of Jesus
  For our pardon cries.

Oft as it is sprinkled
  On our guilty hearts,
Satan in confusion
  Terror-struck departs.

Oft as earth exulting
  Wafts its praise on high,
Hell with horror trembles;
  Heav'n is fill'd with joy.

Lift ye, then, your voices;
  Swell the mighty flood;
Louder still and louder,
  Praise the Precious Blood.

[TR. REV. E. CASWALL]

THE PRECIOUS BLOOD.

96 *Slowly.*

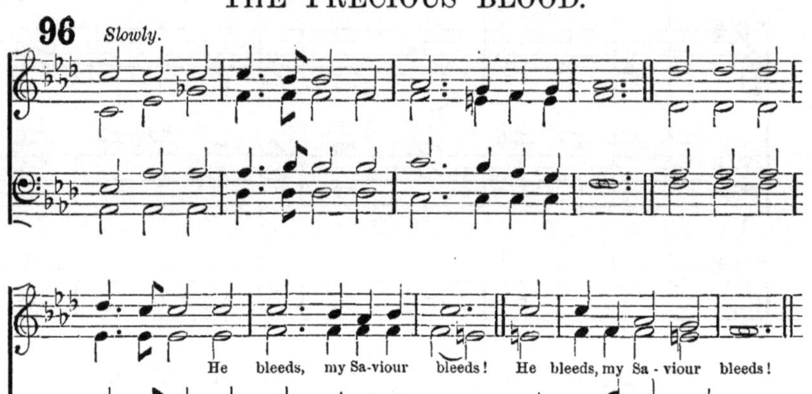

BLOOD is the price of Heaven;
  All sin that price exceeds;
Oh come to be forgiven,—
    He bleeds,
  My Saviour bleeds!

Under the olive boughs,
  Falling like ruby beads,
The Blood drops from His brows,
    He bleeds,
  My Saviour bleeds!

While the fierce scourges fall,
  The Precious Blood still pleads:
In front of Pilate's hall
    He bleeds,
  My Saviour bleeds!

Beneath the thorny crown
  The crimson fountain speeds;
See how it trickles down,—
    He bleeds,
  My Saviour bleeds!

Bearing the fatal wood
  His band of saints He leads,
Marking the way with Blood;
    He bleeds,
  My Saviour bleeds!

On Calvary His shame
  With Blood still intercedes;
His open Wounds proclaim—
    He bleeds,
  My Saviour bleeds!

He hangs upon the tree,
  Hangs there for my misdeeds,
He sheds His Blood for me;
    He bleeds,
  My Saviour bleeds!

His Blood is flowing still;
  My thirsty soul it feeds;
He lets me drink my fill;
    He bleeds,
  My Saviour bleeds!

[REV. F. W. FABER]

97

Salvete Christi vulnera.

THE PRECIOUS BLOOD, LAUDS.

HAIL, wounds! which through eternal
 The love of Jesus show; [years
Hail, wounds! from whence unfailing streams
 Of grace and glory flow.

More precious than the gems of Ind,
 Than all the stars more fair;
Nor honeycomb, nor fragrant rose,
 Can once with you compare.

Through you is open'd to our souls
 A refuge safe and calm,
Whither no raging enemy
 Can reach to work us harm.

What countless stripes did Christ receive
 Naked in Pilate's hall!
From His torn flesh how red a shower
 Did all around Him fall!

How doth th' ensanguined thorny crown
 That beauteous brow transpierce!
How do the nails those hands and feet
 Contract with tortures fierce!

He bows His head, and forth at last
 His loving spirit soars;
Yet even after death His heart
 For us its tribute pours.

Beneath the winepress of God's wrath
 His Blood for us He drains;
Till for Himself, oh, wondrous love!
 No single drop remains.

Oh, come, all ye on whom abide
 The deadly stains of sin!
Come! wash in this encrimson'd tide,
 And ye shall be made clean.

Praise Him, who with the Father sits
 Enthroned upon the skies;
Whose Blood redeems our souls from guilt,
 Whose Spirit sanctifies.

[TR. REV. E. CASWALL]

THE SACRED WOUNDS.

98

THERE is an everlasting home
 Where contrite souls may hide,
Where death and danger dare not come—
 The Saviour's side.

It was a cleft of matchless love
 Opened when He had died;
When mercy hailed in worlds above,
 That wounded side.

Hail, Rock of Ages, pierced for me,
 The grave of all my pride;
Hope, peace and heaven are all in Thee,
 Thy sheltering side.

There issued forth a double flood,
 The sin-atoning tide,
In streams of water and of blood
 From that dear side.

There is the only fount of bliss,
 In joy and sorrow tried;
No refuge for the heart like this—
 A Saviour's side.

Thither the Church, through all her days
 Points as a faithful guide;
And celebrates with ceaseless praise
 That spear-pierced side.

There is the golden gate of heaven,
 An entrance for the Bride,
Where the sweet crown of life is given
 Through Jesus' side.

[M. BRIDGES]

THE SACRED WOUNDS.

99

Cor arca legem continens.

SACRED HEART, LAUDS.

ARK of the Covenant! not that
  Whence bondage came of old;
But that of pure forgiving grace
  And mercies manifold.

Thou Veil of awful mystery!
  Thou Sanctuary sublime!
Thou sacred Temple, holier far
  Than that of olden time!

Blest Heart of Christ! in Thy dear wound
  The hidden depth we see,
Of what were else unguess'd by us,—
  His boundless charity.

Beneath this emblem of pure love,
  'Twas Love Himself that died,
And offer'd up Himself for us,
  A Victim crucified.

Oh, who of His redeem'd will Him
  Their mutual love refuse?
Who would not rather in that Heart
  Their home eternal choose?

To God the Father, with the Son,
  And, Holy Ghost, to Thee,
Be honour, glory, virtue, power,
  Through all eternity.

[TR. REV. E. CASWALL]

THE BLESSED VIRGIN.

100 (First Tune.)

N.B.—The above tune is a corrupted version of a fine melody ("Maria zu lieben"). The tune in its proper form will be found set to Hymn 106.

THE BLESSED VIRGIN.

Omni die dic Mariæ.

DAILY, daily, sing to Mary,
Sing, my soul, her praises due;
All her feasts, her actions worship,
With the heart's devotion true.
Lost in wond'ring contemplation
Be her majesty confest:
Call her mother, call her Virgin,
Happy Mother, Virgin blest.

She is mighty to deliver;
Call her, trust her lovingly:
When the tempest rages round thee,
She will calm the troubled sea.
Gifts of Heaven she has given,
Noble Lady! to our race:
She, the Queen, who decks her subjects
With the light of God's own grace.

Sing, my tongue, the Virgin's trophies,
Who for us her Maker bore;
For the curse of old inflicted,
Peace and blessing to restore.
Sing in songs of praise unending,
Sing the world's majestic Queen.
Weary not nor faint in telling
All the gifts she gives to men.

All my senses, heart, affections,
Strive to sound her glory forth:
Spread abroad the sweet memorials
Of the Virgin's priceless worth.
Where the voice of music thrilling,
Where the tongue of eloquence,
That can utter hymns beseeming
All her matchless excellence?

All our joys do flow from Mary,
All then join her praise to sing;
Trembling sing the Virgin Mother,
Mother of our Lord and King.
While we sing her awful glory,
Far above our fancy's reach,
Let our hearts be quick to offer
Love the heart alone can teach.

[ST. CASIMIR. TR. REV. F. W. FABER]

THE BLESSED VIRGIN.

100 (Second Tune.)

THE BLESSED VIRGIN.

Omni die dic Mariæ.

DAILY, daily, sing to Mary,
  Sing, my soul, her praises due;
All her feasts, her actions worship,
  With the heart's devotion true.
    Lost in wond'ring contemplation
      Be her majesty confest:
    Call her mother, call her Virgin,
      Happy Mother, Virgin blest.

She is mighty to deliver;
  Call her, trust her lovingly:
When the tempest rages round thee,
  She will calm the troubled sea.
    Gifts of Heaven she has given,
      Noble Lady! to our race:
    She, the Queen, who decks her subjects
      With the light of God's own grace.

Sing, my tongue, the Virgin's trophies,
  Who for us her Maker bore;
For the curse of old inflicted,
  Peace and blessing to restore.
    Sing in songs of praise unending,
      Sing the world's majestic Queen.
    Weary not nor faint in telling
      All the gifts she gives to men.

All my senses, heart, affections,
  Strive to sound her glory forth:
Spread abroad the sweet memorials
  Of the Virgin's priceless worth.
    Where the voice of music thrilling,
      Where the tongue of eloquence,
    That can utter hymns beseeming
      All her matchless excellence?

All our joys do flow from Mary,
  All then join her praise to sing;
Trembling sing the Virgin Mother,
  Mother of our Lord and King.
    While we sing her awful glory,
      Far above our fancy's reach,
    Let our hearts be quick to offer
      Love the heart alone can teach.

[ST. CASIMIR. TR. REV. F. W. FABER]

THE BLESSED VIRGIN.

101 (First Tune.)

Salve Regina.

Antiphon, B.V.M.

HAIL, Queen of Heav'n, the ocean Star!
Guide of the wand'rer here below!
Thrown on life's surge, we claim thy care—
Save us from peril and from woe.
Mother of Christ, Star of the sea,
Pray for the wanderer, pray for me.

O gentle, chaste, and spotless Maid,
We sinners make our prayers through thee;
Remind thy Son that He has paid
The price of our iniquity.
Virgin most pure, Star of the sea,
Pray for the sinner, pray for me.

Sojourners in this vale of tears,
To thee, blest advocate, we cry;
Pity our sorrows, calm our fears,
And soothe with hope our misery.
Refuge in grief, Star of the sea,
Pray for the mourner, pray for me.

And while to Him who reigns above,
In Godhead One, in Persons Three,
The Source of life, of grace, of love,
Homage we pay on bended knee;
Do thou, bright Queen, Star of the sea,
Pray for thy children, pray for me.

[Dr. Lingard]

THE BLESSED VIRGIN.

(SECOND TUNE.) **101**

Salve Regina.

ANTIPHON, B.V.M.

HAIL, Queen of Heav'n, the ocean Star!
Guide of the wand'rer here below!
Thrown on life's surge, we claim thy care—
Save us from peril and from woe.
Mother of Christ, Star of the sea,
Pray for the wanderer, pray for me.

O gentle, chaste, and spotless Maid,
We sinners make our prayers through thee;
Remind thy Son that He has paid
The price of our iniquity.
Virgin most pure, Star of the sea,
Pray for the sinner, pray for me.

Sojourners in this vale of tears,
To thee, blest advocate, we cry;
Pity our sorrows, calm our fears,
And soothe with hope our misery.
Refuge in grief, Star of the sea,
Pray for the mourner, pray for me.

And while to Him who reigns above,
In Godhead One, in Persons Three,
The Source of life, of grace, of love,
Homage we pay on bended knee;
Do thou, bright Queen, Star of the sea,
Pray for thy children, pray for me.

[DR. LINGARD]

THE BLESSED VIRGIN.

102 (First Tune.)

MOTHER of Mercy! day by day
  My love of thee grows more and more;
Thy gifts are strewn upon my way,
  Like sands upon the great sea-shore.

Though poverty and work and woe
  The masters of my life may be,
When times are worst, who does not know
  Darkness is light with love of thee?

But scornful men have coldly said
  Thy love was leading me from God;
And yet in this I did but tread
  The very path my Saviour trod.

They know but little of thy worth
  Who speak these heartless words to me;
For what did Jesus love on earth
  One half so tenderly as thee?

Get me the grace to love thee more;
  Jesus will give if thou wilt plead;
And, Mother! when life's cares are o'er,
  Oh, I shall love thee then indeed!

Jesus, when His three hours were run,
  Bequeath'd thee from the cross to me,
And oh! how can I love thy Son,
  Sweet Mother! if I love not thee?

[REV. F. W. FABER]

N.B.—Last line of words repeated.

(SECOND TUNE.) **102**

MOTHER of Mercy! day by day
  My love of thee grows more and more;
Thy gifts are strewn upon my way,
  Like sands upon the great sea-shore.

Though poverty and work and woe
  The masters of my life may be,
When times are worst, who does not know
  Darkness is light with love of thee?

But scornful men have coldly said
  Thy love was leading me from God;
And yet in this I did but tread
  The very path my Saviour trod.

They know but little of thy worth
  Who speak these heartless words to me;
For what did Jesus love on earth
  One half so tenderly as thee?

Get me the grace to love thee more;
  Jesus will give if thou wilt plead;
And, Mother! when life's cares are o'er,
  Oh, I shall love thee then indeed!

Jesus, when His three hours were run,
  Bequeath'd thee from the cross to me,
And oh! how can I love thy Son,
  Sweet Mother! if I love not thee?

[REV. F. W. FABER]

103

Dal tuo celeste.

LOOK down, O Mother Mary,
  From thy bright throne above ;
Cast down upon thy children
  One only glance of love ;
And if a heart so tender
  With pity flows not o'er,
Then turn away, O Mother,
  And look on us no more.

See how, ungrateful sinners,
  We stand before thy Son ;
His loving heart upbraids us
  The evil we have done.
But if thou wilt appease Him,
  Speak for us but one word ;
For thus thou canst obtain us
  The pardon of our Lord.

O Mary, dearest Mother,
  If thou wouldst have us live,
Say that we are thy children,
  And Jesus will forgive.
Our sins make us unworthy
  That title still to bear,
But thou art still our Mother ;
  Then show a Mother's care.

Unfold to us thy mantle,
  There stay we without fear ;
What evil can befall us
  If, Mother, thou art near ?
O kindest, dearest Mother,
  Thy sinful children save ;
Look down on us with pity,
  Who thy protection crave.

[ST. ALPHONSUS. TR. REV. E. VAUGHAN, C.SS.R.]

N.B.—Repeat first four lines of Hymn after each verse.

104

Pulchra tota sine nota.

HOLY Queen! we bend before thee,
  Queen of purity divine!
Make us love thee, we implore thee,
  Make us truly to be thine.

Thou by faith the gates unfolding
  Of the kingdom in the skies,
Hast to us, by faith beholding,
  Shown the land of Paradise.

Thou, when deepest night infernal
  Had for ages shrouded man,
Gavest us that light eternal,
  Promised since the world began.

God in thee hath shower'd plenty
  On the hungry and the weak;
Sending back the mighty empty,
  Setting up on high the meek.

Thine the province to deliver
  Souls that deep in bondage lie;
Thine to crush, and crush for ever,
  Life-destroying heresy.

Thine to show that earthly pleasures,
  All the world's enchanting bloom,
Are outrivall'd by the treasures
  Of the glorious world to come.

Teach, O teach us, Holy Mother!
  How to conquer every sin;
How to love and help each other;
  How the prize of life to win.

Thou, to whom a Child was given
  Greater than the sons of men,
Coming down from highest Heaven
  To create the world again.

Oh, by that Almighty Maker,
  Whom thyself a Virgin bore!
Oh, by thy supreme Creator,
  Link'd with thee for evermore!

By the hope thy name inspires:
  By our doom reversed through thee!
Help us, Queen of Angel-choirs!
  To a blest eternity!

[ST. CASIMIR. TR. REV. E. VAUGHAN, C.SS.R.]

THE BLESSED VIRGIN.

105 (First Tune.)

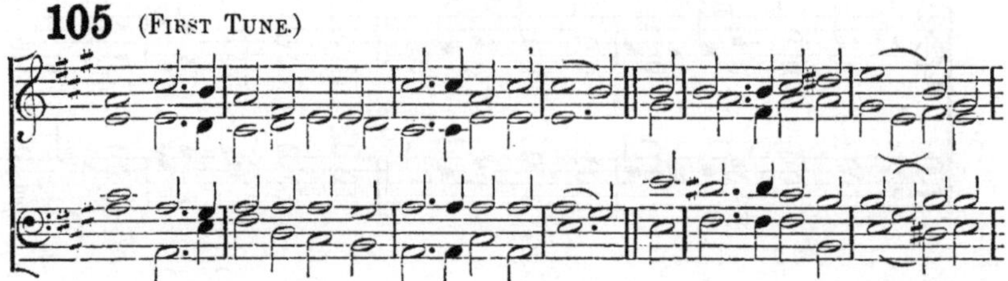

SING, sing, ye Angel Bands,
All beautiful and bright;
For higher still and higher,
Through fields of starry light,
Mary, your Queen, ascends,
Like the sweet moon at night.

Oh, happy angels! look,
How beautiful she is!
See! Jesus bears her up,
Her hand is locked in His;
Oh, who can tell the height
Of that fair Mother's bliss?

And shall I lose thee then,
Lose my sweet right to thee?
Ah! no—the angels' Queen
Man's Mother still will be,
And thou, upon thy throne,
Wilt keep thy love for me.

On—through the countless stars
Proceeds the bright array;
And Love Divine comes forth
To light her on her way,
Through the short gloom of night
Into celestial day.

Hark! hark! through highest Heaven
What sounds of mystic mirth!
Mary by God proclaimed
Queen of Immaculate Birth,
And diademed with stars,
The lowliest of the earth!

See! see! the Eternal Hands
Put on her radiant crown,
And the sweet Majesty
Of Mercy sitteth down,
For ever and for ever,
On her predestined throne.

[REV. F. W. FABER]

THE BLESSED VIRGIN.

(Second Tune.) **105**

Sing, sing, ye Angel Bands,
  All beautiful and bright;
For higher still and higher,
  Through fields of starry light,
Mary, your Queen, ascends,
  Like the sweet moon at night.

Oh, happy angels! look,
  How beautiful she is!
See! Jesus bears her up,
  Her hand is locked in His;
Oh, who can tell the height
  Of that fair Mother's bliss?

And shall I lose thee then,
  Lose my sweet right to thee?
Ah! no—the angels' Queen
  Man's Mother still will be,
And thou, upon thy throne,
  Wilt keep thy love for me.

On—through the countless stars
  Proceeds the bright array;
And Love Divine comes forth
  To light her on her way,
Through the short gloom of night
  Into celestial day.

Hark! hark! through highest Heaven
  What sounds of mystic mirth!
Mary by God proclaimed
  Queen of Immaculate Birth,
And diademed with stars,
  The lowliest of the earth!

See! see! the Eternal Hands
  Put on her radiant crown,
And the sweet Majesty
  Of Mercy sitteth down,
For ever and for ever,
  On her predestined throne.

[Rev. F. W. Faber]

THE BLESSED VIRGIN.

106 (First Tune.)

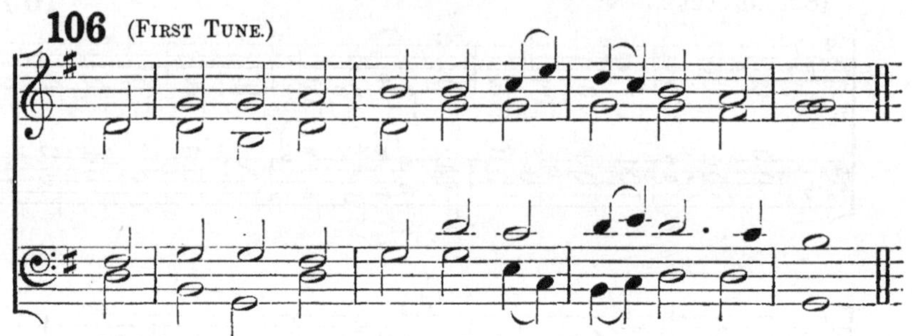

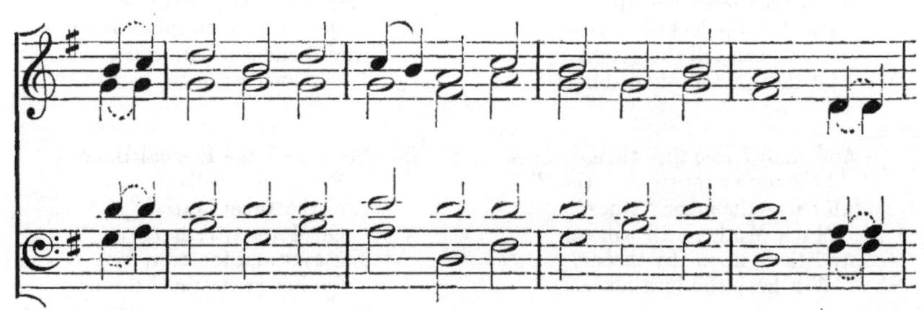

THE BLESSED VIRGIN.

N.B.—This is the original tune, of which a corrupt version is popularly sung to "Daily, daily, sing to Mary."

O PUREST of creatures! sweet Mother! sweet Maid!
The one spotless womb wherein Jesus was laid!
Dark night hath come down on us, Mother! and we
Look out for thy shining, sweet Star of the Sea!

Deep night hath come down on this rough-spoken world,
And the banners of darkness are boldly unfurled:
And the tempest-tost Church—all her eyes are on thee,
They look to thy shining, sweet Star of the Sea!

He gazed on thy soul; it was spotless and fair;
For the empire of sin—it had never been there;
None had e'er owned thee, dear Mother, but He,
And He blessed thy clear shining, sweet Star of the Sea!

Earth gave Him one lodging; 'twas deep in thy breast,
And God found a home where the sinner finds rest;
His home and His hiding-place, both were in thee;
He was won by thy shining, sweet Star of the Sea!

Oh, blissful and calm was the wonderful rest
That thou gavest thy God in thy virginal breast;
For the heaven He left He found heaven in thee,
And He shone in thy shining, sweet Star of the Sea!

[REV. F. W. FABER]

THE BLESSED VIRGIN.

106 (Second Tune.)

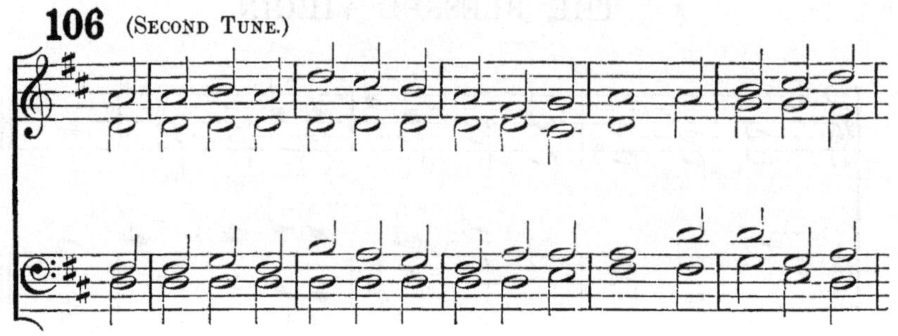

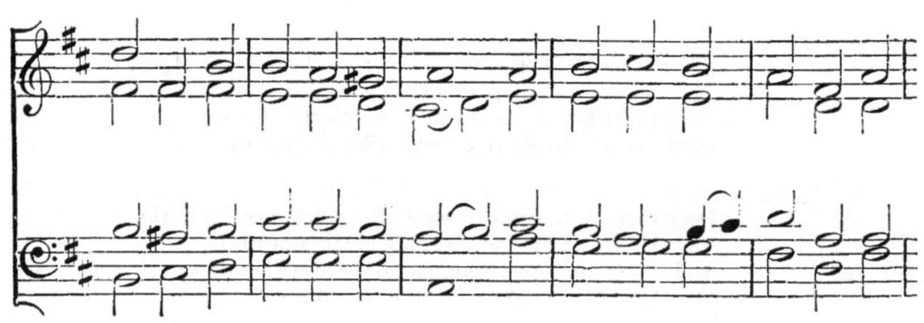

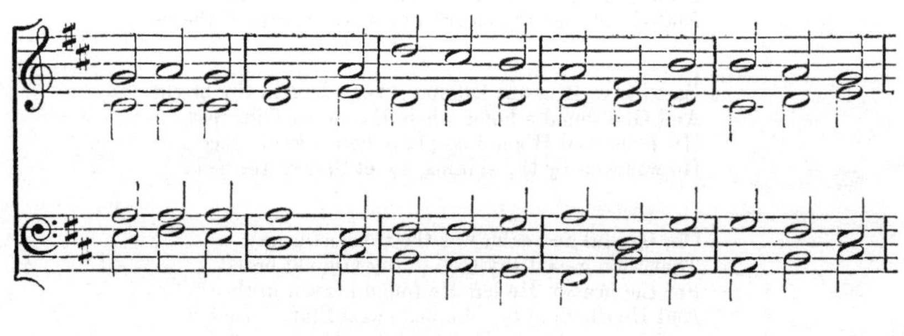

THE BLESSED VIRGIN.

O PUREST of creatures! sweet Mother! sweet Maid!
The one spotless womb wherein Jesus was laid!
Dark night hath come down on us, Mother! and we
Look out for thy shining, sweet Star of the Sea!

Deep night hath come down on this rough-spoken world,
And the banners of darkness are boldly unfurled:
And the tempest-tost Church—all her eyes are on thee,
They look to thy shining, sweet Star of the Sea!

He gazed on thy soul; it was spotless and fair;
For the empire of sin—it had never been there;
None had e'er owned thee, dear Mother, but He,
And He blessed thy clear shining, sweet Star of the Sea!

Earth gave Him one lodging; 'twas deep in thy breast,
And God found a home where the sinner finds rest;
His home and His hiding-place, both were in thee;
He was won by thy shining, sweet Star of the Sea!

Oh, blissful and calm was the wonderful rest
That thou gavest thy God in thy virginal breast;
For the heaven He left He found heaven in thee,
And He shone in thy shining, sweet Star of the Sea!

[REV. F. W. FABER]

N.B.—Repeat last line of each verse.

THE BLESSED VIRGIN.

107 (First Tune.)

HAIL Mary, Pearl of Grace,
Pure flower of Adam's race,
And vessel rare of God's election ;
Unstained as virgin snow,
Serene as sunset glow—
We sinners crave thy sure protection.

Thou Queen of high estate,
Conceived immaculate
To form Incarnate Love's pure dwelling ;
The Spirit found His rest
Within thy sinless breast,
And thence flow joys beyond all telling.

A fairer, purer Eve,
Didst thou her fall retrieve,
For man's debt giving God in payment :
Thy spotless feet are pressed
Upon the serpent's crest—
God's stars thy crown, His sun thy raiment.

Through His dear blood who died,
By sinners crucified,
Art thou preserved, and we forgiven,
Help us to conquer sin,
That we may enter in,
Through thee, the golden gate, to Heaven.

[Dom Bede Camm, O.S.B.]

THE BLESSED VIRGIN.

(SECOND TUNE.) **107**

HAIL Mary, Pearl of Grace,
Pure flower of Adam's race,
And vessel rare of God's election ;
Unstained as virgin snow,
Serene as sunset glow—
We sinners crave thy sure protection.

Thou Queen of high estate,
Conceived immaculate
To form Incarnate Love's pure dwelling ;
The Spirit found His rest
Within thy sinless breast,
And hence flow joys beyond all telling.

A fairer, purer Eve,
Didst thou her fall retrieve,
For man's debt giving God in payment :
Thy spotless feet are pressed
Upon the serpent's crest—
God's stars thy crown, His sun thy raiment.

Through His dear blood who died,
By sinners crucified,
Art thou preserved, and we forgiven,
Help us to conquer sin,
That we may enter in,
Through thee, the golden gate, to Heaven.

[DOM BEDE CAMM, O.S.B.]

THE BLESSED VIRGIN.

108

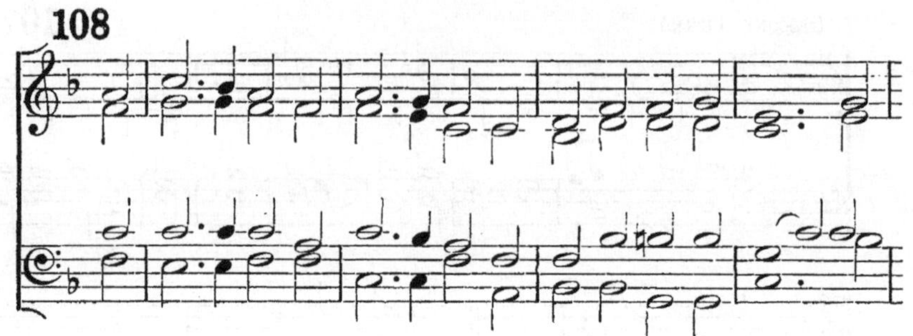

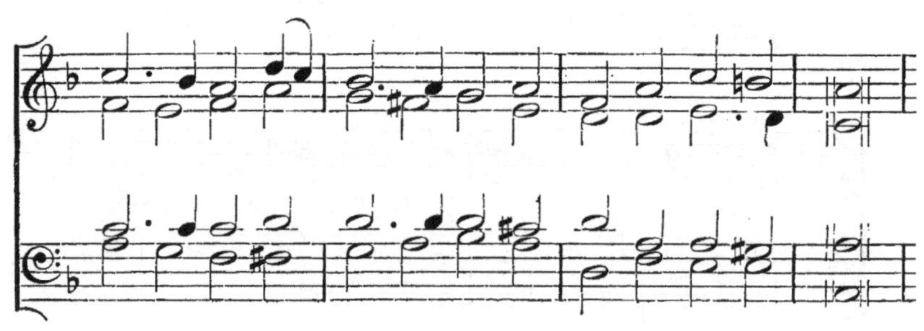

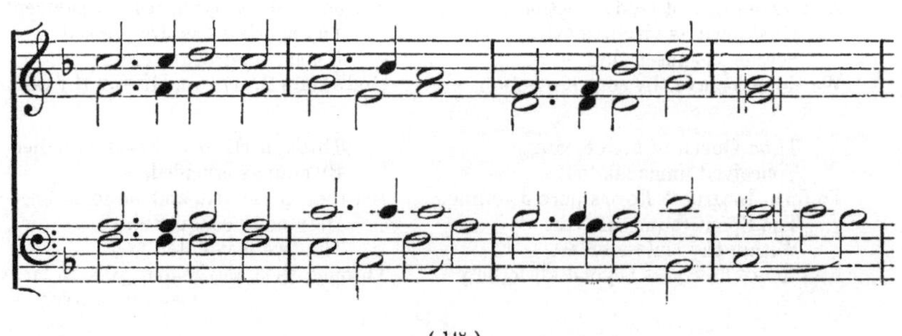

THE BLESSED VIRGIN.

Sei pura sei pia.

O MOTHER blest, whom God bestows
  On sinners and on just,
What joy, what hope thou givest those
  Who in thy mercy trust!
    Thou art clement, thou art chaste,
      Mary, thou art fair;
    Of all mothers sweetest, best;
      None with thee compare.

O heavenly Mother, Mistress sweet!
  It never yet was told
That suppliant sinner left thy feet
  Unpitied, unconsoled.
      Thou art clement, &c.

O Mother pitiful and mild,
  Cease not to pray for me;
For I do love thee as a child,
  And sigh for love of thee.
      Thou art clement, &c.

Most powerful Mother, all men know
  Thy Son denies thee nought;
Thou askest, wishest it, and, lo!
  His power thy will has wrought.
      Thou art clement, &c.

O Mother blest, for me obtain,
  Ungrateful though I be,
To love that God who first could deign
  To show such love to me.
      Thou art clement, &c.

[ST. ALPHONSUS. TR. REV. E. VAUGHAN C.SS.R.]

THE BLESSED VIRGIN.

109

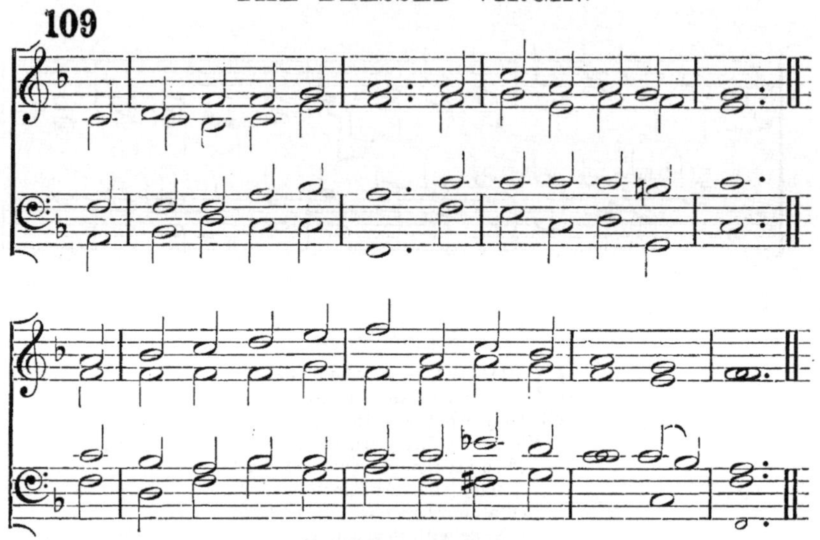

Ave maris stella.

Vespers, B.V.M.

HAIL, thou resplendent star,
  Which shinest o'er the main;
Blest Mother of our God,
  And ever Virgin Queen.

Hail, happy gate of bliss,
  Greeted by Gabriel's tongue;
Negotiate our peace,
  And cancel Eva's wrong.

Loosen the sinner's bands,
  All evils drive away;
Bring light unto the blind,
  And for all graces pray.

Exert the mother's care,
  And thus thy children own:
To Him convey our prayer,
  Who chose to be thy Son.

O pure, O spotless Maid,
  Whose meekness all surpass'd,
Our lusts and passions quell,
  And make us mild and chaste.

Preserve us pure and chaste,
  Through life our safety be,
Till Jesu's sight be given,
  And endless bliss with thee.

Praise to the Father be,
  With Christ His only Son,
And to the Holy Ghost,
  Thrice blessèd Three in One.

[ANON: IN "A SELECTION OF CATHOLIC HYMNS," GLASGOW, 1867]

THE BLESSED VIRGIN.

Vespers, B.V.M.

Ave maris stella.

HAIL, thou Star of ocean!
Portal of the sky!
Ever Virgin Mother
Of the Lord most High!
Oh! by Gabriel's Ave,
Utter'd long ago,
Eva's name reversing,
Stablish peace below.

Break the captive's fetters;
Light on blindness pour;
All our ills expelling,
Every bliss implore.

Show thyself a Mother;
Offer Him our sighs,
Who for us Incarnate
Did not thee despise.

Virgin of all Virgins!
To thy shelter take us;
Gentlest of the gentle!
Chaste and gentle make us.
Still as on we journey,
Help our weak endeavour;
Till with thee and Jesus
We rejoice for ever.

Through the highest Heaven,
To the Almighty Three,
Father, Son, and Spirit,
One same glory be.

[Tr. Rev. E. Caswall]

THE BLESSED VIRGIN.

110 (Second Tune.)

Ave maris stella.

Vespers, B.V.M.

HAIL, thou Star of ocean!
  Portal of the sky!
Ever Virgin Mother
  Of the Lord most High!

Oh! by Gabriel's Ave,
  Utter'd long ago,
Eva's name reversing,
  Stablish peace below.

Break the captive's fetters;
  Light on blindness pour;
All our ills expelling,
  Every bliss implore.

Show thyself a Mother;
  Offer Him our sighs,
Who for us Incarnate
  Did not thee despise.

Virgin of all Virgins!
  To thy shelter take us;
Gentlest of the gentle!
  Chaste and gentle make us.

Still as on we journey,
  Help our weak endeavour;
Till with thee and Jesus
  We rejoice for ever.

Through the highest Heaven,
  To the Almighty Three,
Father, Son, and Spirit,
  One same glory be.

[TR. REV. E. CASWALL]

111

O gloriosa virginum.

Lauds, B.V.M.

O GLORIOUS Maid, enthroned on high,
Above the lights that deck the sky!
O Maid, at whose maternal breast
Thy infant Maker fed, caressed.

Thy Blessèd Seed restores us all
We lost by Eve's unhappy fall,
And bids the gates of Heaven again
Receive the weeping souls of men.

The Great King's Gate art thou, and bright
Abode of everlasting Light:
Ye ransomed nations, hail to Heaven
Our Life-Spring through a Virgin given.

To God the Father, God the Son,
Of Mary born, be homage done;
The like to God the Spirit be;
Eternal Godhead, One in Three.

[Tr. Rev. Francis Trappes]

THE BLESSED VIRGIN.

112 (First Tune.)

THE BLESSED VIRGIN.

I'LL sing a hymn to Mary,
  The Mother of my God,
The Virgin of all virgins,
  Of David's royal blood.
O teach me, holy Mary,
  A loving song to frame,
When wicked men blaspheme thee,
  To love and bless thy name.

O Lily of the Valley,
  O Mystic Rose, what tree,
Or flower, e'en the fairest,
  Is half so fair as thee?
O let me, though so lowly,
  Recite my Mother's fame;
When wicked men blaspheme thee,
  I'll love and bless thy name.

O noble Tower of David,
  Of gold and ivory,
The Ark of God's own promise,
  The gate of Heav'n to me.
To live and not to love thee
  Would fill my soul with shame;
When wicked men blaspheme thee,
  I'll love and bless thy name.

When troubles dark afflict me,
  In sorrow and in care,
Thy light doth ever guide me,
  O beauteous Morning Star.
So I'll be ever ready,
  Thy goodly help to claim,
When wicked men blaspheme thee,
  To love and bless thy name.

The Saints are high in glory,
  With golden crowns so bright;
But brighter far is Mary,
  Upon her throne of light.
Oh, that which God did give thee,
  Let mortal ne'er disclaim;
When wicked men blaspheme thee,
  I'll love and bless thy name

But in the crown of Mary
  There lies a wondrous gem,
As Queen of all the Angels,
  Which Mary shares with them.
"No sin hath e'er defiled thee,"
  So doth our faith proclaim;
When wicked men blaspheme thee,
  I'll love and bless thy name.

And now, O Virgin Mary,
  My Mother and my Queen,
I've sung thy praise—so bless me,
  And keep my heart from sin.
When others jeer and mock thee,
  I'll often think how I,
To shield my Mother Mary,
  Would lay me down and die.

[REV. FR. WYSE]

THE BLESSED VIRGIN.

112 (SECOND TUNE.)

THE BLESSED VIRGIN.

I'LL sing a hymn to Mary,
  The Mother of my God,
The Virgin of all virgins,
  Of David's royal blood.
O teach me, holy Mary,
  A loving song to frame,
When wicked men blaspheme thee,
  To love and bless thy name.

O Lily of the Valley,
  O Mystic Rose, what tree,
Or flower, e'en the fairest,
  Is half so fair as thee?
O let me, though so lowly,
  Recite my Mother's fame;
When wicked men blaspheme thee,
  I'll love and bless thy name.

O noble Tower of David,
  Of gold and ivory,
The Ark of God's own promise,
  The gate of Heav'n to me.
To live and not to love thee
  Would fill my soul with shame;
When wicked men blaspheme thee,
  I'll love and bless thy name.

When troubles dark afflict me,
  In sorrow and in care,
Thy light doth ever guide me,
  O beauteous Morning Star.
So I'll be ever ready,
  Thy goodly help to claim,
When wicked men blaspheme thee,
  I'll love and bless thy name.

The Saints are high in glory,
  With golden crowns so bright;
But brighter far is Mary,
  Upon her throne of light.
Oh, that which God did give thee,
  Let mortal n'er disclaim;
When wicked men blaspheme thee,
  I'll love and bless thy name.

But in the crown of Mary
  There lies a wondrous gem,
As Queen of all the Angels,
  Which Mary shares with them.
"No sin hath e'er defiled thee,"
  So doth our faith proclaim;
When wicked men blaspheme thee,
  I'll love and bless thy name.

And now, O Virgin Mary,
  My Mother and my Queen,
I've sung thy praise—so bless me,
  And keep my heart from sin.
When others jeer and mock thee,
  I'll often think how I,
To shield my Mother Mary,
  Would lay me down and die.

[REV. FR. WYSE]

THE BLESSED VIRGIN.

113

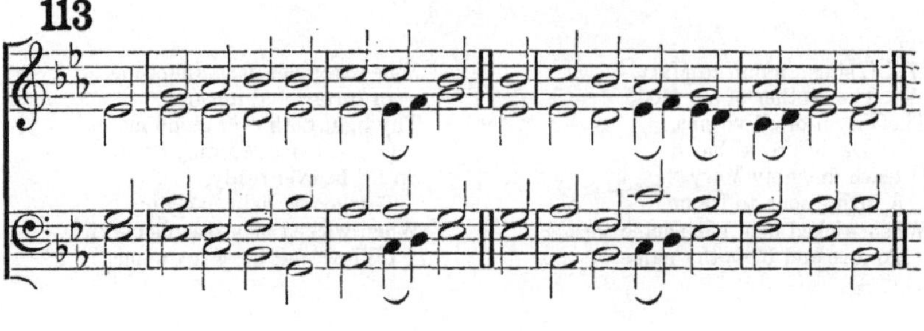

Quem terra, pontus, sidera.

MATINS, B.V.M.

THE Lord whom earth, and air, and sea,
With one adoring voice resound;
Who rules them all in majesty;
In Mary's heart a cloister found.

Lo! in a humble Virgin's womb,
O'ershadowed by Almighty power;
He whom the stars, and sun, and moon,
Each serve in their appointed hour.

O Mother blest! to whom was given
Within thy compass to contain
The Architect of earth and Heaven,
Whose hands the universe sustain:

To thee was sent an Angel down;
In thee the Spirit was enshrined:
From thee came forth that Mighty One,
The long-desired of all mankind.

O Jesu! born of Virgin bright,
Immortal glory be to Thee:
Praise to the Father infinite,
And Holy Ghost eternally.

[TR. REV. E. CASWALL]

114

Quis te canat mortalium?

THE ANNUNCIATION.

WHAT mortal tongue can sing thy praise,
Dear Mother of the Lord?
To Angels only it belongs
Thy glory to record.

Who born of man can penetrate
Thy soul's majestic shrine?
Who can thy mighty gifts unfold,
Or rightly them divine?

Say, Virgin, what sweet force was that,
Which from the Father's breast
Drew forth His co-eternal Son,
To be thy bosom's guest?

'Twas not thy guileless faith alone,
That lifted thee so high;
'Twas not thy pure seraphic love,
Or peerless chastity:

But, oh! it was thy lowliness,
Well pleasing to the Lord,
That made thee worthy to become
The Mother of the Word.

Oh, Loftiest!—whose humility
So sweet it was to see!
That God, forgetful of Himself,
Abased Himself to thee!

Praise to the Father, with the Son,
And Holy Ghost, through whom
The Word eternal was conceived
Within the Virgin's womb.

[TR. REV. E. CASWALL]

THE BLESSED VIRGIN.

115

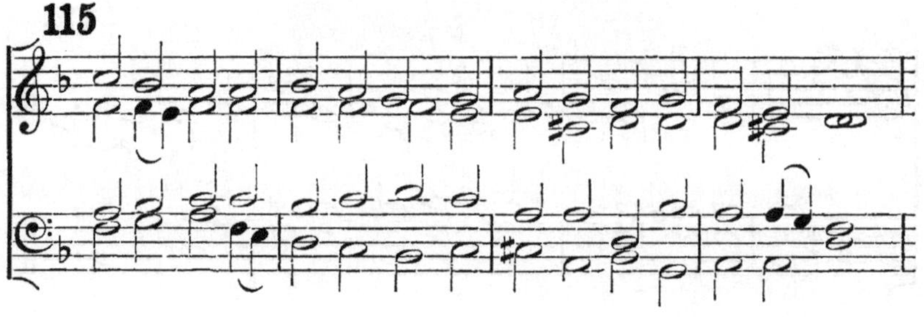

Quo sanctus ardor te rapit.

THE VISITATION.

WHITHER thus, in holy rapture,
  Royal maiden, art thou bent?
Why so fleetly art thou speeding
  Up the mountain's rough ascent?

Fill'd with the eternal Godhead!
  Glowing with the Spirit's flame!
Love it is that bears thee onward,
  And supports thy tender frame.

Lo! thine aged cousin claims thee,
  Claims thy sympathy and care;
God her shame from her hath taken;
  He hath heard her fervent prayer.

Blessèd Mothers! joyful meeting!
  Thou in her, the hand of God,
She in thee, with lips inspired,
  Owns the Mother of her Lord.

As the sun his face concealing,
  In a cloud withdraws from sight,
So in Mary then lay hidden
  He who is the world's true light.

Honour, glory, virtue, merit,
  Be to Thee, O Virgin's Son!
With the Father and the Spirit,
  While eternal ages run.

[TR. REV. E. CASWALL]

116

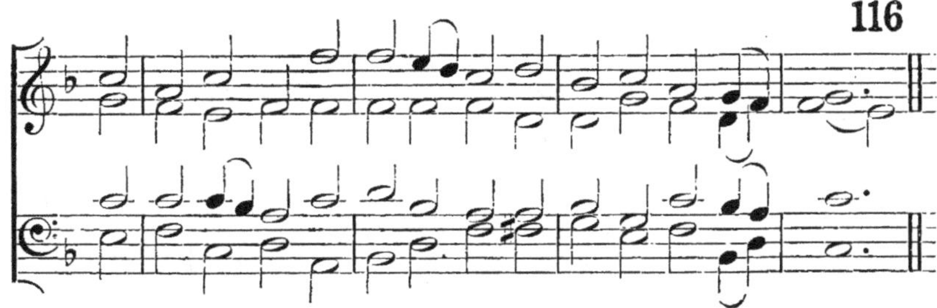

Templi sacratas pande.

THE PURIFICATION.

O SION ! open wide thy gates,
Let figures disappear ;
A Priest and Victim both in one,
The Truth Himself is here.

No more the simple flock shall bleed—
Behold the Father's Son
Himself to His own Altar comes
For sinners to atone.

Conscious of hidden Deity,
The lowly Virgin brings
Her new-born Babe with two young doves,
Her tender offerings.

The hoary Simeon sees at last
His Lord so long desired,
And hails, with Anna, Israel's hope
With sudden rapture fired.

But silent knelt the Mother blest
Of the yet silent Word :
And pondering all things in her heart,
With speechless praise adored.

Praise to the Father with the Son,
And Holy Spirit be ;
Praise to the blessèd Three in One,
Through all eternity.

[TR. REV. E. CASWALL]

THE BLESSED VIRGIN.

117

THE BLESSED VIRGIN.

O vos ætherei plaudite cives.

THE ASSUMPTION.

REJOICE, O ye Spirits and Angels on high!
This day the pure Mother of love
By death was set free; and ascending the sky,
Was welcomed by Jesus, with triumph and joy,
To the Courts of His glory above.

O Virgin divine! what treasures are thine!
What power and splendour untold!
With flesh thou hadst clothed the Lord of all might;—
He clothes thee in turn with His infinite light,
And a vesture of radiant gold.

He, who on thy breast found nurture and rest,
Is now thy ineffable Food;
And He, who from thee in the flesh lay conceal'd,
Now gives thee, beholding His glory reveal'd,
To drink from the fulness of God.

Through thy Virginal womb what graces have come!
What glories encompass thy throne!
Where next to thy Son, thou sittest a Queen,
Exalted on high, above Angels and men!
Inferior to Godhead alone!

Then hear us, we pray, on this blessèd day;
Remember we also are thine;
And deign for thy children with Jesus to plead,
That He may forgive us, and grant us in need
His strength and protection divine.

All praise to the Father, who chose for His Son
A mother, the daughter of Eve;
All praise to the glorious Child of her womb;
All praise to the infinite Spirit, by whom
Her glory it was to conceive!

[TR. REV. E. CASWALL]

THE BLESSED VIRGIN.

118

THE BLESSED VIRGIN

GREEN are the leaves, and sweet the flowers,
  And rich the hues of May;
We see them in the gardens round,
  And market-panniers gay:
And e'en among our streets, and lanes,
  And alleys, we descry,
By fitful gleams, the fair sunshine,
  The blue transparent sky.
    O Mother maid, be thou our aid,
      Now in the opening year;
    Lest sights of earth to sin give birth
      And bring the tempter near.

Green is the grass, but wait awhile,
  'Twill grow and then will wither;
The flow'rets, brightly as they smile,
  Shall perish altogether:
The merry sun, you sure would say,
  It ne'er could set in gloom;
But earth's best joys have all an end,
  And sin, a heavy doom.
    But Mother maid, thou dost not fade;
      With stars above thy brow,
    And the pale moon beneath thy feet,
      For ever throned art thou.

The green, green grass, the glittering grove,
  The heaven's majestic dome,
They image forth a tenderer bower,
  A more refulgent home;
They tell us of that Paradise
  Of everlasting rest,
And that high Tree, all flowers and fruit,
  The sweetest, yet the best.
    O Mary, pure and beautiful,
      Thou art the Queen of May:
    Our garlands wear about thy hair,
      And they will ne'er decay.

[CARDINAL NEWMAN]

THE BLESSED VIRGIN.

119

THE BLESSED VIRGIN.

THIS is the image of the Queen
  Who reigns in bliss above ;
Of her who is the hope of men,
  Whom men and angels love !
    Most holy Mary ! at thy feet
      I bend a suppliant knee ;
    In this thy own sweet month of May,
    Dear Mother of my God, I pray,
      Do thou remember me !

The homage offered at the feet
  Of Mary's image here
To Mary's self at once ascends
  Above the starry sphere.
    Most holy Mary ! at thy feet
      I bend a suppliant knee ;
    In all my joy, in all my pain,
    O Virgin born without a stain,
      Do thou remember me !

How fair soever be the form
  Which here your eyes behold,
Its beauty is by Mary's self
  Excell'd a thousandfold.
    Most holy Mary ! at thy feet
      I bend a suppliant knee ;
    In my temptations each and all,
    From Eve derived in Adam's fall
      Do thou remember me !

Sweet are the flow'rets we have cull'd,
  This image to adorn ;
But sweeter far is Mary's self,
  That rose without a thorn !
    Most holy Mary ! at thy feet
      I bend a suppliant knee :
    When on the bed of death I lie,
    By Him who did for sinners die,
      Do thou remember me.

O Lady, by the stars that make
  A glory round thy head ;
And by thy pure uplifted hands,
  That for thy children plead ;

O Lady, by that face divine
  Which angels joy to see ;
And by the deadly serpent's might,
  Subdued and crush'd by thee ;

And by thy robe of mystic hue,
  More azure than the skies :
And by those lips suffused with grace ;
  And by those pitying eyes ;

And by those freshly-gather'd flowers
  Here offered at thy feet ;
And by thy prayers that evermore
  Ascend as incense sweet ;—
    When at the Judgment-seat I stand,
      And my dread Saviour see ;
    When waves of night around me roll
    And Hell is raging for my soul ;
      Oh, then, remember me !

[REV. E. CASWALL]

THE BLESSED VIRGIN.

120

Lasciate O Vergine.

JOY of my heart! oh let me pay
To thee thine own sweet month of May.
Mary! one gift I beg of thee,
My soul from sin and sorrow free.
Direct my wandering feet aright,
And be thyself mine own true light.
Be love of thee the purging fire,
To cleanse for God my heart's desire.

Mother! be love of thee a ray
From Heaven, to show the heavenward way.
Mary, make haste thy child to win
From sin, and from the love of sin.
Mother of God! let my poor love
A mother's prayers and pity move.
O Mary, when I come to die.
Be thou, thy spouse, and Jesus nigh.

When mute before the Judge I stand,
My holy shield be Mary's hand.
O Mary! let no child of thine
In hell's eternal exile pine.
If time for penance still be mine,
Mother, the precious gift is thine.
Thou, Mary, art my hope and life,
The starlight of this earthly strife.

Oh, for my own and others' sin
Do thou, who canst, free pardon win.
To sinners all, to me the chief,
Send, Mother, send thy kind relief.
To thee our love and troth are given;
Pray for us, pray, bright Gate of Heaven.
Sweet Day-Star! let thy beauty be
A light to draw my soul to thee.

We love thee, light of sinners' eyes!
Oh, let thy prayer for sinners rise.
Look at us, Mother Mary! see
How piteously we look to thee.
I am thy slave, nor would I be
For worlds from this sweet bondage free.
O Jesus, Joseph, Mary, deign
My soul in heavenly ways to train.

Sweet stewardess of God, thy prayers
We beg, who are God's ransomed heirs.
O Virgin-born! O Flesh Divine!
Cleanse us, and make us wholly Thine.
Mary, dear Mistress of my heart,
What thou wouldst have me do, impart.
Thou, who wert pure as driven snow,
Make me as thou wert here below.

O Queen of Heaven! obtain for me
Thy glory there one day to see.
Oh, then and there, on that bright day,
To me thy womb's chaste Fruit display.
Mother of God! to me no less
Vouchsafe a mother's sweet caress.
Be love of thee, my whole life long,
A seal upon my wayward tongue.

Write on my heart's most secret core
The five dear Wounds that Jesus bore.
Oh give me tears to shed with thee
Beneath the cross on Calvary.
One more request, and I have done;—
With love of thee and thy dear Son,
More let me burn, and more each day,
Till love of self is burned away.

[REV. A. MUZZARELLI]

THE BLESSED VIRGIN.

121

OH, vision bright!
The land of light
Beams goldenly beyond the sky!
'Mid heavenly fires,
'Bove angel-choirs,
Mary, our Mother, reigns on high.

Oh, vision bright!
The Father's might
All round His daughter's throne doth lie ·
Where, in the balm
Of endless calm,
Mary, our Mother, reigns on high.

Oh, vision bright!
The eternal light
Of the dear Son may we descry;
Where, brighter far
Than moon or star,
Mary, our Mother, reigns on high.

Oh, vision bright!
Angels' delight!
The Mother sits with Jesus nigh:
Her form He bears,
Her look He wears;
Mary, our Mother, reigns on high.

Oh, vision bright!
Life's darkest night
Is fair as dawn when thou art nigh;
Where, 'mid the throng
Of psalm and song,
Mary, our Mother, reigns on high.

Oh, vision bright!
Oh, land of light!
Thou art our home beyond the sky:
'Tis grand to see
How gloriously
Mary, our Mother, reigns on high.

[REV. F. W. FABER]

122

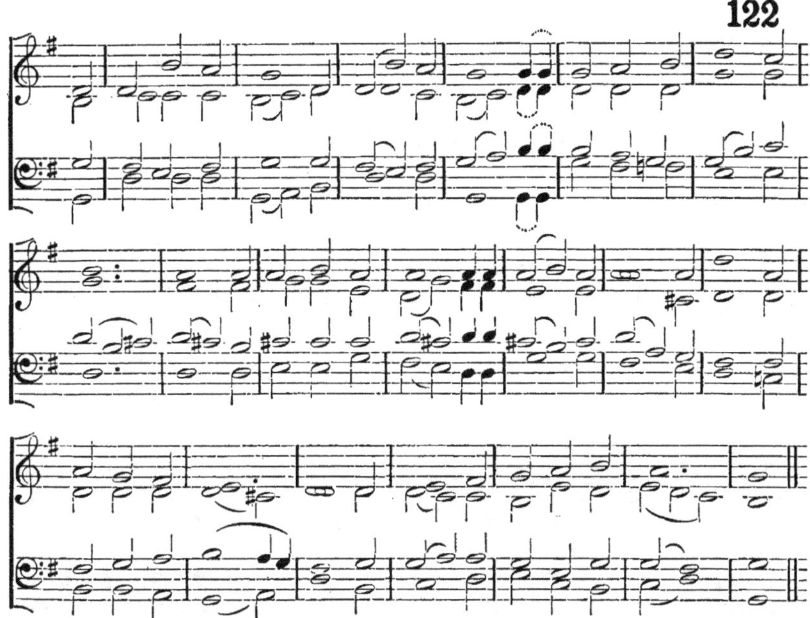

OH! balmy and bright as moonlit night,
Is the love of our Blessèd Mother;
It lies like a beam
Over life's cold stream,
And life knows not such another,
Oh, life knows not such another!

The month of May with a grace a day
Shines bright with our Blessèd Mother;
The angels on high
In the glorious sky,
Oh, they know not such another,
Nay, they know not such another!

The angels' Queen, the beautiful Queen,
Is the sinner's patient Mother;
With pardon and peace
And the soul's release,
Where shall we find such another?
Where shall we find such another?

O Mary's Heart, the Immaculate Heart,
The Heart of the Saviour's Mother!
All Heaven shows bright
In its clear, sweet light,
God hath not made such another,
God hath not made such another!

But Mary's love, her plentiful love,
Lives not in an earthly mother!
'Twill show us at last,
When the strife is past,
Our merciful God as our Brother,
Our merciful God as our Brother!

[REV. F. W. FABER]

THE BLESSED VIRGIN.

123

THE BLESSED VIRGIN.

O FLOWER of Grace! divinest Flower!
God's light thy life, God's love thy dower!
That all alone with virgin ray
Dost make in Heaven eternal May;
Sweet falls the peerless dignity
Of God's eternal choice on thee!
Mother dearest! Mother fairest!
Maiden purest! Maiden rarest!
Help of earth and joy of Heaven!
Love and praise to thee be given,
Blissful Mother! Blissful Maiden!

Choice Flower! that bloomest on the breast
Of Jesus, which is now thy rest,
As thine was once the chosen bed
Of His dear Heart and sacred Head:
O Mary! sweet it is to see
Thy Son's creation graced by thee!
Mother dearest! Mother fairest! &c.

O queenly Flower! enthroned above,
The trophy of Almighty love!
Ah me! how He hath hung thee round
With all love-tokens that abound,
With God's own light, beyond the reach
Of angel song or mortal speech!
Mother dearest! Mother fairest! &c.

O Flower of God! divinest Flower!
Elected from His inmost bower!
Where angels come not, there art thou;
A crown of glory on thy brow!
While far below, all bright and brave,
Their gleamy palms the ransomed wave.
Mother dearest! Mother fairest! &c.

Yet thou didst bloom on earth at first,
In meekness proved, in sorrow nursed;
And Heaven must own its debt to earth,
Sweet flower! for thy surpassing worth;
And angels, for their Queen's dear sake,
Our road to thee more smooth shall make.
Mother dearest! Mother fairest! &c.

O Mary! when we think of thee,
Our hearts grow light as light can be;
For thou hast felt as we have felt,
And thou hast knelt as we have knelt:
And so it is,—that utterly,
Mother of God! we trust in thee!
Mother dearest! Mother fairest! &c.

[REV. F. W. FABER]

THE BLESSED VIRGIN.

124

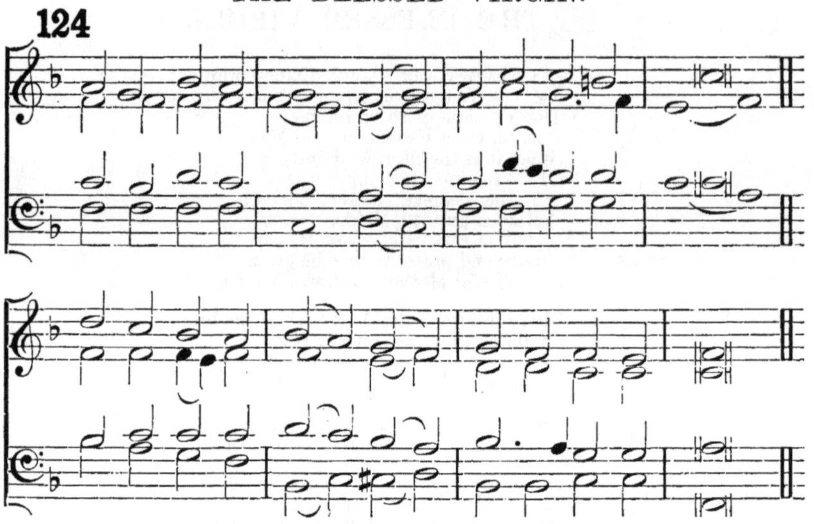

MARY ! dearest Mother !
  From thy heavenly height
Look on us, thy children,
  Lost in earth's dark night.

Mary ! purest creature !
  Keep us all from sin ;
Help us, erring mortals,
  Peace in Heaven to win.

Mary ! Queen and Mother !
  Get us still more grace,
With still greater fervour
  Now to run our race.

Daughter of the Father !
  Lady kind and sweet !
Lead us to our Father,
  Leave us at His Feet.

Mother of our Saviour,
  Joy of God above !
Jesus bade thee keep us
  In His fear and love.

Mary ! Spouse and servant
  Of the Holy Ghost !
Keep for Him His creatures
  Who would else be lost.

Holy Queen of angels !
  Bid thine angels come
To escort us safely
  To our heavenly home.

Bid the saints in Heaven
  Pray for us their prayers ;
They are thine, dear Mother !
  That thou may'st be theirs.

[REV. F. W. FABER]

125

MOTHER Mary! at thine altar
  We thy little daughters kneel;
With a faith that cannot falter,
  To thy goodness we appeal.
We are seeking for a mother
  O'er the earth so waste and wide,
And from off His cross our Brother
  Points to Mary by His side.

We have seen thy picture often
  With thy little Babe in arms,
And it ever seemed to soften
  All our sorrows with its charms;
So we want thee for our Mother,
  In thy gentle arms to rest,
And to share with Him our Brother
  That sweet pillow on thy breast.

We have none but thee to love us
  With a Mother's fondling care;
And our Father, God above us,
  Bids us fly for refuge there.
All the world is dark before us,
  We must out into its strife;
If thy fondness watch not o'er us,
  Oh how sad will be our life!

So we take thee for our Mother,
  And we claim our right to be,
By the gift of our dear Brother,
  Babes and daughters unto thee;
And the orphan's consecration
  Thou wilt surely not despise,
From thy bright and lofty station
  Close to Jesus in the skies.

Mother Mary! to thy keeping
  Soul and body we confide,
Toiling, resting, waking, sleeping,
  To be ever at thy side;
Cares that vex us, joys that please us,
  Life and death we trust to thee;
Thou must make them all for Jesus,
  And for all eternity!

[REV. F. W. FABER]

THE BLESSED VIRGIN.

126 (First Tune.)

THE BLESSED VIRGIN.

AVE Maria! O Maiden, O Mother,
Fondly thy children are calling on thee,
Thine are the graces unclaimed by another,
Sinless and beautiful Star of the Sea!
Mater Amabilis, ora pro nobis!
Pray for thy children who call upon thee;
Ave Sanctissima! Ave purissima!
Sinless and beautiful, Star of the Sea.

Ave Maria! the night shades are falling,
Softly our voices arise unto thee,
Earth's lonely exiles for succour are calling,
Sinless and beautiful, Star of the Sea!
Mater Amabilis, ora pro nobis! &c.

Ave Maria! thy children are kneeling,
Words of endearment are murmured to thee;
Softly thy spirit upon us is stealing,
Sinless and beautiful, Star of the Sea.
Mater Amabilis, ora pro nobis! &c.

Ave Maria! thou portal of Heaven,
Harbour of refuge, to thee do we flee;
Lost in the darkness, by stormy winds driven,
Shine on our pathway, fair Star of the Sea!
Mater Amabilis, ora pro nobis! &c.

[SISTER M.]

THE BLESSED VIRGIN.

126 (Second Tune.)

To be sung in unison.

THE BLESSED VIRGIN.

AVE Maria! O Maiden, O Mother,
Fondly thy children are calling on thee,
Thine are the graces unclaimed by another,
Sinless and beautiful Star of the Sea!
Mater Amabilis, ora pro nobis!
Pray for thy children who call upon thee;
Ave Sanctissima! Ave purissima!
Sinless and beautiful, Star of the Sea.

Ave Maria! the night shades are falling,
Softly our voices arise unto thee,
Earth's lonely exiles for succour are calling,
Sinless and beautiful, Star of the Sea!
Mater Amabilis, ora pro nobis! &c.

Ave Maria! thy children are kneeling,
Words of endearment are murmured to thee;
Softly thy spirit upon us is stealing,
Sinless and beautiful, Star of the Sea.
Mater Amabilis, ora pro nobis! &c.

Ave Maria! thou portal of Heaven,
Harbour of refuge, to thee do we flee;
Lost in the darkness, by stormy winds driven,
Shine on our pathway, fair Star of the Sea!
Mater Amabilis, ora pro nobis!

[SISTER M.]

N 2

THE BLESSED VIRGIN.

127

O MOTHER ! will it always be,
  That every passing year
Shall make thee seem more beautiful,
  Shall make thee grow more dear ?

And art thou really infinite,
  That thou shouldst thus unfold
Fresh glories every feast that comes,
  New grandeurs yet untold ?

We knew thee to be free from stain
  As is the sun's white beam ;
We knew God's Mother must be great
  Above what we could dream.

Yet now it seems we knew thee not ;
  Each feast-day we begin
To know thee in a truer way,
  And truer love to win.

O Mother ! thou art like the life
  The blessèd lead above,
Unchangeable, yet growing still
  In glory and in love.

Thou art, and yet art not, the same ;
  Old things pass not away ;
Yet thou to-morrow wilt be more
  Than the Mary of to-day.

How close to God, how full of God,
  Dear Mother, must thou be !
For still the more we know of God,
  The more we think of thee.

This is thy gift—oh give it us !—
  To make God better known :
Ah Mother ! make Him in our hearts
  More grand and more alone.

[REV. F. W. FABER]

128

O tendre Mère.

O TENDER Mother, Virgin fair,
As none appeal in vain to thee,
With contrite heart in humble prayer
Let this our homage grateful be.
Let this our homage grateful be.

For, when through years gone by we look,
And ponder deeds of mercy o'er,
We find inscribed in mem'ry's book
Of thy dear gifts a boundless store.
Let this our homage grateful be.

Oh, let no cloud this glory veil,
On which with beaming joy we gaze,
As then, may now our prayer avail,
Accept, oh, still accept our praise,*
Let this our homage grateful be.

* *N.B.—This line is repeated in the original. It is inadvisable to sing it so.*

THE BLESSED VIRGIN.

129

Memorare.

REMEMBER, holy Mary,
  'Twas never heard or known
That any one who sought thee
  And made to thee his moan—
That any one who hastened
  For shelter to thy care
Was ever yet abandoned
  And left to his despair.

And so to thee, my Mother,
  With filial faith I call,
For Jesus dying gave thee
  As Mother to us all.
To thee, O Queen of virgins,
  O Mother meek, to thee
I run with trustful fondness,
  Like child to mother's knee.

See at thy feet a sinner,
  Groaning and weeping sore—
Ah! throw thy mantle o'er me,
  And let me stray no more.
Thy Son has died to save me,
  And from His throne on high
His Heart this moment yearneth
  For even such as I.

All, all His love remember,
  And, oh! remember too
How prompt I am to purpose,
  How slow and frail to do.
Yet scorn not my petitions,
  But patiently give ear,
And help me, O my Mother,
  Most loving and most dear.

[ST. BERNARD. TR. REV. M. RUSSELL, S.J.

ALL SAINTS.

130

Placare, Christe, servulis.

VESPERS.

O CHRIST, Thy guilty people spare!
Lo, kneeling at Thy gracious throne,
Thy Virgin Mother pours her prayer,
Imploring pardon for her own.

Ye Angels, happy evermore!
Who in your circles nine ascend,
As ye have guarded us before,
So still from harm our steps defend.

Ye Prophets, and Apostles high!
Behold our penitential tears;
And plead for us when death is nigh,
And our all-searching Judge appears.

Ye Martyrs all! a purple band,
And Confessors, a white-robed train;
Oh, call us to our native land,
From this our exile, back again.

And ye, O choirs of Virgins chaste!
Receive us to your seats on high;
With Hermits whom the desert waste
Sent up of old into the sky.

Drive from the flock, O Spirits blest!
The false and faithless race away;
That all within one fold may rest,
Secure beneath one shepherd's sway.

To God the Father glory be,
And to His sole-begotten Son;
And glory, Holy Ghost, to Thee,
While everlasting ages run.

[TR. REV. E. CASWALL]

ALL SAINTS.

131

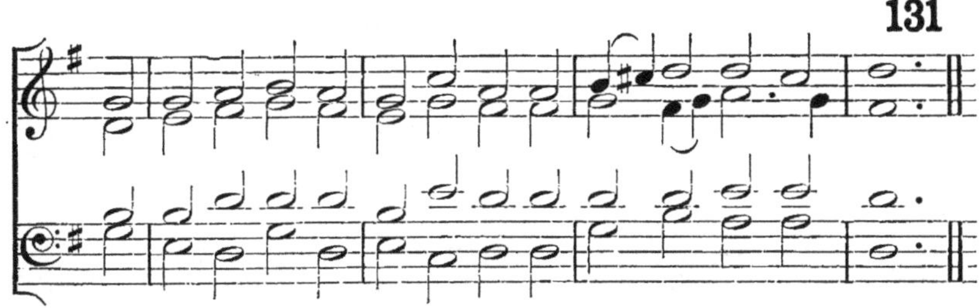

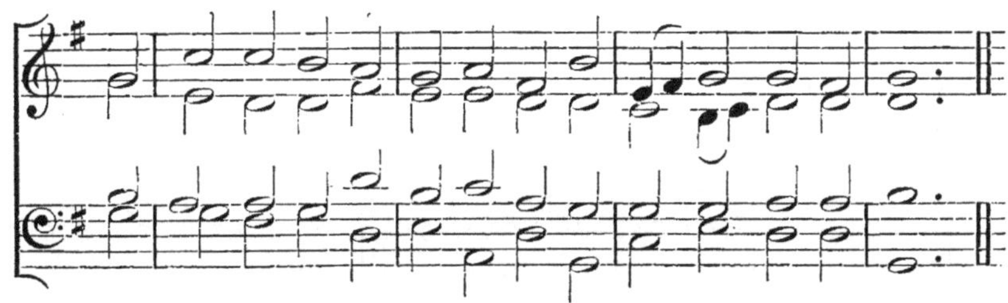

Salutis æternæ dator.

LAUDS.

GIVER of life, eternal Lord!
Thy own redeem'd defend;
Mother of Grace! thy children save,
And help them to the end.

Ye thousand thousand Angel Hosts!
Assist us in our need;
Ye Patriarchs! with the Prophet Choir!
For our forgiveness plead.

Forerunner blest! and thou who still
Dost Heaven's dread keys retain!
Ye glorious Apostles all!
Unloose our guilty chain.

Army of Martyrs! holy Priests
In beautiful array!
Ye happy troops of Virgins chaste!
Wash all our stains away.

All ye who high above the stars
In heavenly glory reign!
May we through your prevailing prayers
Unto your joys attain.

Praise, honour, to the Father be,
Praise to His only Son;
Praise, Holy Paraclete, to Thee,
While endless ages run.

[TR. REV. E. CASWALL]

ALL SOULS.

132

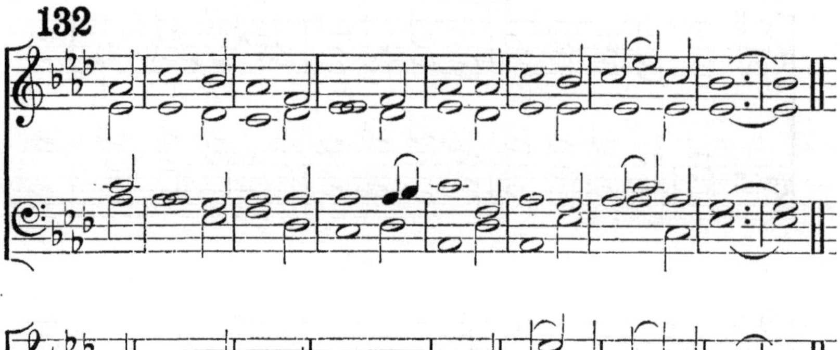

HELP, Lord, the souls which Thou hast
The souls to Thee so dear, [made,
In prison for the debt unpaid
Of sins committed here.

Those holy souls, they suffer on,
Resign'd in heart and will,
Until Thy high behest is done,
And justice has its fill.

For daily falls, for pardon'd crime,
They joy to undergo
The shadow of Thy cross sublime,
The remnant of Thy woe.

Help, Lord, the souls which Thou hast
The souls to Thee so dear, [made,
In prison for the debt unpaid
Of sins committed here.

Oh, by their patience of delay,
Their hope amid their pain,
Their sacred zeal to burn away
Disfigurement and stain;

Oh, by their fire of love, not less
In keenness than the flame;
Oh, by their very helplessness,
Oh, by Thy own great Name;

Good Jesu, help! sweet Jesu, aid
The souls to Thee most dear,
In prison for the debt unpaid
Of sins committed here.

[CARDINAL NEWMAN]

ALL SOULS.

133

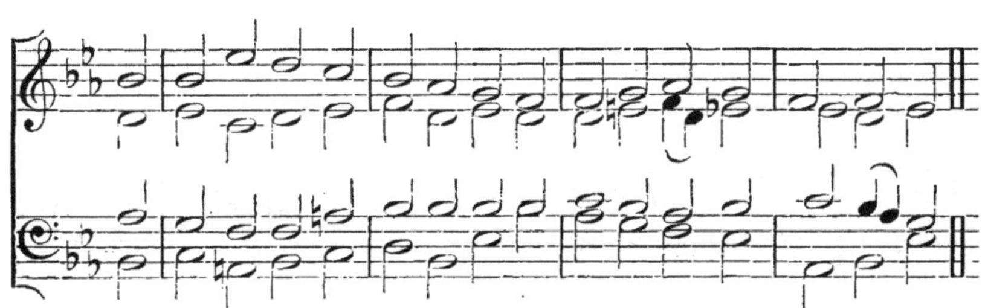

O TURN to Jesus, Mother! turn,
And call Him by His tenderest names;
Pray for the Holy Souls that burn
This hour amid the cleansing flames.

Ah! they have fought a gallant fight:
In death's cold arms they persevered;
And after life's uncheery night,
The arbour of their rest is neared.

In pains beyond all earthly pains,
Favourites of Jesus! there they lie
Letting the fire wear out their stains
And worshipping God's purity.

Spouses of Christ they are, for He
Was wedded to them by His Blood;
And angels o'er their destiny
In wondering adoration brood.

They are the children of thy tears:
Then hasten, Mother, to their aid;
In pity think each hour appears
An age while glory is delayed.

Ah me! the love of Jesus yearns
O'er the abyss of sacred pain,
And, as He looks, His bosom burns
With Calvary's dear thirst again.

O Mary; let thy Son no more
His lingering Spouses thus expect;
God's children to their God restore,
And to the Spirit His elect

[REV. F. W. FABER]

134

ALL SOULS.

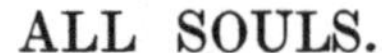

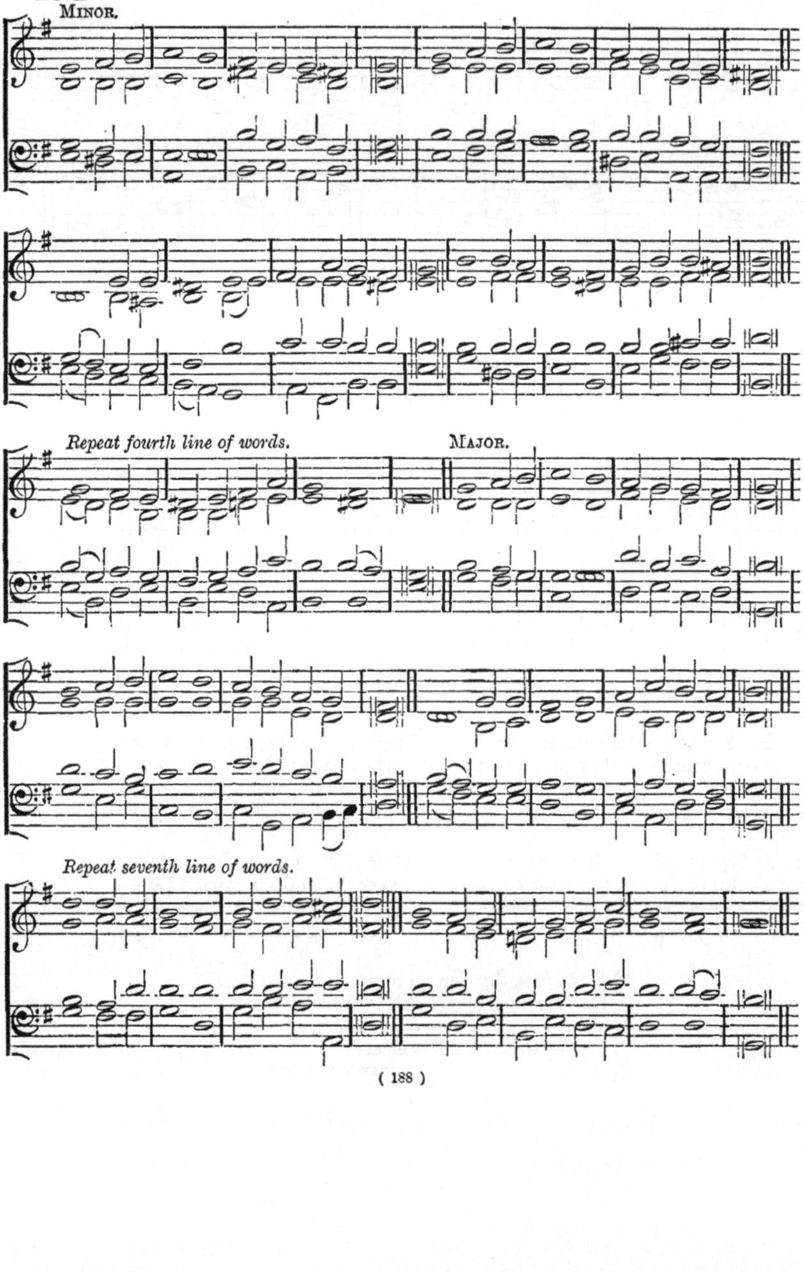
Minor.
Repeat fourth line of words.
Major.
Repeat seventh line of words.

ALL SOULS.

De profundis.

OUT of the depths to Thee, O Lord, I cry,
Lord! gracious turn Thine ear to suppliant sigh;
If sins of man Thou scannest, who may stand
That searching eye of Thine, and chastening hand?
Oh, hear our prayers and sighs, Redeemer blest,
And grant Thy holy souls eternal rest.
And let perpetual light upon them shine;
For though not spotless, still these souls are Thine.

To be appeased in wrath, dear Lord, is Thine;
Thou mercy with Thy justice canst combine;
Thy blood our countless stains can wash away;
This is Thy law, our hope and steadfast stay.
Oh, hear our prayers, &c.

Pledged is Thy word! however foul the sin,
Repentant sinner shall his pardon win;
Our souls shall ever hope, then, Lord, in Thee,
And ne'er despair, though great our crimes may be.
Oh, hear our prayers, &c.

There is no moment of the night or day,
Where sinner contrite may not trustful say,
There is forgiveness! so let Israel sing
An endless song of hope to Israel's King.
Oh, hear our prayers, &c.

For mercy dwells enthroned with God on high,
And spurns not suppliant tear or humble cry;
So countless are the treasures of His store,
He can a thousand worlds redeem, and more.
Oh, hear our prayers, &c.

This God Himself shall come from Heaven above,
The Christ! the God of mercy and of love!
He comes—He comes! the God Incarnate He!
And by His glorious death makes all men free!
Oh, hear our prayers, &c.

THE CHURCH.

135

THE CHURCH.

WHO is she that stands triumphant,
  Rock in strength, upon the Rock,
Like some city crowned with turrets,
  Braving storm and earthquake shock?
Who is she her arms extending,
  Blessing thus a world restored:
All the anthems of creation
  Lifting to creation's Lord?
    Hers the kingdom, hers the sceptre;
      Fall, ye nations, at her feet;
    Hers that Truth whose fruit is Freedom;
      Light her yoke, her burden sweet.

As the moon its splendour borrows
  From a sun unseen all night,
So from Christ, the Sun of Justice,
  Evermore she draws her light.
Touch'd by His, her hands have healing,
  Bread of Life, absolving Key:
Christ Incarnate is her Bridegroom,
  God is hers, His temple she.
    Hers the kingdom, &c.

Empires rise and sink like billows,
  Vanish, and are seen no more;
Glorious as the star of morning
  She o'erlooks the wild uproar.
Hers the Household all-embracing;
  Hers the Vine that shadows earth:
Blest thy children, mighty mother;
  Safe the stranger at thy hearth.
    Hers the kingdom, &c.

[AUBREY DE VERE]

THE CHURCH.

136

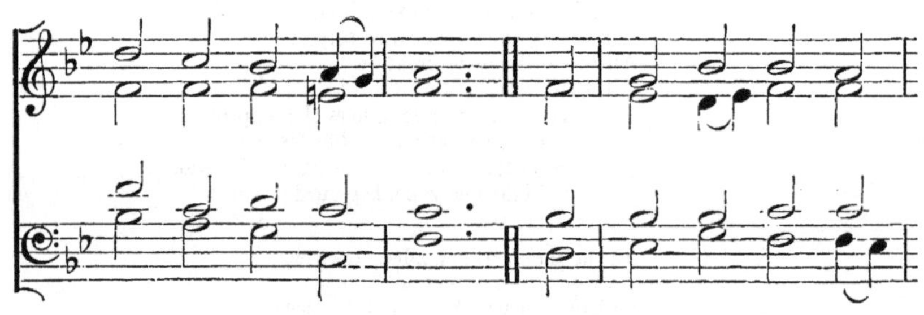

THE CHURCH.

O LORD! behold the suppliant band,
  That kneels before Thy throne;
Come back, come back, unto the land
  That once was all Thine own.

By all Thy toil, by all Thy pain,
  By every sigh and tear,
We pray Thee, let not Satan gain
  The souls that cost so dear.

Remember, Lord, Thy mercies old,
  Thy grace so freely given,
When nations thronged into Thy fold
  Intent on gaining heaven.

Remember how our Lady's Dower,
  Was England's glorious name,
Oh, bid her show her former power,
  Her ancient right reclaim.

Oh, for the sake of saints who prayed
  At altars now laid low,
For deeds of shame, for faith betrayed,
  Thy vengeance, Lord, forego.

And for the sake of those who stood
  Amid the nation's fall,
Who kept their faith and shed their blood,
  Have mercy now on all.

[REV. T. E. BRIDGETT, C.SS.R.]

THE CHURCH.

137

THE CHURCH.

BLEST is the Faith, divine and strong,
  Of thanks and praise an endless fountain,
Whose life is one perpetual song,
  High up the Saviour's holy mountain.
    Oh, Sion's songs are sweet to sing,
      With melodies of gladness laden;
    Hark! how the harps of angels ring,
      Hail, Son of Man! Hail, Mother-Maiden!

Blest is the Hope that holds to God
  In doubt and darkness still unshaken,
And sings along the heavenly road,
  Sweetest when most it seems forsaken.
    Oh, Sion's songs are sweet to sing,
      With melodies of gladness laden;
    Hark! how the harps of angels ring,
      Hail, Son of Man! Hail, Mother-Maiden!

Blest is the Love that cannot love
  Aught that earth gives of best and brightest;
Whose raptures thrill like saints' above,
  Most when its earthly gifts are lightest.
    Oh, Sion's songs are sweet to sing,
      With melodies of gladness laden;
    Hark! how the harps of angels ring,
      Hail, Son of Man! Hail, Mother-Maiden!

[REV. F. W. FABER]

N.B.—Repeat last line of each verse.

138 (First Tune.)

Faith of our Fathers! living still
  In spite of dungeon, fire, and sword:
Oh, how our hearts beat high with joy
  Whene'er we hear that glorious word.
Faith of our Fathers! Holy Faith!
We will be true to thee till death.

Our Fathers, chained in prisons dark,
  Were still in heart and conscience free:
How sweet would be their children's fate,
  If they, like them, could die for thee!
Faith of our Fathers! Holy Faith!
We will be true to thee till death.

Faith of our Fathers! Mary's prayers
  Shall win our country back to thee;
And through the truth that comes from God
  England shall then indeed be free.
Faith of our Fathers! Holy Faith!
We will be true to thee till death.

Faith of our Fathers! we will love
  Both friend and foe in all our strife:
And preach thee too, as love knows how
  By kindly words and virtuous life:
Faith of our Fathers! Holy Faith!
We will be true to thee till death.

[REV. F. W. FABER]

N.B.—Repeat last line of words.

(SECOND TUNE.) **138**

FAITH of our Fathers! living still
In spite of dungeon, fire, and sword:
Oh, how our hearts beat high with joy
Whene'er we hear that glorious word.
Faith of our Fathers! Holy Faith!
We will be true to thee till death.

Our Fathers, chained in prisons dark,
Were still in heart and conscience free:
How sweet would be their children's fate,
If they, like them, could die for thee!
Faith of our Fathers! Holy Faith!
We will be true to thee till death.

Faith of our Fathers! Mary's prayers
Shall win our country back to thee;
And through the truth that comes from [God
England shall then indeed be free.
Faith of our Fathers! Holy Faith!
We will be true to thee till death.

Faith of our Fathers! we will love
Both friend and foe in all our strife:
And preach thee too, as love knows how
By kindly words and virtuous life:
Faith of our Fathers! Holy Faith!
We will be true to thee till death.

[REV. F. W. FABER]

N.B.—Repeat last two lines of words.

THE CHURCH.

139 (First Tune.)

FULL in the panting heart of Rome,
  Beneath the Apostle's crowning dome,
From pilgrims' lips that kiss the ground,
Breathes in all tongues one only sound :
  "God bless our Pope, the great, the good."

The golden roof, the marble walls,
The Vatican's majestic halls,
The note redouble, till it fills
With echoes sweet the seven hills :
  "God bless our Pope," &c.

Then surging through each hallowed gate,
Where martyrs glory, in peace, await,
It sweeps beyond the solemn plain,
Peals over Alps, across the main :
  "God bless our Pope," &c.

From torrid south to frozen north,
That wave harmonious stretches forth,
Yet strikes no chord more true to Rome's,
Than rings within our hearts and homes :
  "God bless our Pope," &c.

For like the sparks of unseen fire,
That speak along the magic wire,
From home to home, from heart to heart,
These words of countless children dart :
  "God bless our Pope," &c.

[CARDINAL WISEMAN]

(Second Tune.) **139**

Full in the panting heart of Rome,
Beneath the Apostle's crowning dome,
From pilgrims' lips that kiss the ground,
Breathes in all tongues one only sound:
"God bless our Pope, the great, the good."

The golden roof, the marble walls,
The Vatican's majestic halls,
The note redouble, till it fills
With echoes sweet the seven hills:
"God bless our Pope," &c.

Then surging through each hallowed gate,
Where martyrs glory, in peace, await,
It sweeps beyond the solemn plain,
Peals over Alps, across the main:
"God bless our Pope," &c.

From torrid south to frozen north,
That wave harmonious stretches forth,
Yet strikes no chord more true to Rome's,
Than rings within our hearts and homes:
"God bless our Pope," &c.

For like the sparks of unseen fire,
That speak along the magic wire,
From home to home, from heart to heart,
These words of countless children dart:
"God bless our Pope," &c.

[Cardinal Wiseman].

N.B.—Repeat last line of words.

140

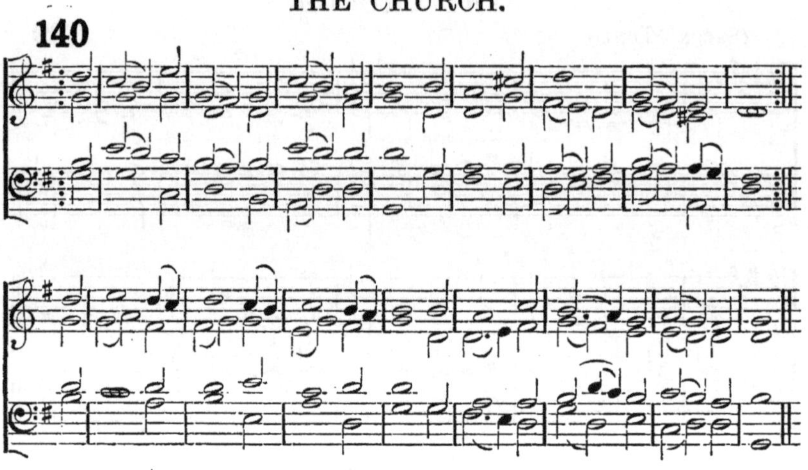

Cœlestis urbs Jerusalem.

FEAST OF DEDICATION.

JERUSALEM, thou City blest!
Dear vision of celestial rest!
Which far above the starry sky,
Piled up with living stones on high,
Art, as a Bride, encircled bright,
With million angel forms of light:

Oh, wedded in a prosperous hour!
The Father's glory was thy dower;
The Spirit all His graces shed,
Thou peerless Queen, upon thy head;
When Christ espoused thee for His Bride,
O City bright and glorified!

Thy gates a pearly lustre pour;
Thy gates are open evermore;
And thither evermore draw nigh
All who for Christ have dared to die;
Or smit with love of their dear Lord,
Have pains endured and joys abhorr'd.

Type of the Church which here we see,
Oh, what a task hath builded thee!
Long did the chisels ring around!
Long did the mallets' blows rebound!
Long work'd the head, and toil'd the hand!
Ere stood thy stones as now they stand!

To God the Father, glory due
Be paid by all the heavenly Host;
And to His only Son most true;
With Thee, O mighty Holy Ghost!
To whom praise, power, and blessing be,
Through th' ages of eternity.

[TR. REV. E. CASWALL]

141

(First Tune.)

HAIL, holy mission, hail!
We sighing turn to thee,
For weary have we found
The path of sin to be.

Hail, holy mission, hail!
Now sent us from above;
When Jesus with His cross
Again wins back our love.

Hail, holy mission, hail!
Blest time of contrite tears;
When to the soul returns
The peace of former years.

Hail, holy mission, hail!
Sweet time of humble prayer;
When rests the soul on God,
Freed from this dark world's care.

Hail, holy mission, hail!
Time of all others blest;
When in the loving soul
Jesus takes up His rest.

Hail, holy mission, hail!
Foretaste of joys above;
Oh, Jesus, make our hearts
Inflam'd and pure with love.

[BISHOP CHADWICK]

MISSIONS.

141 (Second Tune.)

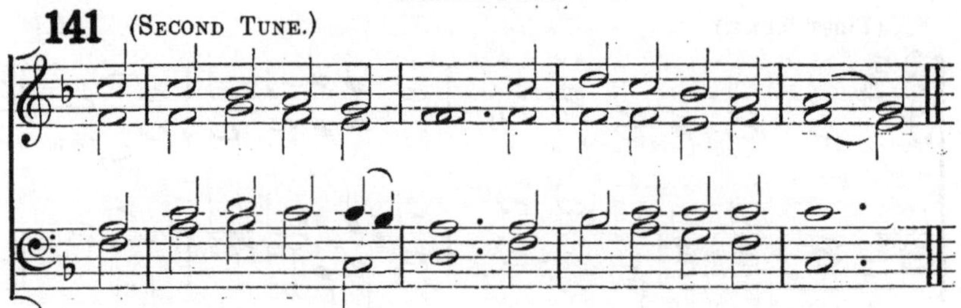

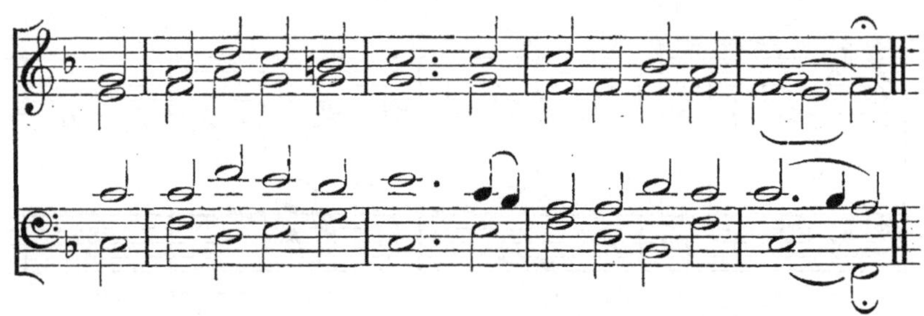

HAIL, holy mission, hail!
  We sighing turn to thee
For weary have we found
  The path of sin to be.

Hail, holy mission, hail!
  Now sent us from above;
When Jesus with His cross
  Again wins back our love.

Hail, holy mission, hail!
  Blest time of contrite tears
When to the soul returns
  The peace of former years.

Hail, holy mission, hail!
  Sweet time of humble prayer;
When rests the soul on God,
  Freed from this dark world's care.

Hail, holy mission, hail!
  Time of all others blest;
When in the loving soul
  Jesus takes up His rest.

Hail, holy mission, hail!
  Foretaste of joys above;
Oh, Jesus, make our hearts
  Inflam'd and pure with love.

[BISHOP CHADWICK]

142

Renewal of Baptismal Vows.

O Father, Son, and Holy Ghost,
One God in Persons Three,
We come in faith to cóunt the cost,
And give ourselves to Thee.
In hope and love Thy name we bless
For countless mercies given ;
To make our earthly burdens less,
And smooth our way to heaven.

But most we thank Thee for the grace
Of that thrice-blessèd day,
Which sped us in our Christian race,
And wash'd our sin away.
Then we were free from guilty stain,
Tho' sad and sinful *now* ;
With contrite hearts we come again
To make our solemn vow.

Dear Lord, before Thy wounded feet
Weeping Thy children fall ;
Hear us, kind Jesus, Saviour sweet,
Our Life, our Love, our All.
We seek to serve no other king,
Follow no other guide,
Nor earth, nor any earthly thing,
Shall tear us from Thy side.

We seek to know no other love,
Save what we love in Thee ;
And Thee we choose all else above
Our chiefest love to be.
Thy Blood our only treasure is,
Thy Cross our chosen part ;
Thyself and Mary all our bliss ;
Our home, Thy Sacred Heart.

[Anon. "Catholic Hymnal," 1860]

MISSIONS.

143

MISSIONS.

WE come to Thee, sweet Saviour,
Just because we need Thee so;
None need Thee more than we do;
Nor are half so vile or low.
O bountiful salvation!
O life eternal won!
O plentiful redemption!
O Blood of Mary's Son!

We come to Thee, sweet Saviour!
None will have us, Lord! but Thee;
And we want none but Jesus,
And His grace that makes us free.
O bountiful, &c.

We come to Thee, sweet Saviour!
With our broken faith again:
We know Thou wilt forgive us,
Nor upbraid us, nor complain.
O bountiful, &c.

We come to Thee, sweet Saviour!
For to whom, Lord! can we go?
The words of life eternal
From Thy lips ever flow.
O bountiful, &c.

We come to Thee, sweet Saviour!
We have tried Thee, oft before;
And now we come more wholly,
With the heart to love Thee more.
O bountiful, &c.

We come to Thee, sweet Saviour!
And Thou wilt not ask us why:
We cannot live without Thee,
And still less without Thee die.
O bountiful, &c.

[REV. F. W. FABER]

MISSIONS.

144

SOULS of men! why will ye scatter
  Like a crowd of frightened sheep?
Foolish hearts! why will ye wander
  From a love so true and deep?

Was there ever kindest shepherd
  Half so gentle, half so sweet,
As the Saviour who would have us
  Come and gather round His Feet?

There's a wideness in God's mercy,
  Like the wideness of the sea;
There's a kindness in His justice,
  Which is more than liberty.

There is no place where earth's sorrows
  Are more felt than up in Heaven;
There is no place where earth's failings
  Have such kindly judgment given.

For the love of God is broader
  Than the measures of man's mind;
And the Heart of the Eternal
  Is most wonderfully kind.

There is plentiful redemption
  In the Blood that has been shed;
There is joy for all the members
  In the sorrows of the Head.

Pining souls! come nearer Jesus,
  And oh, come not doubting thus,
But with faith that trusts more bravely
  His huge tenderness for us.

If our love were but more simple,
  We should take Him at His word;
And our lives would be all sunshine
  In the sweetness of our Lord.

[REV. F. W. FABER]

145

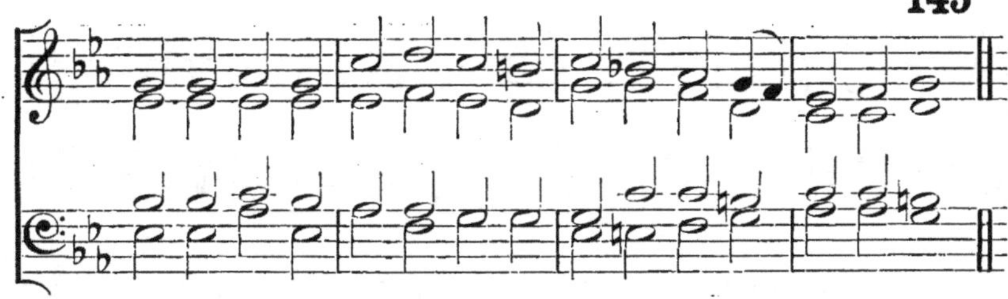

DAYS and moments quickly flying,
  Blend the living with the dead;
Soon will you and I be lying
  Each within our narrow bed.

Soon our souls to God who gave them
  Will have sped their rapid flight;
Able now by grace to save them,
  Oh, that, while we can, we might!

Jesu, infinite Redeemer,
  Maker of this mighty frame!
Teach, O teach us to remember
  What we are, and whence we came;

Whence we came and whither wending,
  Soon we must through darkness go,
To inherit bliss unending,
  Or eternity of woe.

[REV. E. CASWALL]

MISSIONS.

146

JESUS, my Lord, behold at length the time
When I resolve to turn away from crime.
Oh, pardon me, Jesus ;
Thy mercy I implore ;
I will never more offend Thee,
No, never more.

Since my poor soul Thy precious Blood has cost,
Suffer it not for ever to be lost.
Oh, pardon, &c.

Kneeling in tears, behold me at Thy feet ;
Like Magdalene, forgiveness I entreat.
Oh, pardon, &c.

[BISHOP CHADWICK]

147

GOD of mercy and compassion,
Look with pity upon me;
Father, let me call Thee Father,
'Tis Thy child returns to Thee.
Jesus, Lord, I ask for mercy;
Let me not implore in vain;
All my sins I now detest them,
Never will I sin again.

By my sins I have deserved
Death and endless misery,
Hell with all its pains and torments,
And for all eternity.
Jesus, Lord, &c.

By my sins I have abandon'd
Right and claim to Heav'n above,
Where the Saints rejoice for ever
In a boundless sea of love.
Jesus, Lord, &c.

See our Saviour, bleeding, dying,
On the cross of Calvary;
To that cross my sins have nail'd Him,
Yet He bleeds and dies for me.
Jesus, Lord, I ask for mercy;
Let me not implore in vain;
All my sins I now detest them,
Never will I sin again.

[REV. E. VAUGHAN, C.SS.R.]

MISSIONS.

148

MISSIONS.

OH, come to the merciful Saviour who calls you,
  Oh, come to the Lord who forgives and forgets;
Though dark be the fortune on earth that befalls you,
  There's a bright home above where the sun never sets.

Oh come, then, to Jesus, whose arms are extended
  To fold His dear children in closest embrace;
Oh come, for your exile will shortly be ended,
  And Jesus will show you His beautiful Face.

Ye sons of dear England, your Saviour is calling
  You back to His Fold and your forefathers' faith;
Ah, love Him, then, love Him; for the dark night is falling,
  And the light of His love shall be with you in death.

Yes, come to the Saviour, whose mercy grows brighter
  The longer you look at the depths of His love;
And fear not! 'tis Jesus, and life's cares grow lighter,
  As you think of the home and the glory above.

Have you sinned as none else in the world have before you?
  Are you blacker than all other creatures in guilt?
Oh, fear not, and doubt not! the mother who bore you
  Loves you less than the Saviour whose Blood you have spilt.

Oh come, then, to Jesus, and say how you love Him,
  And vow at His feet you will keep in His grace;
For one tear that is shed by a sinner can move Him,
  And your sins will drop off in His tender embrace.

Come, come to His feet, and lay open your story
  Of suffering and sorrow, of guilt and of shame;
For the pardon of sin is the crown of His glory,
  And the joy of our Lord to be true to His Name.

Come quickly to Jesus for graces and pardons,
  Come now, for who needs not His mercy and love?
Believe me, dear children, that England's fair gardens
  Are dull to the bright land that waits you above.

[REV. F. W. FABER]

149

OH, the priceless love of Jesus!
Oh, the strength of grace divine!
All His gifts are showered upon me,
All His blessings may be mine.
He is throned in Heavenly glory
Where no sin nor death can be;
Yet He loves me in this darkness,
Yet He does not turn from me.

I am blind and poor and wretched,
By temptations sorely tried;
Yet His watchful care abounding
Keeps me ever at His side.
He is God and King Eternal,
Higher than all height can be;
Yet His Heart is with me always,
Yet He stoopeth down to me.

Storms of sorrow roll around me,
Darkling clouds above me meet;
But I hasten to my refuge
At my Saviour's wounded Feet.
Oh, how lovingly, my Jesus,
Thou dost with me ever bear;
I can never, never thank Thee
For Thy goodness and Thy care.

When the clouds of darkness hide me
Bitter tears of pain I weep:
But Thou loving One, Thou healest
All my sorrow dark and deep.
O Thy priceless love, my Jesus,
Human love and love divine;
Thou art gentle, Thou art mighty;
All Thy Sacred Heart is mine.

150

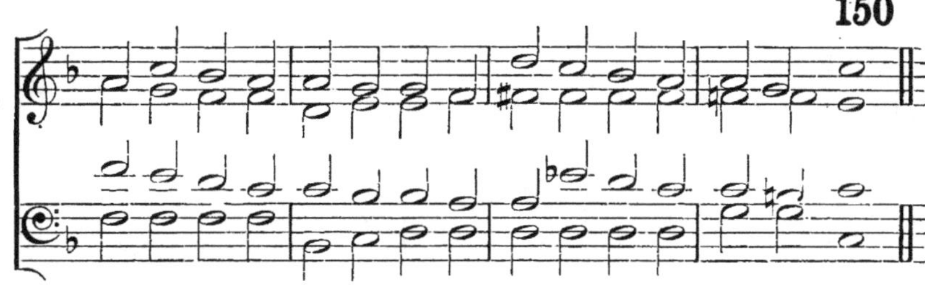

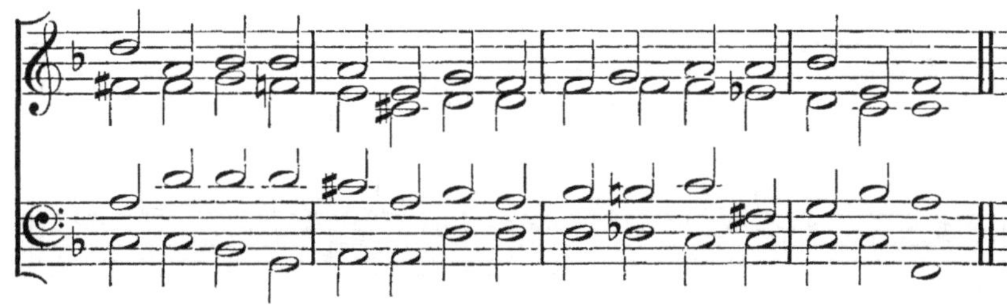

HEAR Thy children, gentle Jesus,
While we breathe our evening prayer,
Save us from all harm and danger,
Take us 'neath Thy shelt'ring care.

Save us from the wiles of Satan,
'Mid the lone and sleepful night,
Sweetly may bright Guardian Angels
Keep us 'neath their watchful sight.

Gentle Jesus, look in pity,
From Thy great white throne above,
All the night Thy Heart is wakeful;
In Thy Sacrament of love.

Shades of even fast are falling,
Day is fading into gloom.
When the shades of death fall round us,
Lead Thine exiled children home.

[REV. F. STANFIELD]

FOR CHILDREN.

151

HEAR thy children, gentlest Mother,
  Prayerful hearts to thee arise;
Hear us while our evening Ave
  Soars beyond the starry skies.

Darkling shadows fall around us,
  Stars their silent watches keep;
Hush the heart oppressed with sorrow,
  Dry the tears of those who weep.

Hear, sweet Mother, hear the weary,
  Borne upon life's troubled sea;
Gentle guiding Star of Ocean,
  Lead thy children home to thee.

Still watch o'er us, dearest Mother,
  From thy beauteous throne above;
Guard us from all harm and danger,
  'Neath thy sheltering wings of love.

[REV. F. STANFIELD]

152

O SING a joyous carol
  Unto the holy Child,
And praise with gladsome voices
  His Mother undefiled :
Our infant voices greeting
  Shall hail our infant King ;
And our sweet Lady listens
  When infant voices sing.

Who is there meekly lying
  In yonder stable poor ?
Dear children, it is Jesus ;
  He bids you now adore.
Who is there kneeling by Him,
  In virgin beauty fair ?
It is our mother Mary ;
  She bids you all draw near.

Who is there near the cradle,
  That guards the holy Child ?
It is our father Joseph,
  Chaste spouse of Mary mild.
Dear children, oh, how joyful
  With them in Heaven to be !
God grant that none be missing
  From that festivity.

[SISTER M. B.]

FOR CHILDREN.

153

I LOVE those precious Christmas words,
  That come but once a year;
They fall, at midnight's silent hour,
  Like music on mine ear:
The heav'nly choirs who filled the air
  With praises from above,
All glory be to God on high
  And peace to men of love!

Then come, ye children, haste with me,
  Behold this gracious sight,
The world's Creator from His throne
  Descending in the night;
Not arm'd with terrors, nor in robes
  Of majesty array'd,
But meekly wrapt in swaddling-clothes,
  And in a manger laid.

Our God, whom Heaven and earth obey,
  Was poorer far than we;
Shall poverty, so dear to Him,
  Seem grief to you or me?
Then let us run with cheerful hearts
  Our Heaven-appointed race;
For He, who once was poor for us,
  Shall make us rich in grace.

[ANON. "HYMNS FOR THE YEAR," 1867]

154

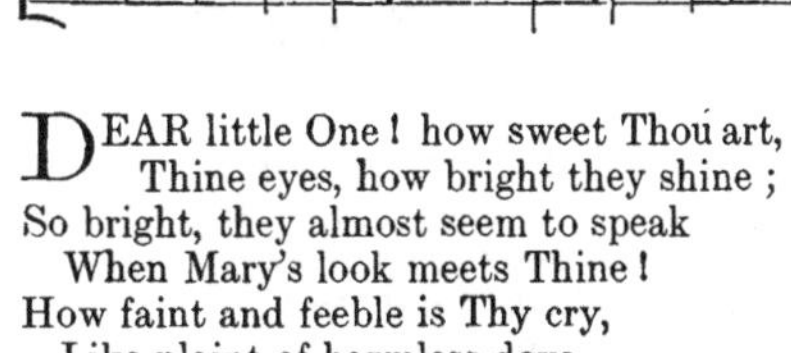

DEAR little One! how sweet Thou art,
Thine eyes, how bright they shine;
So bright, they almost seem to speak
When Mary's look meets Thine!
How faint and feeble is Thy cry,
Like plaint of harmless dove,
When Thou dost murmur in Thy sleep
Of sorrow and of love.

When Mary bids Thee sleep Thou sleep'st:
Thou wakest when she calls;
Thou art content upon her lap,
Or in the rugged stalls.
Simplest of Babes! with what a grace
Thou dost Thy Mother's will!
Thine infant fashions well betray
The Godhead's hidden skill.

When Joseph takes Thee in his arms,
And smoothes Thy little cheek,
Thou lookest up into his face
So helpless and so meek.
Yes! Thou art what Thou seem'st to be,
A thing of smiles and tears;
Yet Thou art God, and Heaven and earth
Adore Thee with their fears.

Yes, dearest Babe! those tiny hands
That play with Mary's hair,
The weight of all the mighty world
This very moment bear.
Art Thou, weak Babe! my very God?
Oh I must love Thee, then,
Love Thee, and yearn to spread Thy love
Among forgetful men.

[REV. F. W. FABER]

FOR CHILDREN.

155

MOTHER Mary, at thine altar
  We thy loving children kneel;
With a faith that cannot falter
  To thy goodness we appeal.
We are seeking for a mother
  O'er the earth so waste and wide;
And from off the Cross our Brother
  Points to Mary by His side.

Thou wilt love us, thou wilt guide us,
  With a mother's fondest care:
And our Father, God above us,
  Bids us fly for refuge there.
Life's temptations are before us,
  We must mingle in the strife;
If thy fondness watch not o'er us,
  All unsafe will be our life.

So we take thee for our Mother,
  And we claim our right to be,
By the gift of our dear Brother,
  Loving children unto thee;
And our humble consecration
  Thou wilt surely not despise,
From Thy high and lofty station
  Close to Jesus in the skies.

Mother Mary, to thy keeping
  We ourselves to thee confide;
Toiling, resting, waking, sleeping,
  To be ever at thy side.
Cares that vex us, joys that please us,
  Life and death we trust to thee;
Thou wilt make them all for Jesus,
  And for all eternity.

[REV. F. W. FABER]

156

O divine Enfance.

COME, ye little children,
Unto Me draw nigh;
For 'tis such as you
That dwell with Me on high;
Who in love and meekness,
From all malice free,
Serve their dear Redeemer
With simplicity.

I, who pride and greatness
Evermore abase,
On the poor and lowly
Lavish all My grace;
And to humble spirits
Heavenly things reveal,
Which My secret judgments
From the proud conceal.

This, O sweetest Jesus,
Seemest Thou to say,
Ah then, wretched earthlings,
Cast your pride away;
If the God of glory
So Himself abase,
How shall man presume
To choose the highest place?

Sacred charms of childhood,
Unto Christ so dear,
Bright in generous frankness,
Innocence sincere,
Love serene, unselfish,
Void of worldly stain,
Would that in my bosom
Ye might ever reign!

[REV. FR. LAMBILOTTE. TR. REV. E. CASWALL]

FOR CHILDREN.

157

O JESUS ! God and man ! for love
  Of children, once a child ;
O Jesus ! God and man ! we hail
  Thee, Saviour sweet and mild.
O Jesus ! God and man ! make us
  Poor children dear to Thee ;
And lead us to Thyself to love
  Thee for eternity.

O Mary, Mother-Maid ! thou art
  The Mother of the poor ;
Mary, to thee we look to make
  Our souls' salvation sure.
O Mary, Mother dear ! thank God
  For us for all His love ;
And pray that in our faith we all
  May true and steadfast prove.

O Jesus ! Mary's Son ! on Thee
  For grace we children call ;
Make us all men to love, but Thee
  To love beyond them all.
O Jesus, bless us in our work,
  And all our sins forgive ;
O happy, happy they who in
  The Church of Jesus live !

[ANON. "HYMNS FOR THE YEAR," 1867]

158

DEAR God of orphans, hear our prayer,
  Bless Thou our orphans' home,
And let the children Thou dost love,
  To Thee, their true love, come.
How sweetly, Jesus, did Thine eye
  On children ever rest,
When by the lure of Thy sweet voice
  They fondly round Thee prest!

Oh, plead the children's cause with them,
  Whose cause Thy cross did plead;
Make sinners' hearts with pity melt,
  For whom Thine own did bleed.
Thou lovest most the hearts that bring
  Most little ones to Thee;
But most of all the hearts that bring
  Thy babes most lovingly.

We all are orphans, outcasts all,
  Until to Thee we come;
On earth, in Heaven, dear Jesus, Thou,
  Thou art Thyself our home.
One only joy there is on earth—
  It is, to have Thy grace;
One only joy can be in Heaven—
  It is, to see Thy face.

[REV. F. W. FABER]

FOR CHILDREN.

159

FOR CHILDREN.

GUARDIAN Angel,
  From Heaven so bright,
Watching beside me,
  To lead me aright,
Fold thy wings round me,
  O guard me with love,
Softly sing songs to me,
  Of Heav'n above.
    Beautiful Angel,
      My guardian so mild,
    Tenderly guide me,
      For I am thy child.

Angel so holy,
  Whom God sends to me,
Sinful and lowly,
  My guardian to be.
Wilt thou not cherish
  The child of thy care?
Let me not perish,—
  My trust is thy prayer.
    Beautiful Angel,
      My guardian so mild,
    Tenderly guide me,
      For I am thy child.

O may I never,
  Forget thou art near;
But keep me for ever,
  In love and in fear.
Waking and sleeping,
  In labour and rest,
In thy sweet keeping,
  My life shall be blest,
    Beautiful Angel,
      My guardian so mild,
    Tenderly guide me,
      For I am thy child.

FOR CHILDREN.

160

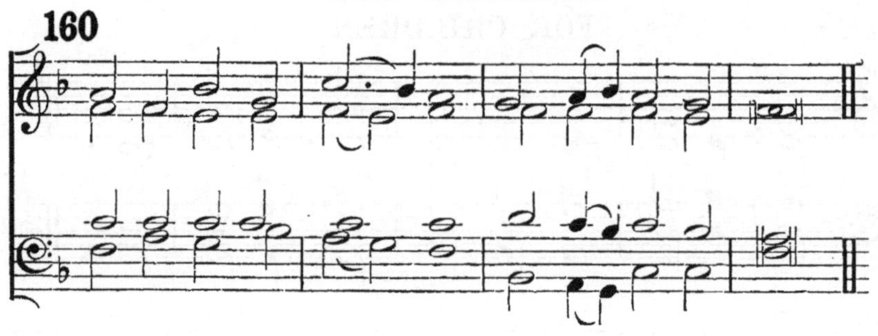

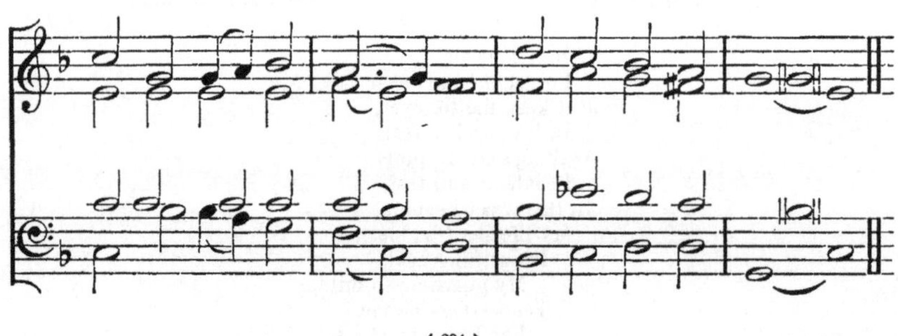

FOR CHILDREN.

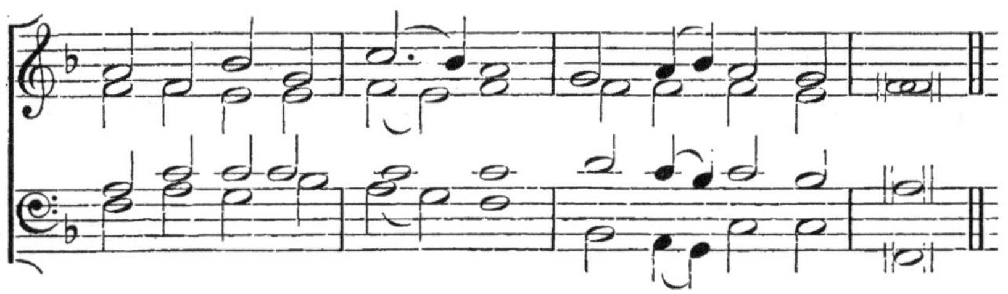

Before Communion.

Adoration and Faith.

JESUS ! Thou art coming,
  Holy as Thou art,
Thou, the God who made me,
  To my sinful heart.
Jesus ! I *believe* it,
  On Thy only word ;
Kneeling, I adore Thee
  As my King and Lord.

Humility and Sorrow.

Who am I, my Jesus,
  That Thou com'st to me ?
I have sinned against Thee,
  Often, grievously ;
I am very *sorry*
  I have caused Thee pain,
I will never, never,
  Wound Thy Heart again.

Trust.

Put Thy kind arms round me,
  Feeble as I am ;
Thou art my Good Shepherd,
  I, Thy little lamb ;
Since Thou comest, Jesus,
  Now to be my Guest,
I can *trust* Thee always,
  Lord, for all the rest.

Love and Desire.

Dearest Lord, I *love* Thee,
  With my whole, whole heart,
Not for what Thou givest,
  But for what Thou art.
Come, oh, come, sweet Saviour !
  Come to me, and stay,
For I *want* Thee, Jesus,
  More than I can say.

Offering and Petition.

Ah ! what gift or present,
  Jesus, can I bring ?
I have nothing worthy
  Of my God and King ;
But Thou art my Shepherd,
  I, Thy little lamb ;
Take *myself*, dear Jesus,
  All I have and am.

Take my body, Jesus,
  Eyes, and ears, and tongue ;
Never let them, Jesus,
  Help to do Thee wrong.
Take my heart, and fill it
  Full of love for Thee ;
All I have I give Thee,
  Give Thyself to me.

FOR CHILDREN.

161

FOR CHILDREN.

LITTLE King, so fair and sweet,
See us gathered round Thy feet;
Be Thou Monarch of our school,
It shall prosper 'neath Thy rule.
We will be Thy subjects true,
Brave to suffer, brave to do,
All our hearts to Thee we bring,
Take them, keep them, little King.

Be our Leader in the fight,
In the darkness be our Light,
O'er the rough, and o'er the smooth,
Safely guide our wayward youth.
Wheresoe'er our path may be,
We will try to follow Thee,
To Thy mantle we will cling,
Help us, save us, little King.

Raise Thy little hand to bless
All our childhood's happiness;
Bless our sorrow and our pain,
That each cross may be our gain.
By Thine own sweet childhood, Lord,
Sanctify each thought and word,
Set Thy seal on everything
Which we do, O little King.

Little King, so dear, so sweet,
Here we cast before Thy feet
All we are or yet may be,
Every sense and faculty:
All our body, all our soul,
We subject to Thy control,
Let them all Thy praises sing,
Now and always, little King.

Be our Teacher when we learn,
All the hard to easy turn;
Be our Playmate when we play,
So we shall indeed be gay.
Keep us happy, keep us pure,
While our childhood shall endure,
All its days to Thee we bring,
Bless them, guard them, little King.

Let us in the noisy world
Keep Thy banner broad unfurled,
In an age of ease and pride
Leading Christian lives denied,
In an age which seeks its way,
Glad and cheerful to obey,
While Thy simple truth shall ring
In word and act, O little King.

And when holidays have come,
Call Thy children to Thy home,
In that gentle voice of Thine,
Which we know, sweet Child Divine.
At the gate, oh! meet us thus,
As we loved Thee—Child like us:
Stretch Thine hands in welcoming
To Thine own, O little King.

[S. N. D.]

FOR CHILDREN.

162

Act of Faith.

Act of Hope.

FOR CHILDREN.

Act of Charity.

[ANON. ST. PATRICK'S HYMN BOOK]

163

FOR CHILDREN.

O JESUS! on Thy Mother's breast,
  How beautiful Thou art;
Winning with those sweet looks of Thine,
  The love of my young heart.
    O Jesus! on Thy Mother's breast,
      How beautiful Thou art;
    Oh, may Thy love grow day by day
      Within my youthful heart.

The tender light within Thine eyes
  Forbids my soul to fear;
And though Thou art a mighty God,
  I to Thy feet draw near.
    O Jesus! &c.

The shepherds have before me been,
  Their humble gifts I see;
And kings have bowed their royal heads,
  Dear Little One, to Thee.
    O Jesus! &c.

I have no costly things to lay
  Before Thee—can I dare,
A little child with empty hands,
  Approach to Thee in prayer?
    O Jesus! &c.

Oh, dost Thou ask me for my heart?
  Yes, I will give it Thee;
Alas! that it is not more pure
  For Thy sweet eyes to see.
    O Jesus! &c.

O Mary, give it thou to Him,
  He'll take it for thy sake;
A richer gift than this poor heart,
  Oh, would that I could make.
    O Jesus! &c.

Tho' pain and poverty may blight
  My life—yet still to Thee
My heart shall turn, and Holy Child!
  Thou shalt my comfort be.
    O Jesus! &c.

ANGELS.

164

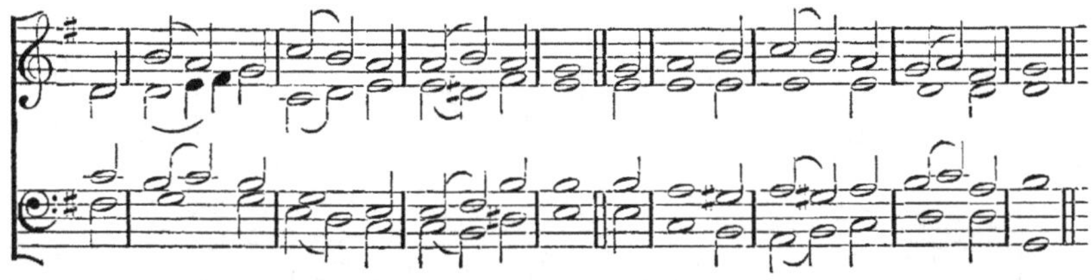

KIND Angel Guardian, thanks to thee
For thy so watchful care of me;
Oh, lead me still in ways of truth,
Dear guide of childhood and of youth.

Kind Angel Guardian, let my tears
Implore thee too for riper years;
Oh, keep me safe in wisdom's way,
And bring me back if I should stray.

When angry passions fill my soul,
Subdue them to thy meek control;
Through good and ill, oh, ever be
A guide, a guard, a friend to me.

And when death's hand shall seal mine eyes,
Oh, bear my spirit to the skies,
And teach me there my voice to raise
In hymns of never-ending praise.

[SISTER M. J.]

ANGELS.

165

MY oldest friend, mine from the hour
When first I drew my breath;
My faithful friend, that shall be mine,
Unfailing, till my death;

Thou hast been ever at my side;
My Maker to thy trust
Consign'd my soul, what time He framed
The infant child of dust.

No beating heart in holy prayer,
No faith, inform'd aright,
Gave me to Joseph's tutelage,
Or Michael's conquering might.

Nor patron Saint, nor Mary's love,
The dearest and the best,
Has known my being, as thou hast known,
And blest, as thou hast blest.

Thou wast my sponsor at the font;
And thou, each budding year,
Didst whisper elements of truth
Into my childish ear.

And when, ere boyhood yet was gone,
My rebel spirit fell,
Ah! thou didst see, and shudder too,
Yet bear each deed of Hell.

And then in turn, when judgments came,
And scared me back again,
Thy quick soft breath was near to soothe
And hallow every pain.

Oh! who of all thy toils and cares
Can tell the tale complete,
To place me under Mary's smile,
And Peter's royal feet!

And thou wilt hang about my bed,
When life is ebbing low;
Of doubt, impatience, and of gloom,
The jealous sleepless foe.

Mine, when I stand before the Judge,
And mine, if spared to stay
Within the holy furnace till
My sin is burn'd away.

And mine, O Brother of my soul,
When my release shall come;
Thy gentle arms shall lift me then,
Thy wings shall waft me home.

[CARDINAL NEWMAN]

ANGELS.

166

DEAR Angel! ever at my side,
How loving must thou be,
To leave thy home in Heaven to guard
A sinful child like me.

Thy beautiful and shining face
I see not, though so near;
The sweetness of thy soft low voice
I am too deaf to hear.

But I have felt thee in my thoughts
Fighting with sin for me;
And when my heart loves God, I know
The sweetness is from thee.

And when, dear Spirit! I kneel down
Morning and night to prayer,
Something there is within my heart
Which tells me thou art there.

Yes! when I pray thou prayest too,
Thy prayer is all for me;
But when I sleep, thou sleepest not,
But watchest patiently.

Then, for thy sake, dear Angel! now
More humble will I be;
But I am weak, and when I fall,
Oh weary not of me:

Oh weary not, but love me still,
For Mary's sake, thy Queen;
She never tired of me, though I
Her worst of sons have been.

Then love me, love me, Angel dear!
And I will love thee more;
And help me when my soul is cast
Upon the eternal shore.

[REV. F. W. FABER]

ANGELS.

167

Christe, sanctorum decus angelorum.

St. Raphael, Lauds.

O CHRIST, the glory of the angel choirs !
Author and Ruler of the human race !
Grant us one day to climb the happy hills
And see Thy blissful face.

And oh, Thy Raphael, physician blest,
Send down to us from yon celestial height,
To heal our soul's diseases, and direct
Our lifelong course aright.

Thou too, O Mary, Mother of our God !
And happy Queen of Angels, hither speed,
Drawing with thee the Army of the Saints
To help us in our need.

This grace on us bestow, O Father blest,
And Thou, O Son by an eternal birth ;
With Thee, from both proceeding, Holy Ghost !
Whose glory fills the earth.

[TR. REV. E. CASWALL]

ANGELS.

168

Te Splendor et virtus.

APPARITION OF ST. MICHAEL, VESPERS.

O JESU! life-spring of the soul!
The Father's Power, and Glory bright!
Thee with the Angels we extol;
From Thee they draw their life and light.

Thy thousand thousand hosts are spread,
Embattled o'er the azure sky;
But Michael bears Thy standard dread,
And lifts the mighty Cross on high.

He in that Sign the rebel powers
Did with their Dragon Prince expel;
And hurl'd them from the Heaven's high tower
Down like a thunderbolt to hell.

Grant us with Michael still, O Lord,
Against the Prince of Pride to fight;
So may a crown be our reward,
Before the Lamb's pure throne of light.

To God the Father, and the Son,
Who rose from death, all glory be;
With Thee, O blessèd Paraclete,
Henceforth through all eternity.

(*Within Octave of the Ascension, the following in place of v.* 5.)

Glory to Jesus, who returns
In pomp triumphant to the sky,
To Thee, O Father, and with Thee,
O Holy Ghost, eternally.

[TR. REV. E. CASWALL]

ANGELS.

169

Tibi Christe splendor.

ST. RAPHAEL, VESPERS.

JESU, brightness of the Father!
  Life and strength of all who live!
In the presence of the Angels,
  Glory to Thy Name we give;
And Thy wondrous praise rehearse,
Singing in alternate verse.

Hail, all ye angelic Princedoms!
  Hail, ye thrones celestial!
Hail, Physician of Salvation!
  Guide of life, blest Raphael!
Binding fast the fiend of night
In the glory of thy might.

Oh, may Christ beneath thy pinions
  Shield us from all harm this day;
Keep us pure in flesh and spirit;
  Save us from the enemy;
And vouchsafe us, of His grace,
In His Paradise a place.

Glory to th' Almighty Father,
  Sing we now in anthems sweet;
Glory to the great Redeemer;
  Glory to the Paraclete;
Godhead sole and Persons three!
In eternal unity!

[TR. REV. E. CASWALL]

ANGELS.

170

Custodes hominum psallimus.

GUARDIAN ANGELS.

PRAISE we those ministers celestial
  Whom the dread Father chose
To be defenders of our nature frail,
  Against our scheming foes.

For, since that from his glory in the skies
  Th' Apostate Angel fell,
Burning with envy, evermore he tries
  To drown our souls in Hell.

Then hither, watchful Spirit, bend thy wing,
  Our country's Guardian blest!
Avert her threatening ills; expel each thing
  That hindereth her rest.

Praise to the trinal Majesty, whose strength
  This mighty fabric sways;
Whose glory reigns beyond the utmost length
  Of everlasting days.

[TR. REV. E. CASWALL]

HEAVEN.

171

To be sung in unison.

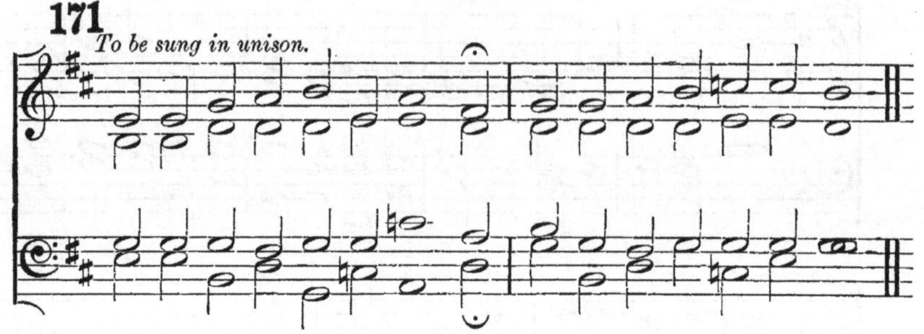

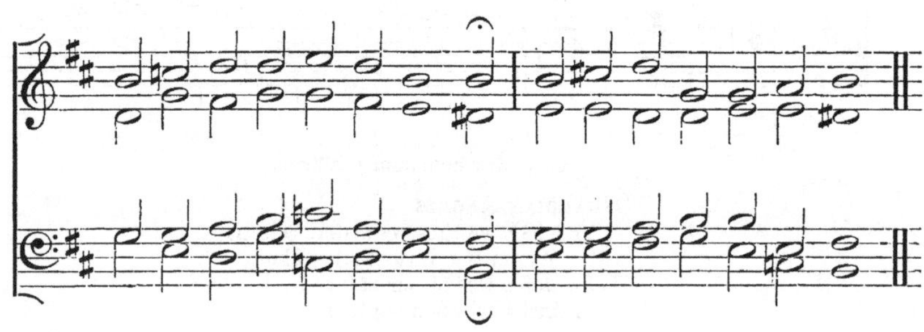

N.B.—Tune 169 can also be used for this hymn.

HEAVEN.

Ad perennis vitæ fontem.

WHO can paint that lovely city,
  City of true peace divine,
Whose pure gates, for ever open,
  Each in pearly lustre shine;
Whose abodes of glory clear
Nought defiling cometh near?

There no stormy winter rages;
  There no scorching summer glows;
But through one perennial spring-tide
  Bloom the lily and the rose,
With the myrrh and balsam sweet,
And the fadeless violet.

There a paradisal perfume
  Breathes upon the air serene;
There crystalline waters flowing
  Keep the grass for ever green;
And the golden orchards show
Fruits that ne'er corruption know.

There no sun his circuit wheeleth;
  There no moon or stars appear;
Thither night and darkness come not;
  Death hath no dominion there;
But the Lamb's pure beaming ray
Scatters round eternal day.

There the saints of God, resplendent
  As the sun in all his might,
Evermore rejoice together,
  Crown'd with diadems of light,
And from peril safe at last
Reckon up their triumphs past.

Happy he who with them seated
  Doth in all their glory share!
O that I, my days completed,
  Might be but admitted there!
There with them the praise to sing
Of my beauteous God and King.

[ST. PETER DAMIAN. TR. REV. E. CASWALL]

HEAVEN.

172 (First Tune.)

HEAVEN.

O PARADISE! O Paradise!
  Who doth not crave for rest?
Who would not seek the happy land,
  Where they that loved are blest;
    Where loyal hearts, and true,
      Stand ever in the light,
    All rapture through and through
      In God's most holy sight?

O Paradise! O Paradise!
  The world is growing old;
Who would not be at rest and free
  Where love is never cold,
    Where loyal hearts, &c.

O Paradise! O Paradise!
  Wherefore doth death delay,
Bright death, that is the welcome dawn
  Of our eternal day;
    Where loyal hearts, &c.

O Paradise! O Paradise!
  'Tis weary waiting here;
I long to be where Jesus is,
  To feel, to see Him near;
    Where loyal hearts, &c.

O Paradise! O Paradise!
  I want to sin no more;
I want to be as pure on earth
  As on thy spotless shore;
    Where loyal hearts, &c.

O Paradise! O Paradise!
  I greatly long to see
The special place my dearest Lord
  Is destining for me;
    Where loyal hearts, &c.

O Paradise! O Paradise!
  I feel 'twill not be long;
Patience! I almost think I hear
  Faint fragments of thy song;
    Where loyal hearts, &c.

[REV. F. W. FABER]

HEAVEN.

172 (Second Tune.)

HEAVEN.

O PARADISE! O Paradise!
  Who doth not crave for rest?
Who would not seek the happy land,
  Where they that loved are blest;
    Where loyal hearts, and true,
      Stand ever in the light,
    All rapture through and through
      In God's most holy sight?

O Paradise! O Paradise!
  The world is growing old;
Who would not be at rest and free
  Where love is never cold,
    Where loyal hearts, &c.

O Paradise! O Paradise!
  Wherefore doth death delay,
Bright death, that is the welcome dawn
  Of our eternal day;
    Where loyal hearts, &c.

O Paradise! O Paradise!
  'Tis weary waiting here;
I long to be where Jesus is,
  To feel, to see Him near;
    Where loyal hearts, &c.

O Paradise! O Paradise!
  I want to sin no more;
I want to be as pure on earth
  As on thy spotless shore;
    Where loyal hearts, &c.

O Paradise! O Paradise!
  I greatly long to see
The special place my dearest Lord
  Is destining for me;
    Where loyal hearts, &c.

O Paradise! O Paradise!
  I feel 'twill not be long;
Patience! I almost think I hear
  Faint fragments of thy song;
    Where loyal hearts, &c.

[REV. F. W. FABER]

R

173

ST. JOSEPH.

HAIL! holy Joseph, hail!
Husband of Mary, hail!
Chaste as the lily flower
In Eden's peaceful vale.

Hail! holy Joseph, hail!
Father of Christ esteemed,
Father be thou to those
Thy Foster-Son redeemed.

Hail! holy Joseph, hail!
Prince of the House of God,
May His best graces be
By thy sweet hands bestowed.

Hail! holy Joseph, hail!
Comrade of angels, hail!
Cheer thou the hearts that faint,
And guide the steps that fail.

Hail! holy Joseph, hail!
God's choice wert thou alone!
To thee the Word made flesh
Was subject as a Son.

Hail! holy Joseph, hail!
Teach us our flesh to tame,
And, Mary, keep the hearts
That love thy husband's name.

Mother of Jesus! bless,
And bless, ye saints on high,
All meek and simple souls
That to Saint Joseph cry.

[REV. F. W. FABER]

Tune 109 *or the Second Tune to Hymn* 141 *may also be used.*

174

St. Joseph.

DEAR Husband of Mary! dear Nurse of her Child!
Life's ways are full weary, the desert is wild;
Bleak sands are all round us, no home can we see;
Sweet Spouse of our Lady! we lean upon thee.

For thou to the pilgrim art Father and Guide,
And Jesus and Mary felt safe by thy side;
Ah, blessèd Saint Joseph, how safe should I be,
Sweet Spouse of our Lady! if thou wert with me!

O blessèd Saint Joseph! how great was thy worth
The one chosen shadow of God upon earth,
The Father of Jesus—ah then wilt thou be,
Sweet Spouse of our Lady! a father to me?

When the treasures of God were unsheltered on earth,
Safe keeping was found for them both in thy worth,
O Father of Jesus, be father to me,
Sweet Spouse of our Lady! and I will love thee.

[REV. F. W. FABER]

SAINTS.

175

Dei qui gratiam impotes.

St. Joseph.

SEEK ye the grace of God,
And mercies from on high ?—
Invoke Saint Joseph's holy name,
And on his aid rely.

So shall the Lord well pleased
Your earnest prayer fulfil ;
The guilty cleanse from guilt ; and make
The holy holier still.

So shall His tender care
To you through life be nigh ;
So shall His love with triumph crown
Your dying agony.

Safe in the virgin arms
Of Mary and her Son,
Embracing each in speechless joy,
And sweetest union ;

O Joseph, in what peace
Was breathed thy latest sigh,
Dear pattern of all those to come,
Who should in Jesus die !

Hail, mightiest of Saints !
To whom submissive bent
He whose Creator-hand outstretch'd
To starry firmament !

Hail, Mary's Spouse elect !
Hail, Guardian of the Word !
Nurse of the Highest ! and esteem'd
The Father of the Lord !

Blest Trinity ! to Thee
One God of earth and Heaven,
And to Saint Joseph's holy name,
Be praise and honour given !

[TR. REV. E. CASWALL]

176

Giacchè tu vuoi chiamarmi padre.

St. Joseph.

"JESUS! let me call Thee son,
Since Thou dost call me father;
How I love Thee, sweetest One,
My God and son together."
Blessèd Saint Joseph, to thee do we pray;
Offer our hearts to thy Jesus to-day.

"Since Thy guardian I must be,
My treasure I will make Thee;
Do not Thou abandon me,
And I will ne'er forsake Thee."
Blessèd Saint Joseph, to thee do we pray;
Offer our hearts to thy Jesus to-day.

"As my God I Thee adore,
And as my son embrace Thee;
Let me love Thee more and more,
And in my bosom place Thee."
Blessèd Saint Joseph, to thee do we pray;
Offer our hearts to thy Jesus to-day.

"All my love henceforth is Thine,
My very life I proffer,
And my heart no more is mine,
For all I am I offer."
Blessèd Saint Joseph, to thee do we pray;
Offer our hearts to thy Jesus to-day.

"Since to share Thy presence sweet
To choose me here Thou deignest,
Shall we not in heaven meet,
Where Thou for ever reignest?"
Blessèd Saint Joseph, to thee do we pray;
Offer our hearts to thy Jesus to-day.

[ST. ALPHONSUS. TR. REV. E. VAUGHAN]

177

Te Joseph celebrent agmina cœlitum.

St. Joseph, Vespers.

JOSEPH, pure Spouse of that immortal Bride,
Who shines in ever-virgin glory bright,
Through all the Christian climes thy praise be sung,
Through all the realms of light.

Thee, when amazed concern for thy betrothed
Had fill'd thy righteous spirit with dismay,
An Angel visited, and, with blest words,
Scatter'd thy fears away.

Thine arms embraced thy Maker newly born ;
With Him to Egypt's desert didst thou flee ;
Him in Jerusalem didst seek and find ;
Oh grief, oh joy for thee!

Not until after death their blissful crown
Others obtain ; but unto thee was given,
In thine own lifetime to enjoy thy God,
As do the blest in Heaven.

Grant us, great Trinity, for Joseph's sake,
Unto the starry mansions to attain ;
There, with glad tongues, Thy praise to celebrate
In one eternal strain.

[TR. REV. E. CASWALL]

178

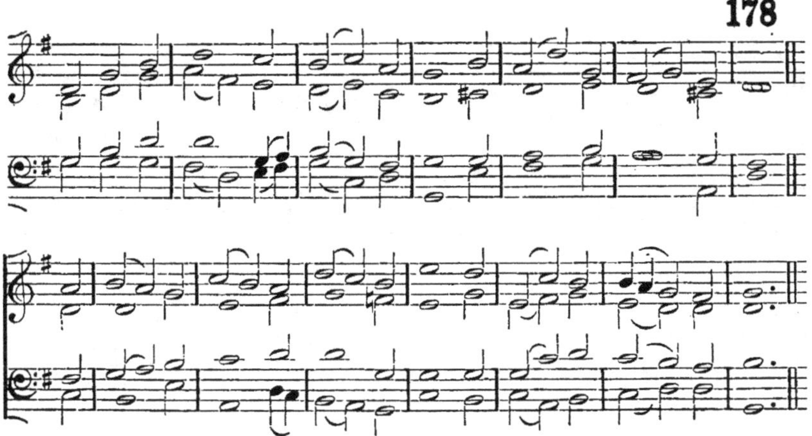

Cœlitum Joseph decus atque nostræ.

St. Joseph, Matins.

Joseph! our certain hope below!
  Glory of earth and Heaven!
Thou Pillar of the world! to thee
  Be praise immortal given.

Thee, as Salvation's minister,
  The mighty Maker chose;
As Foster-father of the Word;
  As Mary's spotless Spouse.

With joy thou sawest Him new born
  Of whom the Prophets sang;
Him in a manger didst adore,
  From whom Creation sprang.

The Lord of lords, and King of kings,
  Ruler of sky and sea,
Whom Heaven, and Earth, and Hell obey,
  Was subject unto thee.

Praise to the sacred Trine who thee
  So glorifies on high,
And for thy merits' sake may we
  Be sharers in thy joy.

[TR. REV. E. CASWALL]

SAINTS.

179

Du aus David's Stamm.

St. Joseph.

GREAT Saint Joseph! Son of David,
  Foster-father of our Lord,
Spouse of Mary ever Virgin,
  Keeping o'er them watch and ward!
In the stable thou didst guard them
  With a father's loving care;
Thou by God's command didst save them
  From the cruel Herod's snare.

Three long days in grief and anguish
  With His Mother, sweet and mild,
Mary Virgin, didst thou wander
  Seeking the belovèd Child.
In the temple thou didst find Him:
  Oh! what joy then filled thy heart!
In thy sorrows, in thy gladness
  Grant us, Joseph, to have part.

Clasped in Jesus' arms and Mary's,
  When death gently came at last,
Thy pure spirit sweetly sighing
  From its earthly dwelling passed.
Dear Saint Joseph! by that passing
  May our death be like to thine;
And with Jesus, Mary, Joseph,
  May our souls for ever shine. Amen.

[TR. BISHOP CASARTELLI]

180

Antra deserti teneris.

NATIVITY OF ST. JOHN BAPTIST, MATINS.

IN caves of the lone wilderness thy youth
Thou hiddest, shunning the rude throng of men,
So the pure treasure of thy soul to guard
From the least touch of sin.

There to thy sacred limbs the camel gave
A garment; the hard rock a bed supplied;
The stream thy thirst, locusts and honey wild
Thy hunger satisfied.

Oh, blest beyond the Prophets of old time!
They of the Saviour sang that was to be:
Him present to announce, and show to all,
Thy God reserved for thee!

Through the wide earth was never mortal man
Born holier than John; to whom was given
The guilty world's Baptizer to baptize,
And ope the door of Heaven.

Glory immortal to the Father be,
Praise to the sole-begotten sovereign Son,
With Thee, co-equal Spirit, One in Three,
While endless ages run.

[TR. REV. E. CASWALL]

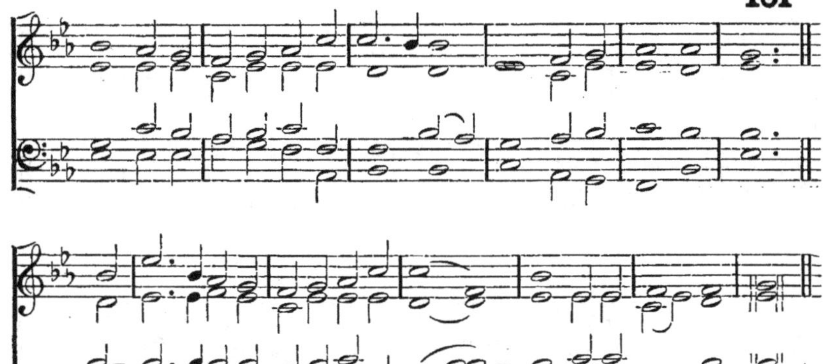

O nimis felix meritique celsi.

St. John Baptist, Lauds.

O BLESSÈD Saint, of snow-white purity!
  Dweller in wastes forlorn!
O mightiest of the Martyr host on high!
  Greatest of Prophets born!

Of all the diadems that on the brows
  Of Saints celestial shine,
Not one with brighter, purer, halo glows,
  In Heaven's high Court, than thine.

Oh! then on us a tender pitying gaze
  Cast from thy glory's throne;
Straighten our crooked, smooth our rugged ways,
  And break our hearts of stone.

So may the world's Redeemer find us meet
  To offer Him a place,
Where He may deign to set His sacred feet,
  Coming with gifts of grace.

Praise in the Heav'ns to Thee, O First and Last,
  The Trine eternal God!
Spare, Jesu, spare Thy people, whom Thou hast
  Redeem'd with Thine own blood.

[TR. REV. E. CASWALL]

SAINTS.

182

SAINTS.

Si vis Patronum quærere.

ST. PETER.

SEEK ye a Patron to defend
  Your cause?—then, one and all,
Without delay upon the Prince
  Of the Apostles call.
    Blest Holder of the heavenly Keys!
      Thy prayers we all implore:
    Unlock to us the sacred bars
      Of Heaven's eternal door.

By penitential tears thou didst
  The path of life regain;
Teach us with thee to weep our sins
  And wash away their stain.
    Blest Holder of the heavenly Keys!
      Thy prayers we all implore:
    Unlock to us the sacred bars
      Of Heaven's eternal door.

The Angel touch'd thee, and forthwith
  Thy chains from off thee fell;
Oh, loose us from the subtle coils
  That link us close with Hell.
    Blest Holder of the heavenly Keys!
      Thy prayers we all implore:
    Unlock to us the sacred bars
      Of Heaven's eternal door.

Firm Rock whereon the Church is based!
  Pillar that cannot bend!
With strength endue us; and the Faith
  From heresy defend.
    Blest Holder of the heavenly Keys!
      Thy prayers we all implore:
    Unlock to us the sacred bars
      Of Heaven's eternal door.

Save Rome, which from the days of old
  Thy blood hath sanctified;
And help the nations of the earth,
  That in thy help confide.
    Blest Holder of the heavenly Keys!
      Thy prayers we all implore;
    Unlock to us the sacred bars
      Of Heaven's eternal door.

Oh, worshipp'd by all Christendom!
  Her realms in peace maintain;
Let no contagion sap her strength,
  No discord rend in twain.
    Blest Holder of the heavenly Keys!
      Thy prayers we all implore
    Unlock to us the sacred bars
      Of Heaven's eternal door.

The weapons which our ancient foe
  Against us doth prepare,
Crush thou; nor suffer us to fall
  Into his deadly snare.
    Blest Holder of the heavenly Keys!
      Thy prayers we all implore:
    Unlock to us the sacred bars
      Of Heaven's eternal door.

Guard us through life; and in that hour
  When our last fight draws nigh,
O'er Death, o'er Hell, o'er Satan's power,
  Gain us the victory.
    Blest Holder of the heavenly Keys!
      Thy prayers we all implore:
    Unlock to us the sacred bars
      Of Heaven's eternal door.

Praise to the Lord and Father be;
  Praise to the Son who rose;
Praise to the Spirit Paraclete;
  While ages on ages flows.
    Blest Holder of the heavenly Keys!
      Thy prayers we all implore:
    Unlock to us the sacred bars
      Of Heaven's eternal door.

[TR. REV. E. CASWALL]

183

Decora lux æternitatis.

SS. PETER AND PAUL.

THE beauteous light of God's eternal Majesty
Streams down in golden rays to grace this holy day
Which crowned the princes of the Apostles' glorious choir,
And unto guilty mortals showed the heavenward way.

The teacher of the world and keeper of heaven's gate,
Rome's founders twain and rulers too of every land,
Triumphant over death by sword and shameful cross,
With laurel crowned are gathered to the eternal band.

O happy Rome! who in thy martyr princes' blood,
A twofold stream, art washed and doubly sanctified.
All earthly beauty thou alone outshinest far,
Empurpled by their outpoured life-blood's glorious tide.

All honour, power, and everlasting jubilee
To Him who all things made and governs here below,
To God, in essence One, and yet in persons Three,
Both now and ever, while unending ages flow.

[TR. MGR. CANON HALL]

184

Miris modis repente liber ferrea.

St. Peter's Chains.

THE Lord commands ; and, lo, his iron chains,
Falling from Peter, the behest obey :
Peter, blest shepherd ! who, to verdant plains,
And life's immortal springs, from day to day,
Leads on his tender charge, driving all wolves away.

Praise to the Father, through all ages be ;
Praise, blessing to the co-eternal Son,
And Holy Ghost, One glorious Trinity ;
To whom all majesty and might belong ;
So sing we now, and such be our eternal song.

[TR. REV. E. CASWALL]

185

Beate Pastor Petre clemens accipe.

St. Peter's Chair.

PETER, blest Shepherd! hearken to our cry,
And with a word unloose our guilty chain;
Thou! who hast power to ope the gates on high
To men below, and power to shut them fast again.

Praise, blessing, majesty, through endless days,
Be to the Trinity immortal given;
Who in pure Unity profoundly sways
Eternally alike all things in earth and Heaven.

[TR. REV. E. CASWALL]

186

Exultet orbis gaudiis.

VESPERS AND LAUDS OF APOSTLES.

NOW let the earth with joy resound;
And Heav'n the chant re-echo round;
Nor Heav'n nor earth too high can raise
The great Apostles' glorious praise.

O ye who, throned in glory dread,
Shall judge the living and the dead!
Lights of the world for evermore!
To you the suppliant prayer we pour.

Ye close the sacred gates on high;
At your command apart they fly:
Oh! loose for us the guilty chain
We strive to break, and strive in vain.

Sickness and health your voice obey:
At your command they go or stay:
From sin's disease our souls restore;
In good confirm us more and more.

So when the world is at its end,
And Christ to judgment shall descend,
May we be call'd those joys to see
Prepared from all eternity.

Praise to the Father, with the Son,
And Holy Spirit, Three in One;
As ever was in ages past,
And so shall be while ages last.

[TR. REV. E. CASWALL]

187

Æterna Christi munera.

APOSTLES, MATINS.

THE Lord's eternal gifts,
Th' Apostles' mighty praise,
Their victories, and high reward,
Sing we in joyful lays.

Theirs was the Saints' high Faith;
And quenchless Hope's pure glow;
And perfect Charity which laid
The world's fell tyrant low.

Lords of the Churches they;
Triumphant Chiefs of war;
Brave Soldiers of the Heavenly Camp;
True lights for evermore.

In them the Father shone;
In them the Son o'ercame;
In them the Holy Spirit wrought,
And fill'd their hearts with flame.

Praise to the Father, Son,
And Spirit, One and Three;
As evermore hath been before
And shall for ever be.

[TR. REV. E. CASWALL]

N.B.—The second Tune to Hymn 175 *is also suitable.*

188

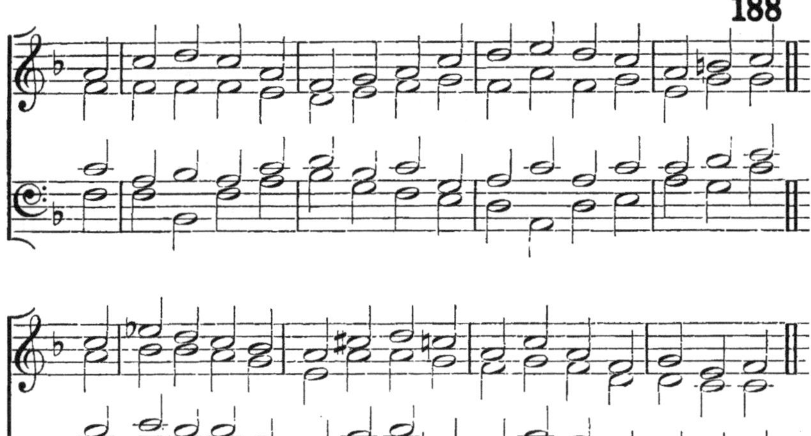

Tristes erant Apostoli.

APOSTLES, PASCHALTIME, VESPERS.

WHEN Christ, by His own servants
Had died upon the cruel Cross, [slain,
Th' Apostles of their joy bereft,
Were weeping their dear Master's loss :

Meanwhile, an Angel at the tomb
To holy women hath foretold,
" The faithful flock with joy shall soon
Their Lord in Galilee behold."

Who, as they run the news to bring, [meet,
Lo, straightway Christ Himself they
All radiant bright with heavenly light,
And falling, clasp His sacred feet.

To Galilee's lone mountain height
The Apostolic band retire :
There blest with their dear Saviour's sight,
Enjoy in full their soul's desire.

O Jesu ! from the death of sin
Keep us, we pray ; so shalt Thou be
The everlasting Paschal joy
Of all the souls new-born in Thee.

To God the Father, with the Son,
Who from the grave immortal rose ;
And Thee, O Paraclete, be praise,
While age on endless ages flows.

[TR. REV. E. CASWALL]

189

Paschale mundo gaudium.

APOSTLES, PASCHALTIME, LAUDS.

NOW daily shines the sun more fair,
Recalling that blest time,
When Christ on His Apostles shone,
In radiant light sublime.

They in His Body see the wounds
Like stars divinely glow;
Then forth, as His true Witnesses,
Throughout the world they go.

O Christ! Thou King most merciful!
Our inmost hearts possess;
So may our canticles of praise
Thy name for ever bless.

Keep us, O Jesu! from the death
Of sin; and deign to be
The everlasting Paschal joy
Of all new-born in Thee.

Praise to the Father, and the Son,
Who from the dead arose;
Praise to the blessèd Paraclete,
While age on ages flows.

[TR. REV. E. CASWALL]

190

St. John.

SAINT of the Sacred Heart,
  Sweet teacher of the Word,
Partner of Mary's woes,
  And favourite of thy Lord!
Thou to whom grace was given
  To stand where Peter fell;
Whose heart could brook the Cross
  Of Him it loved so well!

We know not all thy gifts;
  But this Christ bids us see,
That He who so loved all
  Found more to love in thee.
When the last evening came,
  Thy head was on His breast,
Pillowed on earth, where now
  In Heaven the saints find rest.

Dear Saint! I stand far off,
  With vilest sins opprest;
Oh may I dare, like thee,
  To lean upon His breast?
His touch could heal the sick,
  His voice could raise the dead!
Oh that my soul might be
  Where He allows thy head.

The gifts He gave to thee
  He gave thee to impart:
And I, too, claim with thee
  His Mother and His Heart.
Ah teach me, then, dear Saint!
  The secrets Christ taught thee,
The beatings of His Heart,
  And how it beat for me.

[REV. F. W. FABER]

N.B.—The Tunes to Hymns 141 *and* 173 *are also suitable.*

191

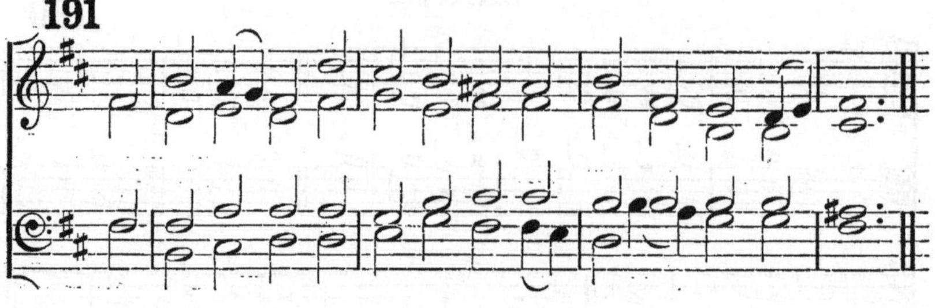

Quæ dixit, egit, pertulit.

OLD OFFICE OF ST. JOHN.

THE life which God's Incarnate Word
 Lived here below with men,
Three blest Evangelists record
 With Heav'n-inspired pen:

John penetrates on eagle wing
 The Father's dread abode;
And shows the mystery wherein
 The Word subsists with God.

Pure Saint! upon his Saviour's breast,
 Invited to recline,
'Twas thence he drew, in moments blest,
 His knowledge all divine:

There too, with that angelic love
 Did he his bosom fill,
Which, once enkindled from above,
 Breathes in his pages still.

Oh, dear to Christ!—to thee upon
 His Cross, of all bereft,
Thou virgin soul! the Virgin Son
 His Virgin Mother left.

To Jesus, born of Virgin bright,
 Praise with the Father be;
Praise to the Spirit Paraclete,
 Through all eternity.

[TR. REV. E. CASWALL]

192

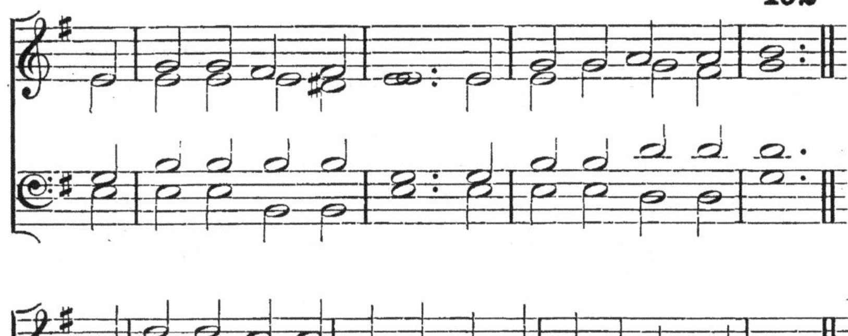

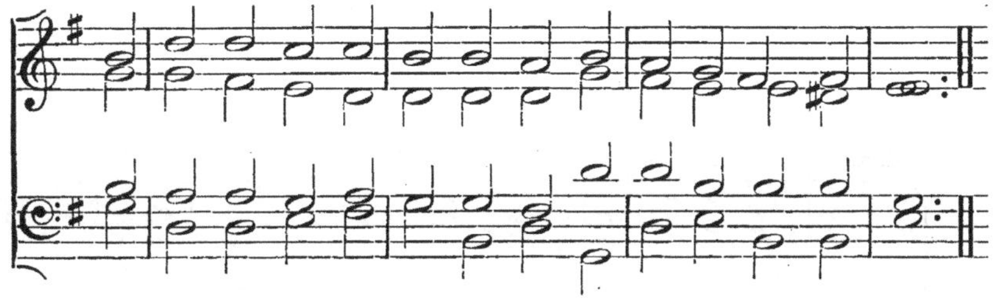

Jussu tyranni pro fide.

St. John.

AN exile for the Faith
Of thy Incarnate Lord,
Beyond the stars,—beyond all space,
Thy soul unprison'd soar'd:

There saw in glory Him
Who liveth, and was dead;
There Juda's Lion, and the Lamb
That for our ransom bled:

There of the Kingdom learnt
The mysteries sublime,
How, sown in Martyrs' blood, the Faith
Should spread from clime to clime.

There the new City, bathed
In her dear Spouse's light,
Pure seat of bliss, thy spirit saw,
And gloried in the sight.

Now to the Lamb's clear fount,
To drink of life their fill
Thou callest all;—O Lord, in me
This blessèd thirst instil.

To Jesus, Virgin-born,
Praise with the Father be;
Praise to the Spirit Paraclete,
Through all eternity.

[NICHOLAS LE TOURNEAUX. TR. REV. E. CASWALL]

SAINTS.

193

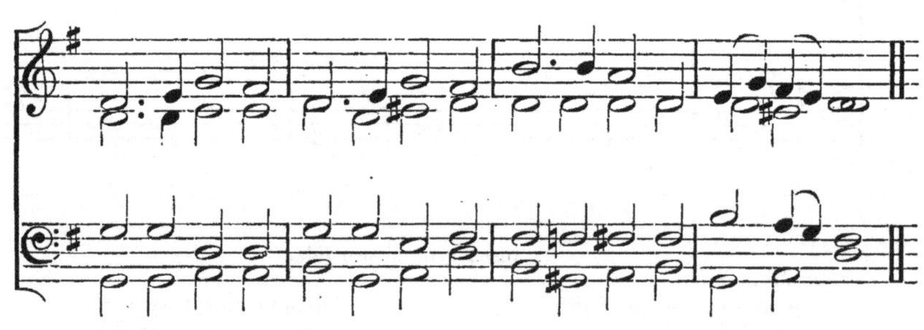

SAINTS.

St. Andrew.

GREAT Saint Andrew, Friend of Jesus,
  Lover of His glorious Cross,
Early by His voice effective
  Called from ease to pain and loss,
Sweet Saint Andrew, Simon's brother,
  Who with haste fraternal flew,
Fain with him to share the treasure
  Which, at Jesus' lips, he drew.

Blest Saint Andrew, Jesus' herald,
  Meek Apostle, Martyr bold,
Who, by deeds his words confirming,
  Seal'd with blood the truth he told.
Ne'er to king was crown so beauteous,
  Ne'er was prize to heart so dear,
As to him the Cross of Jesus
  When its promised joys drew near.

Loved Saint Andrew, Scotland's patron,
  Watch thy land with heedful eye,
Rally round the Cross of Jesus
  All her storied chivalry!
To the Father, Son, and Spirit,
  Fount of sanctity and love,
Give we glory, now and ever,
  With the saints who reign above.

[Canon Oakeley]

194

Deus tuorum militum.

VESPERS FOR ONE MARTYR.

O THOU, of all Thy warriors Lord,
Thyself the crown and sure reward;
Set us from sinful fetters free,
Who sing Thy Martyr's victory.

Right manfully his cross he bore,
And ran his race of torments sore:
For Thee he pour'd his life away;
With Thee he lives in endless day.

In selfish pleasures' worldly round
The taste of bitter gall he found;
But sweet to him was Thy dear Name,
And so to heavenly joys he came.

We, then, before Thee bending low,
Intreat Thee, Lord, Thy love to show
On this the day Thy Martyr died,
Who in Thy Saints art glorified!

To God the Father, with the Son,
And Holy Spirit, Three in One,
Be praise and glory evermore,
As in th' eternity before!

[TR. REV. E. CASWALL]

195

Rex gloriose martyrum.

Lauds for Many Martyrs.

O THOU, the Martyrs' glorious King!
  Of Confessors the crown and prize;
Who dost to joy celestial bring
  Those who the joys of earth despise;

By all the praise Thy Saints have won;
  By all their pains in days gone by;
By all the deeds which they have done;
  Hear Thou Thy suppliant people's cry.

Thou dost amid Thy Martyrs fight;
  Thy Confessors Thou dost forgive;
May we find mercy in Thy sight,
  And in Thy sacred presence live.

To God the Father glory be,
  And to His sole begotten Son;
And glory, Holy Ghost, to Thee!
  While everlasting ages run.

[TR. REV. E. CASWALL]

SAINTS.

196

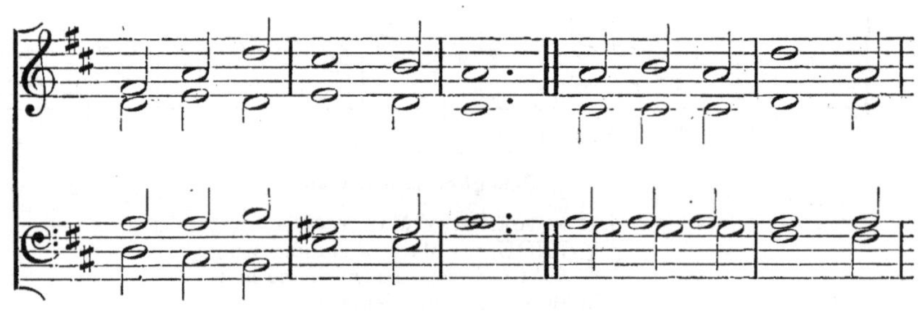

SAINTS.

English Martyrs.

MARTYRS of England! standing on high
  Warrior-band of the great White Throne—
Martyrs of England! list to our cry,
  Pray for the country you called your own.

Not as strangers of far-off land;
  Not as heroes of long ago;
Our English speech ye can understand:
  Our cities, and hills, and fields ye know.

Nighest to us of the White-robed Host;
  Bound to us as our kith and kin;
Get us the love that counts no cost,
  That knows no fear but the fear of sin.

Martyrs of England! keep us true,
  True to Jesus, whate'er the pain;
Martyrs of England! we look to you;
  Win our country to Christ again.

Many, alas! your blood forget;
  Many your combat do not know;
We, your children, will pay the debt
  Our thankless country to you doth owe.

Few are the shrines o'er your scattered dust,
  Grateful hearts are your living fane;
Your incense, our love, and prayer, and trust
  Till England honour her Saints again.

Jesus, Master! how long, how long
  Shall the nation's rage Thy glory foil?
The blood of Thy Martyrs—a mighty throng—
  Cries to Thee from our hallowed soil.

Lord of glory, holy and true,
  Honour those that have honour'd Thee;
Bid Thy people, the whole world through,
  Hail them as Saints on bended knee.

King of the Martyrs! these are they
  Whose blood for Thee in our land was given;
King of the Martyrs! their children pray,
  Crown them on earth as Thou hast in Heaven.

[SISTER MARY XAVIER]

SAINTS.

197

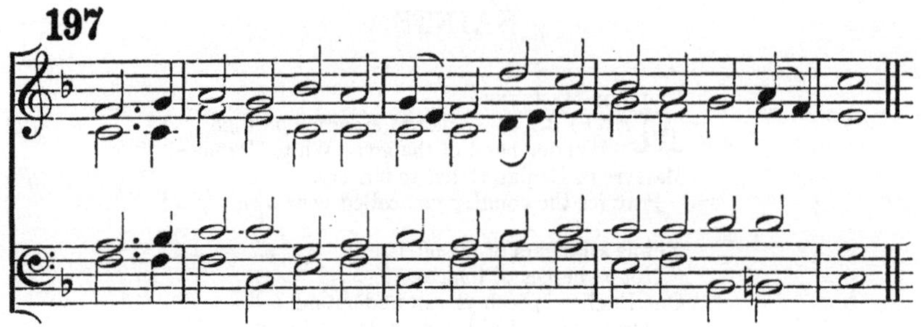

SAINTS.

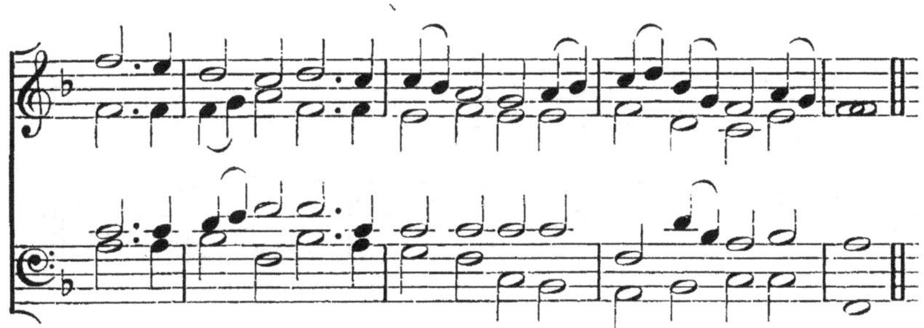

ENGLISH MARTYRS.

TYBURN'S days are long forgiven, unforgotten is the pain ;
 Time can never dim the traces of the cruel blood-red stain ;
And the Martyrs' cry for vengeance rises up before Thy throne :—
" Save the land we love so well, Lord ! claim its children for Thine own."

For the blood they shed so gladly must bear living fruit one day :
Let that day be swift in coming, for we cannot brook delay ;
Precious lives are daily shipwrecked on the sea of doubt and strife ;
Human souls are ever hungry for the word that giveth life.

And the labourers are few, Lord, while the fields are growing white
With their human harvest, waiting for God's sickle keen and bright,—
For the sickle of the Gospel, keener than the victor's sword,
That shall gather in the harvest to the storehouse of the Lord.

Look upon this land, deep watered with the blood of Martyrs slain ;
Surely these who were our kinsmen have not bled for us in vain ;
We, like them, are stoutly fighting for the souls of men to-day,
And we claim them for our brothers who have fallen in the fray.

So for ever through the ages as they stand before Thy throne
May the glory of their triumph for our sinful past atone ;
May the wounds they bore for Thee, Lord, ever flashing ruby bright,
Guide us through the darksome future, till we rest within Thy sight.

[REV. J. REEKS]

N.B.—Tune 198 *may also be sung to this Hymn.*

SAINTS.

198

SAINTS.

St. George.

LEADER now on earth no longer,
  Soldier of th' eternal King,
Victor in the fight for Heaven,
  We thy loving praises sing.
    Great Saint George, our patron, help us,
      In the conflict be thou nigh;
    Help us in that daily battle,
      Where each one must win or die.

Praise him who in deadly battle
  Never shrank from foeman's sword,
Proof against all earthly weapon,
  Gave his life for Christ the Lord.
    Great Saint George, &c.

Who, when earthly war was over,
  Fought, but not for earth's renown;
Fought, and won a nobler glory—
  Won the martyr's purple crown.
    Great Saint George, &c.

Help us when temptation presses,
  We have still our crown to win;
Help us when our soul is weary
  Fighting with the powers of sin.
    Great Saint George, &c.

Clothe us in thy shining armour,
  Place thy good sword in our hand;
Teach us how to wield it, fighting
  Onward towards the heavenly land.
    Great Saint George, &c.

Onward, till, our striving over,
  On life's battlefield we fall,
Resting then, but ever ready,
  Waiting for the angel's call.
    Great Saint George, &c.

[REV. J. REEKS]

199

St. George.

ARM! arm! for the struggle approaches,
  Prepare for the combat of life;
Saint George! be our watchword in battle,
  Saint George! be our strength in the strife.

Great Saint, from the throne of thy splendour,
  Look down on thy own chosen isle,
Soon, soon may they share in thy glory,
  Who faithfully strive here awhile.

The land of thy love is a desert,
  Its temples and altars are bare,
The finger of death is upon it,
  The footprints of Satan are there.

Arise in the might of thy power,
  And scatter the foes of the Lord;
As the idols of Rome in their temple
  Were crushed at the sound of thy word.

Oh, bring back the faith that we cherish,
  For which thou hast nobly withstood
The tortures and rack of the tyrant,
  That faith which thou seal'dst with thy blood.

200

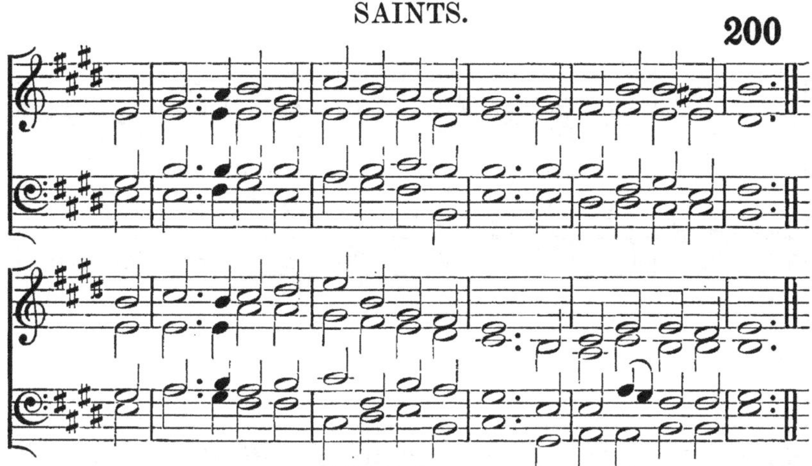

Iste Confessor Domini.

Confessors, Vespers.

THE Confessor of Christ, from shore to shore
 Worshipp'd with solemn rite ;
This day with merits full, his labours o'er,
 Went to his seat in light.

(If it be not the day of his death.)

This day receives those honours which are his,
 High in the realms of light.

Holy and innocent were all his ways ;
 Sweet, temperate, unstain'd ;
His life was prayer—his every breath was praise,
 While breath to him remain'd.

Ofttimes have miracles in many a land
 His sanctity displayed ;
And still doth health return at his command
 To many a frame decay'd.

Therefore to him triumphant praise we pay,
 And yearly songs renew ;
Praying our glorious Saint for us to pray,
 All the long ages through.

To God, of all the centre and the source,
 Be power and glory given ;
Who sways the mighty world through all its course,
 From the bright throne of Heaven.

[TR. REV. E. CASWALL]

SAINTS.

201

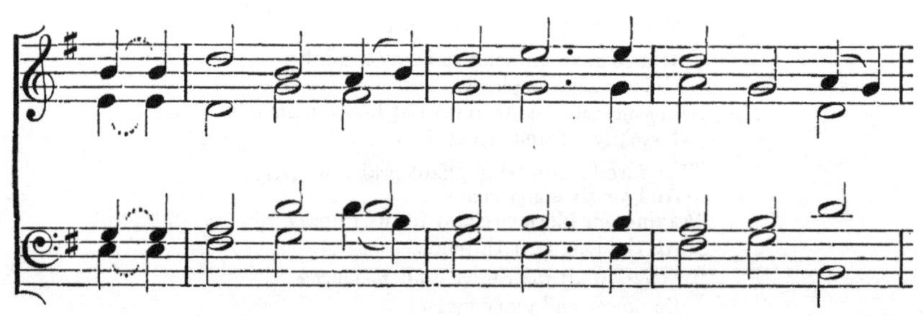

SAINTS.

St. Patrick.

HAIL, glorious Saint Patrick, dear Saint of our isle,
On us thy poor children bestow a sweet smile :
And now thou art high in the mansions above,
On Erin's green valleys look down in thy love.

Hail, glorious Saint Patrick ! thy words were once strong
Against Satan's wiles and a heretic throng ;
Not less is thy might where in Heaven thou art ;
Oh, come to our aid, in our battle take part.

In the war against sin, in the fight for the faith,
Dear Saint, may thy children resist unto death ;
May their strength be in meekness, in penance, in prayer,
Their banner the Cross which they glory to bear.

Thy people, now exiles on many a shore,
Shall love and revere thee till time be no more ;
And the fire thou hast kindled shall ever burn bright,
Its warmth undiminished, undying its light.

Ever bless and defend the sweet land of our birth,
Where the shamrock still blooms as when thou wert on earth,
And our hearts shall yet burn, wheresoever we roam,
For God and Saint Patrick, and our native home.

[SISTER AGNES]

202 SAINTS.

Boldly (in march time).

SAINTS.

St. Patrick.

SAINT Patrick, for our country pray,
  Our ever-faithful land,
Whose martyred hosts so gloriously
  Before God's great throne stand ;
Look down upon thy children here,
  Look down upon our race,
And bless, dear Saint, this little isle
  And each one's native place.

Oh, hear, Saint Patrick, while we pray ,
  Thou art our own dear Saint ;
Uphold the weak, protect the young,
  Give strength to souls that faint ;
Thou know'st how we are tempted still,
  Thou know'st how we are tried,
Thou know'st that we are faithful too,
  Whatever ills betide.

Oh, help our poor in patient love
  To bear their suffering life,
To think of that great victory
  Which cometh after strife ;
Keep from them all revengeful thoughts
  Whene'er they suffer wrong—
The meek alone are crowned in Heav'n,
  And Heav'n will come ere long.

We are thy children, blessèd Saint,
  The children of thy love ;
We know how mighty is thy prayer,
  How it was heard above ;
Pray for us now, for priest and nun,
  For rich men and for poor,
That to the end, however tried,
  Our faith may still endure.

[ANON. "HYMNS FOR ECCLESIASTICAL YEAR"]

203

SAINTS.

Very slowly. In unison.

SAINTS.

N.B.—Criticism of this Tune is disarmed by the fact that Faber wrote his words for it.

St. Patrick.

ALL praise to Saint Patrick who brought to our mountains
  The gifts of God's faith, the sweet light of His love !
All praise to the shepherd who showed us the fountains
  That rise in the Heart of the Saviour above !
    For hundreds of years,
    In smiles and in tears,
Our Saint has been with us, our shield and our stay ;
    All else may have gone,
    Saint Patrick alone,
He hath been to us light when earth's lights were all set,
  For the glories of faith they can never decay ;
And the best of our glories is bright with us yet,
  In the faith and the feast of Saint Patrick's Day.

There is not a saint in the bright courts of Heaven
  More faithful than he to the land of his choice ;
Oh, well may the nation to whom he was given,
  In the feast of their sire and apostle rejoice !
    In glory above,
    True to his love,
He keeps the false faith from his children away ;
    The dark false faith,
    That is worse than death,
Oh, he drives it far off from the green sunny shore,
  Like the reptiles which fled from his curse in dismay ;
And Erin, when error's proud triumph is o'er,
  Will still be found keeping Saint Patrick's Day.

Then what shall we do for thee, Heaven-sent Father ?
  What shall the proof of our loyalty be ?
By all that is dear to our hearts, we would rather
  Be martyred, sweet Saint ! than bring shame upon thee !
    But oh, he will take
    The promise we make,
So to live that our lives by God's help may display
    The light that he bore
    To Erin's shore :
Yes ! Father of Ireland ! no child wilt thou own,
  Whose life is not lighted by grace on its way ;
For they are true Irish, oh yes ! they alone,
  Whose hearts are all true on Saint Patrick's Day.

[REV. F. W. FABER]

204

St. Gregory the Great.

LORD, receive our thankful homage,
  Who, from toils of error freed,
Bless Thee for the hand that saved us,
  And the heart that felt our need—
For Saint Gregory our father,
  Vigilant in name and deed.

For our own, our dear apostle,
  Gregory the Great, the Blest,
Who, while England lay in darkness,
  Spared no labour, knew no rest;
For the gracious love he bore us,
  Be Thy holy name confessed!

Love that grew, since first those children,
  Fettered in a Roman mart,
With their bright young beauty won him
  Help and comfort to impart—
From that day he bore our England
  Graven ever on his heart.

Lovingly he looks upon them,
  Sighing, as he sets them free:
"If these little ones are Angles,
  Surely angels shall they be,
Singing joyous Alleluias,
  Saved from wrath, dear Lord, to Thee!"

When on Peter's throne uplifted,
  All the churches claim his care,
Yet his heart is most in England
  With his sons who battle there,
And he aids them in the conflict
  By the arm of ceaseless prayer.

Thus our own we joy to name him,
  Though our shores he never trod:
Though our sins have marred his life-work,
  And we bow beneath Thy rod,
Jesu, may our father's pleading
  Gain the land once more for God.

[DOM BEDE CAMM, O.S.B.]

205

Doctors.

O qui perpetuus nos monitor doces.

O THOU, th' eternal Father's Word!
What though on earth Thy voice is [heard
No longer, as of yore;
Still, age by age, dost Thou supply
With holy teachers from on high
Thy Church for evermore.

They, in Thy stead, the truth maintain,
And guard the Christian Faith from stain,
Against its deadly foes;
Which, under such protecting care,
For ever fresh, for ever fair,
In virgin beauty glows.

Remnants of superstition old,
Falsehood and error from the fold
'Tis theirs to drive away;
Theirs to recover to the Lord
The souls, whom heresy and fraud
Have made a wretched prey.

They, to the long hoar-headed line
Of Fathers, pointing,—as they shine
Far in the ages deep,—
Preserve the ancient doctrines pure;
Confute the novel; and secure
The great deposit keep.

All praise to Thee, who by the pen
Of saintly doctors, teaching men
Thy truths, O Truth sublime!
Without a word, without a sound,
Thy grace diffusest all around,
Thy glory through all time.

[TR. REV. E. CASWALL]

206

Jesu corona Virginum.

VIRGINS.

DEAR Crown of all the Virgin-choir!
That holy Mother's Virgin Son!
Who is, alone of womankind,
Mother and Virgin both in one.

Encircled by Thy virgin band
Amid the lilies Thou art found;
For Thy pure brides with lavish hand
Scattering immortal graces round.

And still wherever Thou dost bend
Thy lovely steps, O glorious King,
Virgins upon Thy steps attend,
And hymns to Thy high glory sing.

Keep us, O Purity divine,
From every least corruption free;
Our every sense from sin refine,
And purify our souls for Thee.

To God the Father, and the Son,
All honour, glory, praise be given;
With Thee, co-equal Paraclete!
For evermore in earth and Heaven.

[TR. REV. E. CASWALL]

207

ST. AGNES.

SWEET Agnes, holy child,
  All purity,
Oh, may we, undefiled,
  Be pure as thee :
Ready our blood to shed
Forth as the martyrs led,
The path of pain to tread,
  And die like thee.

O gentle patroness
  Of holy youth,
Ask God all those to bless
  Who love the truth :
Oh, guide us on our way
Unto th' eternal day,
With hearts all pure and gay,
  Dear Saint, like thine.

Look down and hear our prayer
  From realms above,
Show us thy tender care,
  Thy guiding love :
Oh, keep us in thy sight,
Till in th' unclouded light
Of Heaven's pure vision bright
  We dwell with thee.

208

St. Cecilia.

LET the deep organ swell the lay,
In honour of this festive day;
Let the harmonious choirs proclaim
Cecilia's ever-blessèd name.

Rome gave the virgin martyr birth,
Whose holy name hath filled the earth;
And from the early dawn of youth,
She fixed her heart on God and truth.

Then from the world's bewildering strife,
In peace she spent her holy life—
Teaching the organ to combine
With voice, to praise the Lamb divine.

Cecilia, with a twofold crown
Adorned in Heaven, we pray look down
Upon thy fervent votaries here,
And hearken to their humble prayer.

[REV. C. PISE]

209

Virgo vernans velut rosa.

St. Winifred.

MORE fair than all the vernal flowers
 Embosom'd in the dales,
Saint Winifred in beauty bloom'd,
 The rose of ancient Wales.

With every loveliest grace adorn'd,
 The Lamb's unsullied bride,
Apart from all the world she dwelt
 Upon this mountain side.

Till Caradoc, with impious love,
 Her fleeing steps pursued,
And in her sacred maiden blood
 His cruel hands imbrued.

He straight the debt of vengeance paid,
 Ingulf'd in yawning flame;
But God a deed of wonder work'd
 To her immortal fame.

For where the grassy sward received
 The Martyr's sever'd head,
This holy fountain upward gush'd,
 Of crystal vein'd with red.

Here miracles of might are wrought;
 Here all diseases fly;
Here see the blind, and speak the dumb,
 Who but in faith draw nigh.

Assist us, glorious Winifred,
 Dear Virgin, ever blest!
The passions of our hearts appease,
 And lull each storm to rest.

[TR. REV. E. CASWALL]

U

SAINTS.

210

Claræ dici gaudiis.

St. Anne.

SPOTLESS Anna! Juda's glory!
  Through the Church from East to West,
Every tongue proclaims thy praises,
  Holy Mary's Mother blest.
    Under thy protecting banner
      Here assembled in thy name,
    Mary's Mother, gracious Anna,
      Grace and help of thee we claim.

Saintly Kings and priestly Sires
  Blended in thy sacred line;
Thou in virtue, all before thee
  Didst excel by grace divine.
    Under thy protecting banner, &c.

Link'd in bonds of purest wedlock,
  Thine it was for us to bear,
By the favour of High Heaven,
  Our auroral Virgin Star.
    Under thy protecting banner, &c.

From thy stem in beauty budded
  Ancient Jesse's mystic rod;
Earth from thee received the Mother
  Of th' Almighty Son of God.
    Under thy protecting banner, &c.

All the human race benighted
  In the depths of darkness lay;
When in Anne it saw the dawning
  Of the long-expected day.
    Under thy protecting banner, &c.

Honour, glory, virtue, merit,
  Be to Thee, O Virgin's Son!
With the Father and the Spirit,
  While eternal ages run.
    Under thy protecting banner, &c.

[TR. REV. E. CASWALL]

U

211

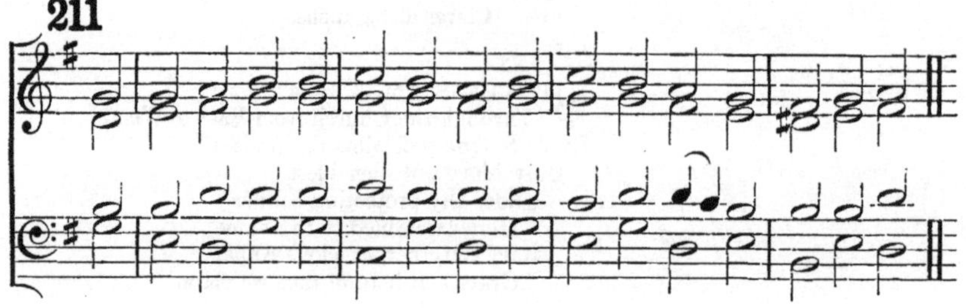

Pater superni luminis.

ST. MARY MAGDALENE.

FATHER of light! one glance of Thine,
 Whose eyes the Universe control,
Fills Magdalene with holy love,
 And melts the ice within her soul.

Her precious ointment forth she brings,
 Upon those sacred feet to pour;
She washes them with burning tears;
 And with her hair she wipes them o'er.

Impassion'd to the Cross she clings,
 Nor fears beside the tomb to stay;
Nought of its ruffian guard she recks,
 For love has cast all fear away.

O Christ, Thou very Love itself! [given!
 Blest hope of man, through Thee for-
So touch our spirits from above,
 So purify our souls for Heaven.

To God the Father with the Son
 And Holy Paraclete, with Thee,
As evermore hath been before,
 Be glory through eternity.

[CARDINAL BELLARMINE. TR. REV. E. CASWALL]

212

MY God! how wonderful Thou art,
  Thy Majesty how bright,
How beautiful Thy Mercy-seat
  In depths of burning light!

How dread are Thine eternal years,
  O everlasting Lord!
By prostrate spirits day and night
  Incessantly adored!

How beautiful, how beautiful
  The sight of Thee must be,
Thine endless wisdom, boundless power,
  And awful purity!

Oh, how I fear Thee, Living God!
  With deepest, tenderest fears,
And worship Thee with trembling hope,
  And penitential tears.

Yet I may love Thee too, O Lord!
  Almighty as Thou art,
For Thou hast stooped to ask of me
  The love of my poor heart.

Oh, then, this worse than worthless heart
  In pity deign to take,
And make it love Thee, for Thyself
  And for Thy glory's sake.

No earthly father loves like Thee,
  No mother half so mild
Bears and forbears, as Thou hast done,
  With me, Thy sinful child.

Only to sit and think of God,
  Oh, what a joy it is!
To think the thought, to breathe the Name,
  Earth has no higher bliss!

Father of Jesus, love's Reward!
  What rapture will it be,
Prostrate before Thy Throne to lie,
  And gaze and gaze on Thee!

[REV. F. W. FABER]

213 GENERAL.

With dignity.

PRAISE we our God with joy
And gladness never ending;
Angels and saints with us
Their grateful voices blending.
He is our Father dear,
With Parent's love o'erflowing;
Mercies unsought, unknown,
On wayward hearts bestowing.

He is our Shepherd true;
With watchful care unsleeping,
On us, His erring sheep,
An eye of pity keeping.
He with a mighty arm
The bonds of sin hath broken,
And to our burden'd hearts
The words of peace hath spoken.

Graces in copious stream
From that pure fount are welling,
Where, in our heart of hearts,
Our God hath set His dwelling.
His word our lantern is,
His peace our consolation,
His sweetness all our rest,
Himself our great salvation.

[CANON OAKELEY]

214

LOVING Shepherd of Thy sheep,
  Keep me, Lord, in safety keep;
Nothing can Thy power withstand,
  None can pluck me from Thy hand.

Loving Shepherd, Thou didst give
  Thine own life that I might live;
May I love Thee day by day,
  Gladly Thy sweet will obey.

Loving Shepherd, ever near,
  Teach me still Thy voice to hear;
Suffer not my step to stray
  From the strait and narrow way.

Where Thou leadest may I go,
  Walking in Thy steps below;
Then before Thy Father's throne,
  Jesu, claim me for Thine own.

[MISS LEESON]

GENERAL.

215

GENERAL.

SWEET Saviour! bless us ere we go;
  Thy word into our minds instil;
And make our lukewarm hearts to glow
  With lowly love and fervent will.
Through life's long day and death's dark night,
O gentle Jesus! be our light.

The day is done; its hours have run;
  And Thou hast taken count of all,
The scanty triumphs grace has won,
  The broken vow, the frequent fall.
Through life's long day and death's dark night,
O gentle Jesus! be our light.

Grant us, dear Lord! from evil ways
  True absolution and release;
And bless us more than in past days
  With purity and inward peace.
Through life's long day and death's dark night,
O gentle Jesus! be our light.

Do more than pardon; give us joy,
  Sweet fear and sober liberty,
And loving hearts without alloy,
  That only long to be like Thee.
Through life's long day and death's dark night,
O gentle Jesus! be our light.

Labour is sweet, for Thou hast toiled,
  And care is light, for Thou hast cared;
Let not our works with self be soiled,
  Nor in unsimple ways ensnared.
Through life's long day and death's dark night,
O gentle Jesus! be our light.

For all we love—the poor, the sad,
  The sinful—unto Thee we call;
Oh let Thy mercy make us glad;
  Thou art our Jesus and our All.
Through life's long day and death's dark night,
O gentle Jesus! be our light.

[REV. F. W. FABER]

GENERAL.

216

GENERAL.

WHY art thou sorrowful, servant of God?
And what is this dulness that hangs o'er thee now?
Sing the praises of Jesus, and sing them aloud,
And the song shall dispel the dark cloud from thy brow.

For is there a thought in the wide world so sweet,
As that God has so cared for us, bad as we are,
That He thinks for us, plans for us, stoops to entreat,
And follows us, wander we ever so far?

Then how can the heart e'er be drooping or sad,
Which God hath once touched with the light of His grace?
Can the child have a doubt who but lately hath laid
Himself to repose in his father's embrace?

And is it not wonderful, servant of God!
That He should have honoured us so with His love,
That the sorrows of life should but shorten the road
Which leads to Himself and the mansion above?

Oh then, when the spirit of darkness comes down,
With clouds and uncertainties into thy heart,
One look to thy Saviour, one thought of thy crown,
And the tempest is over, the shadows depart.

That God hath once whispered a word in thine ear,
Or sent thee from Heaven one sorrow for sin,
Is enough for a life both to banish all fear,
And to turn into peace all the troubles within.

[REV. F. W. FABER]

GENERAL.

217 *Briskly.*

YES, Heaven is the prize
My soul shall strive to gain;
One glimpse of Paradise
Repays a life of pain.
'Tis Heaven; yes, Heaven; yes,
Heaven is the prize;
'Tis Heaven; 'tis Heaven; yes,
Heaven is the prize.

Yes, Heaven is the prize!
My soul, oh think of this;
All earthly goods despise
For such a crown of bliss.
'Tis Heaven, &c.

Yes, Heaven is the prize!
When sorrows press around,
Look up beyond the skies,
Where hope and strength are found.
'Tis Heaven, &c.

Yes, Heaven is the prize!
Oh, 'tis not hard to gain;
He surely wins who tries,
For hope can conquer pain.
'Tis Heaven, &c.

Yes, Heaven is the prize!
The strife will soon be past:
Faint not, but raise your eyes
And struggle to the last.
'Tis Heaven, &c.

Yes, Heaven is the prize!
Faith shows the crown to gain;
Hope lights the way and dies;
But love will always reign.
'Tis Heaven, &c.

Yes, Heaven is the prize!
Too much cannot be given;
And he alone is wise
Who gives up all for Heaven.
'Tis Heaven, &c.

Yes, Heaven is the prize!
Death opens wide the door,
And then the spirit flies
To God for evermore.
'Tis Heaven; yes, Heaven; yes,
Heaven is the prize;
'Tis Heaven; 'tis Heaven; yes,
Heaven is the prize.

[REV. E. VAUGHAN, C.SS.R.]

GENERAL.

218

GENERAL.

JESUS, ever-loving Saviour,
  Thou didst live and die for me;
Living, I will live to love Thee,
  Dying, I will die for Thee.
    Jesus! Jesus!
By Thy life and death and sorrow
  Help me in my agony.

Mary, thou canst not forsake me,
  Virgin-mother undefiled;
Thou didst not abandon Jesus,
  Dying, tortured, and reviled.
    Jesus! Jesus!
Send Thy Mother to console me:
  Mary, help thy guilty child.

When the last dread hour approaching
  Fills my guilty soul with fear,
All my sins rise up before me,
  All my virtues disappear.
    Jesus! Jesus!
Turn not Thou in anger from me;
  Mary, Joseph, then be near.

Jesus, when in cruel anguish
  Dying on the shameful tree,
All abandoned by Thy Father,
  Thou didst writhe in agony.
    Jesus! Jesus!
By those three long hours of sorrow
  Thou didst purchase hope for me.

Kindest Jesus, Thou wert standing
  By Thy foster-father's bed
While Thy Mother, softly praying,
  Held her dying Joseph's head.
    Jesus! Jesus!
By that death so calm and holy
  Soothe me in that hour of dread.

When the priest, with holy unction,
  Prays for mercy and for grace,
May the tears of deep compunction
  All my guilty stains efface.
    Jesus! Jesus!
Let me find in Thee a refuge,
  In Thy heart a resting-place.

Then, by all that Thou didst suffer,
  Grant me mercy in that day;
Help me, Mary, my sweet Mother,
  Holy Joseph, near me stay.
    Jesus! Jesus!
Let me die, my lips repeating,
  Jesus, mercy! Mary, pray!

[ANON. "HOLY FAMILY HYMNS," 1860]

219

LORD, for to-morrow and its needs
I do not pray;
Keep me, my God, from stain of sin,
Just for to-day.

Let me both diligently work,
And duly pray;
Let me be kind in word and deed,
Just for to-day.

Let me be slow to do my will,
Prompt to obey;
Help me to mortify my flesh,
Just for to-day.

Let me no wrong or idle word
Unthinking say;
Set Thou a seal upon my lips,
Just for to-day.

Let me in season, Lord, be grave,
In season, gay;
Let me be faithful to Thy grace,
Just for to-day.

And if to-day my tide of life
Should ebb away,
Give me Thy sacraments divine
Sweet Lord, to-day.

In Purgatory's cleansing fires
Brief be my stay;
Oh, bid me, if to-day I die,
Go home to-day.

So, for to-morrow and its needs,
I do not pray;
But keep me, guide me, love me, Lord,
Just for to-day.

[SISTER M. XAVIER]

220

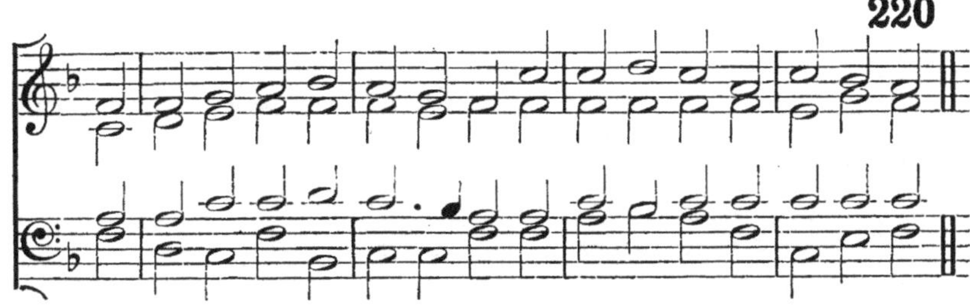

OH, say not thou art left of God,
  Because His tokens in the sky
Thou canst not read: this earth He trod
  To teach thee He was ever nigh.

He sees, beneath the fig-tree green,
  Nathaniel con His sacred lore;
Shouldst thou thy chamber seek, unseen,
  He enters through the unopen'd door.

And when thou liest, by slumber bound,
  Outwearied in the Christian fight,
In glory, girt with Saints around,
  He stands above thee through the night.

When friends to Emmaus bend their course,
  He joins, although He holds their eyes:
Or, shouldst thou feel some fever's force,
  He takes thy hand, He bids thee rise.

Or on a voyage, when storms prevail,
  And threaten thee upon the sea,
He walks the wave, He wings the sail,
  The shore is gain'd, and thou art free.

[CARDINAL NEWMAN]

221

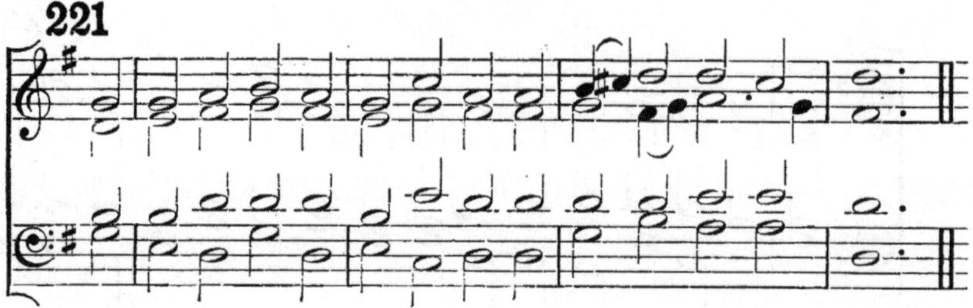

UNVEIL, O Lord, and on us shine,
In glory and in grace;
This gaudy world grows pale before
The beauty of Thy face.

Till Thou art seen, it seems to be
A sort of fairy ground,
Where suns unsetting light the sky,
And flowers and fruits abound.

But when Thy keener, purer beam
Is pour'd upon our sight,
It loses all its power to charm,
And what was day is night.

Its noblest toils are then the scourge
Which made Thy blood to flow;
Its joys are but the treacherous thorns
Which circled round Thy brow.

And thus, when we renounce for Thee
Its endless aims and fears,
The tender memories of the past,
The hopes of coming years,

Poor is our sacrifice, whose eyes
Are lighted from above;
We offer what we cannot keep,
What we have ceased to love.

[CARDINAL NEWMAN]

222

WHEN I sink down in gloom or fear,
  Hope blighted or delay'd,
Thy whisper, Lord, my heart shall cheer,
  "'Tis I ; be not afraid!"

Or, startled at some sudden blow,
  If fretful thoughts I feel,
"Fear not, it is but I!" shall flow,
  As balm my wound to heal.

Nor will I quit Thy way, though foes
  Some onward pass defend ;
From each rough voice the watchword goes,
  "Be not afraid! . . . a friend!"

And oh! when judgment's trumpet clear
  Awakes me from the grave,
Still in its echo may I hear,
  "'Tis Christ! He comes to save."

[CARDINAL NEWMAN]

GENERAL.

223

GENERAL.

Dies iræ.

THE day of wrath, that awful day,
Shall all the world in ashes lay,
David and Sibyls prophesy;
And oh! what trembling will there be,
When the Judge comes in Majesty,
To try the world unsparingly.

The trumpet sends its wondrous sound
Through all the tombs beneath the ground,
And brings all to the Judgment Seat;
Nature and Death shall stand amazed,
When they behold the creature raised,
The Judge's questioning to meet.

Now shall the written Book appear,
In which all actions are made clear,
That to this Judgment are assigned;
The Judge His Judgment Seat shall take,
All hidden things shall public make,
Nothing impunity shall find.

Unhappy me, what shall I say,
And to what patron shall I pray,
When e'en the just might quake with dread?
O King of fearful Majesty,
Thou savest freely, O save me,
Thou art sweet pity's Fountain Head.

For love of me, sweet Jesus kind,
Thou cam'st on earth; call this to mind,
And save me in that day of pain;
Thou soughtest me with weary care,
To save me Thou the Cross didst bear;
Let not such labour be in vain.

Thou, who dost righteous vengeance take,
A grant of free forgiveness make,
Before the accounting day arrives;
With blushes deep and heartfelt moan,
O God, oppressed with guilt, I groan,
Spare one, who for Thy pardon strives.

Who Mary didst absolve from sin,
From whom the thief did pardon win,
Thou givest hope to me in turn;
Good Jesus, worthless is my prayer,
Yet deign to grant, that I may ne'er
In hell's avenging fire burn.

Give me a place among Thy sheep,
Far from the goats, oh, let me keep,
And station me on Thy right hand;
When the accursed confess their shames,
And are condemned to biting flames,
Among the Blessèd bid me stand.

Prostrate before Thy Feet I fall,
On Thee with contrite heart I call,
Of my last end, oh, take the care:
Tearful will be that day of woe,
When, from his ashes rising now,
Frail man to Judgment must repair;
Spare him, O God, in mercy spare!
Jesus, Love reigns within Thy breast,
Grant to the dead eternal rest. Amen.

[ARCHBISHOP BAGSHAWE]

N.B.—For music to the last three lines of verse 9, repeat from asterisk.

GENERAL.

224

GENERAL.

Act of Faith.

GREAT God, whatever through Thy Church
    Thou teachest to be true,
I firmly do believe it all,
    And will confess it too.
Thou never canst deceivèd be,
    Thou never canst deceive,
For Thou art truth itself, and Thou
    Dost tell me to believe.

Act of Hope.

My God, I firmly hope in Thee,
    For Thou art great and good ;
Thou gavest us Thine only Son
    To die upon the Rood.
I hope through Him for grace to live
    As Thy commandments teach,
And through Thy mercy, when I die
    The joys of Heaven to reach.

Act of Love.

With all my heart and soul and strength
    I love Thee, O my Lord,
For Thou art perfect, and all things
    Were made by Thy blest Word.
Like me to Thine own image made,
    My neighbour Thou didst make,
And as I love myself, I love
    My neighbour for Thy sake.

Act of Contrition.

Most holy God, my very soul
    With grief sincere is moved,
Because I have offended Thee,
    Whom I should e'er have loved.
Forgive me, Father ; I am now
    Resolved to sin no more,
And by Thy holy grace to shun
    What made me sin before.

[ANON. "HYMNS FOR THE YEAR" 1[illegible]]

GENERAL.

225

GENERAL.

THE HOLY FAMILY.

HAPPY we, who thus united
  Join in cheerful melody;
Praising Jesus, Mary, Joseph,
  In the "Holy Family."
    Jesus, Mary, Joseph, help us,
      That we ever true may be,
    To the promises that bind us
      To the "Holy Family."

Jesus, whose almighty bidding
  All created things fulfil,
Lives on earth in meek subjection
  To His earthly parents' will.
    Sweetest Infant, make us patient
      And obedient for Thy sake;
    Teach us to be chaste and gentle,
      All our stormy passions break.

Mary! thou alone wert chosen
  To be Mother of thy Lord:
Thou didst guide the early footsteps
  Of the Great Incarnate Word.
    Dearest Mother! make us humble;
      For thy Son will take His rest
    In the poor and lowly dwelling
      Of a humble sinner's breast.

Joseph! thou wert called the father
  Of thy Maker and thy Lord;
Thine it was to save thy Saviour
  From the cruel Herod's sword.
    Suffer us to call thee father;
      Show to us a father's love;
    Lead us safe through every danger
      Till we meet in Heaven above.

[REV. E. VAUGHAN, C.SS.R.]

GENERAL.

226

GENERAL.

THE HOLY FAMILY.

LET those who seek the world to please
Do all for honour, wealth, and ease;
But in the Holy Family
A nobler motive far have we.
Living, we will say joyfully each day,
All for Jesus, Mary, Joseph!
Dying, we will cry, till our latest sigh,
All for Jesus, Mary, Joseph!

O wicked world! we know thee well;
Thy works and maxims lead to hell;
We were thy slaves, but now are free,
We serve the Holy Family.
Living, we will say, &c.

What matter though we sometimes bear
A little suffering, toil, and care;
We serve a good and bounteous Lord,
And Heaven will soon be our reward.
Living, we will say, &c.

What though despised and poor we be,
We're like the Holy Family:
If They could poverty endure,
We should be proud to be as poor.
Living, we will say, &c.

And when this wretched life is past,
And every moment seems the last,
Oh, then the Holy Family
Our sweetest hope in death will be!
Living, we will say, &c.

[REV. E. VAUGHAN, C.SS.R.]

GENERAL.

227 (Part I.)

The Joyful Mysteries.

The Rosary.

i. *The Annunciation.—Humility.*

Hail, full of grace and purity!
  Meek Handmaid of the Lord,
Hail, model of humility!
  Chaste Mother of the Word.

ii. *The Visitation.—Charity to our Neighbours.*

By that pure love which prompted thee
  To seek thy cousin blest,
Pray that the fires of Charity
  May burn within our breast.

iii. *The Birth of Our Lord.—Poverty.*

This blessing beg, O Virgin Queen,
  From Jesus through His birth,
By holy poverty to wean
  Our hearts from things of earth.

iv. *Presentation in the Temple.—Obedience.*

Most Holy Virgin, Maiden mild,
  Obtain for us, we pray,
To imitate thy Holy Child,
  By striving to obey.

v. *The finding of Our Lord—Love of Him and of His Service.*

By thy dear Son, restored to thee,
  This grace for us implore,
To serve our Lord most faithfully,
  And love Him more and more.

Concluding verse.

Queen of the Holy Rosary,
  With tender love look down,
And bless the hearts that offer thee
  This chaplet for thy crown.

(PART II.) **227**

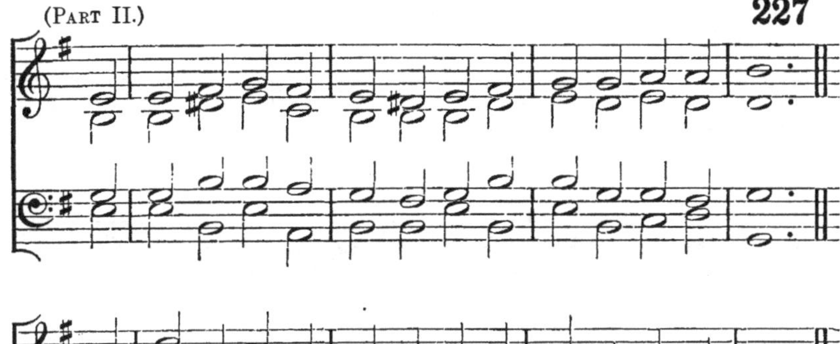

The Sorrowful Mysteries.

THE ROSARY.

I. *The Prayer of Our Lord.—Prayer.*

LORD, by Thy prayer in agony,
  On Olivet, alone,
Teach us to pray, resigned like Thee,
  And say, "Thy will be done."

II. *The Scourging.—Mortification.*

Sweet Saviour! who didst bear for me
  The scourge's pains intense,
Help me to fly all luxury,
  And mortify each sense.

III. *The Crowning with Thorns.—Fortitude.*

By the sharp thorns so meekly borne,
  And scoffs and buffets rude,
Teach us to bear all pain and scorn
  With holy fortitude.

IV. *The carrying the Cross.—Patience.*

Lord, by Thy cross Thy people spare,
  And on us pity take,
Help us our daily cross to bear
  With patience for Thy sake.

V. *The Crucifixion.—Spirit of Self-Sacrifice.*

O Jesu, victim for man's fall,
  Lamb slain on Calvary,
Accept henceforth our lives, our all,
  In sacrifice to Thee.

Concluding verse.

Queen of the Holy Rosary,
  With tender love look down,
And bless the hearts that offer thee
  This chaplet for thy crown.

227 (Part III.)

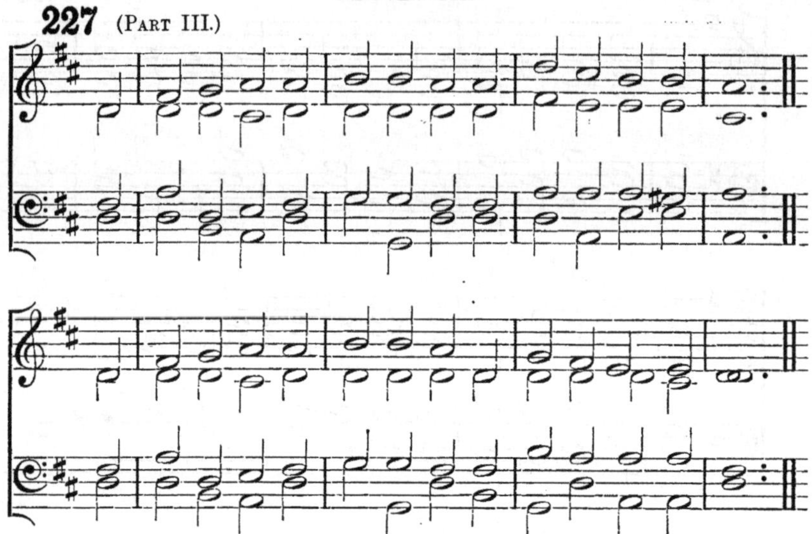

The Glorious Mysteries.

The Rosary.

I. *The Resurrection.—Faith.*

All hail, great Conqueror, to Thee,
Arisen from the dead!
Grant us the light of faith, that we
May in Thy footsteps tread.

II. *The Ascension.—Hope.*

To Heaven Thou dost ascend again,
Sweet Saviour of our race,
With hope our fainting hearts sustain
To see in Heaven Thy face.

III. *The Descent of the Holy Ghost.—Zeal for Souls.*

O Holy Ghost, who didst descend
In cloven tongues of fire,
Our souls, which all to earthward tend,
With burning zeal inspire.

IV. *The Assumption.—Devotion to Our Lady.*

Mother of God, enthroned above,
Beseech thy Son anew,
To fill our hearts with childlike love
For thee our Mother too.

V. *The Coronation of Our Lady.—Perseverance.*

All gracious Queen of Angels, deign
Our last request to hear,
For us this crowning gift obtain
In grace to persevere.

Concluding verse.

Queen of the Holy Rosary.
With tender love look down,
And bless the hearts that offer thee
This chaplet for thy crown.

[Rev. Fr. Conway, O.P.]

(Part I.) **228**

The Joyful Mysteries.

The Rosary.

By the Archangel's word of love
That announced Thee from above;
By the grace to Mary given;
By Thy first descent from Heaven;
Child of Mary, hear our cry;
Thou wert helpless once as we;
Now enthroned in majesty,
Countless angels sing to Thee.

By that journey made in haste
O'er the desert mountain waste;
By that voice whose heav'nly tone
Thrill'd the Baptist in the womb;
Child of Mary, hear our cry, &c.

By Thy poor and lowly lot,
By the manger and the grot;
By Thy tender feet and hands
Folded in their swaddling bands;
Child of Mary, hear our cry, &c.

By the joy of Simeon blest
When he clasp'd Thee to his breast;
By the widow'd Anna's song
Pour'd amid the wandering throng,
Child of Mary, hear our cry, &c.

By our Lady's glad delight,
In her temple, at the sight
Of her Child so young and fair,
Wiser than the wisest there;
Child of Mary, hear our cry, &c.

GENERAL.

228 (Part II.)

The Sorrowful Mysteries.

THE ROSARY.
BY the blood that flow'd from Thee
In Thy grievous agony ;
By the traitor's guileful kiss,
Filling up Thy bitterness ;
    Jesu, Saviour, hear our cry :
        Thou wert suff'ring once as we ;
    Now enthroned in majesty
        Countless angels sing to Thee.

By the cords that, round Thee cast,
Bound Thee to the pillar fast ;
By the scourge so meekly borne ;
By Thy purple robe of scorn ;
    Jesu, Saviour, hear our cry, &c.

By the thorns that crown'd Thy head ;
By Thy sceptre of a reed ;
By Thy foes on bending knee,
Mocking at Thy royalty ;
    Jesu, Saviour, hear our cry, &c.

By the people's cruel jeers ;
By the holy women's tears ;
By Thy footsteps faint and slow,
Weigh'd beneath Thy cross of woe ;
    Jesu, Saviour, hear our cry, &c.

By Thy weeping Mother's woe ;
By the sword that pierced her through,
When in anguish standing by,
On the cross she saw Thee die ;
    Jesu, Saviour, hear our cry, &c.

GENERAL.

228 (Part III.)

The Glorious Mysteries.

THE ROSARY.

BY the first bright Easter-day,
When the stone was roll'd away;
By the glory round Thee shed
At Thy rising from the dead;
King of glory, hear our cry;
Make us soon Thy joys to see,
Where enthron'd in majesty
Countless angels sing to Thee.

By Thy parting blessing giv'n
As Thou didst ascend to Heaven;
By the cloud of living light
That received Thee out of sight;
King of glory, hear our cry, &c.

By that rushing sound of might
Coming down from Heaven's height;
By the clóven tongue of fire,
Holy Ghost, our hearts inspire.
King of glory, hear our cry, &c.

See the Virgin Mother rise,
Angels bear her to the skies:
Mount aloft, imperial Queen,
Plead on high the cause of men.
King of glory, hear our cry, &c.

Mary reigns upon the throne
Pre-ordain'd for her alone;
Saints and angels round her sing,
Mother of our God and King.
King of glory, hear our cry, &c.

[C. M. CADDELL]

GENERAL.

229

Lucis Creator optime.

SUNDAY VESPERS.

O BLEST Creator of the light! [bring;
Who dost the dawn from darkness
And framing Nature's depth and height,
Didst with the light Thy work begin;

Who gently blending eve with morn,
And morn with eve, did'st call them day;—
Thick flows the flood of darkness down;
Oh, hear us as we weep and pray!

Keep Thou our souls from schemes of crime,
Nor guilt remorseful let them know;
Nor, thinking but on things of time,
Into eternal darkness go.

Teach us to knock at Heaven's high door;
Teach us the prize of life to win;
Teach us all evil to abhor,
And purify ourselves within.

Father of mercies! hear our cry;
Hear us, co-equal Son!
Who reignest with the Holy Ghost
While endless ages run.

[TR. REV. E. CASWALL]

230

Te lucis ante terminum.

COMPLINE.

NOW with the fast-departing light,
Maker of all! we ask of Thee,
Of Thy great mercy, through the night
Our guardian and defence to be.

Far off let idle visions fly:
No phantom of the night molest:
Curb Thou our raging enemy,
That we in chaste repose may rest.

Father of mercies! hear our cry;
Hear us, O sole-begotten Son!
Who, with the Holy Ghost most high,
Reignest while endless ages run.

[TR. REV. E. CASWALL]

231

O BREAD of Heaven, beneath this veil
  Thou dost my very God conceal :
My Jesus, dearest treasure, hail ;
  I love Thee, and adoring kneel ;
Each loving soul by Thee is fed
With Thy own Self in form of bread.

O Food of life, Thou who dost give
  The pledge of immortality ;
I live ; no, 'tis not I that live ;
  God gives me life, God lives in me :
He feeds my soul, He guides my ways,
And every grief with joy repays.

O bond of love, that dost unite
  The servant to his loving Lord ;
Could I dare live, and not requite
  Such love,—then death were meet reward:
I cannot live unless to prove
Some love for such unmeasur'd love.

Belovèd Lord, in Heaven above,
  There, Jesus, Thou awaitest me ;
To gaze on Thee with changeless love ;
  Yes, thus, I hope, thus shall it be :
For how can He deny me Heaven
Who here on earth Himself hath given ?

[ST. ALPHONSUS. TR. REV. E. VAUGHAN, C.SS.R.]

232

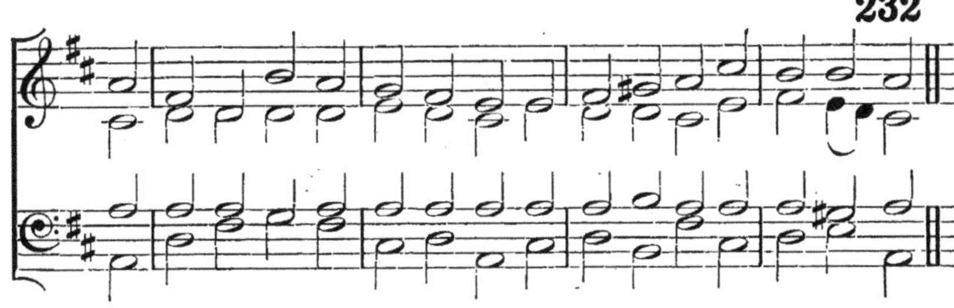

WHAT happiness can equal mine?
  I've found the object of my love.
My Saviour and my Lord divine
  Is come to me from Heaven above.

He makes my heart His own abode,
  His flesh becomes my daily bread,
He pours on me His healing blood,
  And with His life my soul is fed.

My Love is mine, and I am His;
  In me He dwells, in Him I live;
Where could I taste a purer bliss?
  What greater boon could Jesus give?

O royal banquet! heavenly feast!
  O flowing Fount of life and grace!
Where God the giver, man the guest,
  Meet and unite in sweet embrace.

Dear Jesus, now my heart is Thine,
  Oh, may it never from Thee fly;
My God, be Thou for ever mine,
  And I Thine own eternally.

No more, O Satan, thee I fear!
  O world, thy charms I now despise,
For Christ Himself is with me here,
  My joy, my life, my Paradise!

[REV. F. W. FABER]

GENERAL.

233

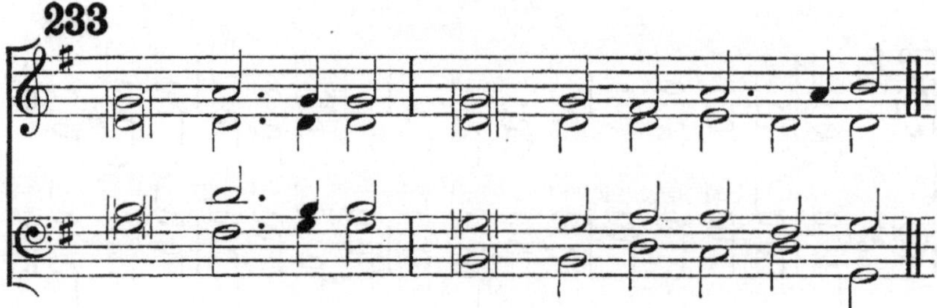

Jam lucis orto sidere.

PRIME.

NOW doth the sun ascend the sky,
And wake creation with its ray;
Keep us from sin, O Lord most high!
Through all the actions of the day.

Oh, may our hearts be pure within!
No cherish'd madness vex the soul!
May abstinence the flesh restrain,
And its rebellious pride control.

Curb Thou for us th' unruly tongue;
Teach us the way of peace to prize;
And close our eyes against the throng
Of earth's absorbing vanities.

So when the evening stars appear,
And in their train the darkness bring;
May we, O Lord, with conscience clear,
Our praise to Thy pure glory sing.

To God the Father glory be,
And to His sole-begotten Son;
Glory, O Holy Ghost! to Thee,
While everlasting ages run.

[TR. REV. E. CASWALL]

234

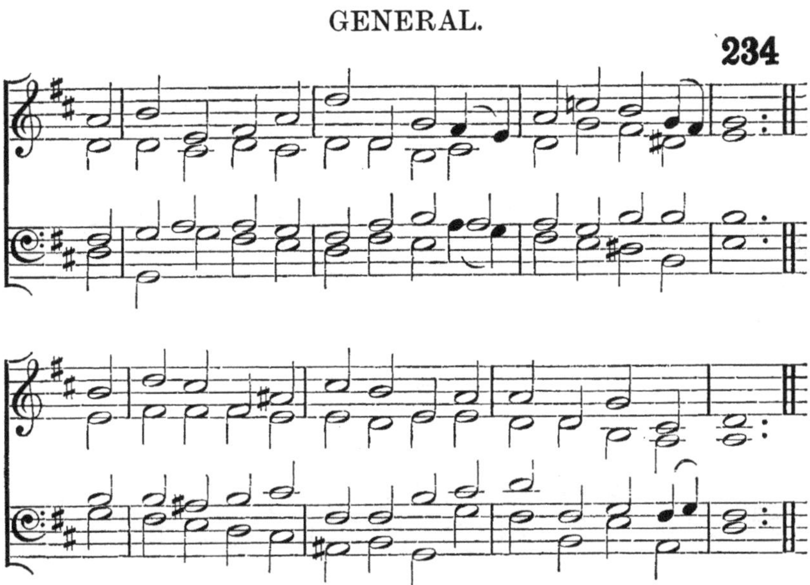

For Use at Sea.

ALL night the Apostles toiled amain
And stoutly plied the oar;
Against the gale they strove in vain
To reach the distant shore.

At dawn they saw a startling sight,
A ghost they seemed to spy;
'Twas Jesus walking on the sea:
"Fear not," He said, "'tis I."

He went up to them in their ship,
Straightway the tempest died;
"Thou truly art the Son of God,"
Adoring Him they cried.

Temptation's storm our hearts may shake
As Heaven to reach we try:
In darkest hour our Help will come,
And say: "Fear not, 'tis I."

When death's dark flood shall whelm our soul,
And judgment dread be nigh,
May Jesus come across the wave,
And say: "Fear not, 'tis I."

[MGR. CANON HALL]

235

For Use at Sea.

THE fierce gale struck the ship that
The sea of Galilee; [sailed
While Jesus slept, the Apostles wept
And prayed on bended knee.

"Arise, O Lord," they fearful cried,
"Arise, O Lord, and save!
Help, Jesus, help! or else we sink
Beneath the angry wave."

"O ye of little faith," He said,
"Why tremble thus with fear?
What evil thing can you befall,
When I, your help, am near?"

"Be still," He cried, "ye winds and waves!
My loved ones do not harm.
Be still, ye winds! ye waves, be still!"
When lo! a sudden calm.

When sailing life's uncertain sea,
The storm our hearts may scare;
And God, to test our faith, may seem
Of us to have no care.

He watches over Israel;
He slumbers not nor sleeps:
He loveth all, and in His hand
His loved ones safely keeps.

[MGR. CANON HALL]

236

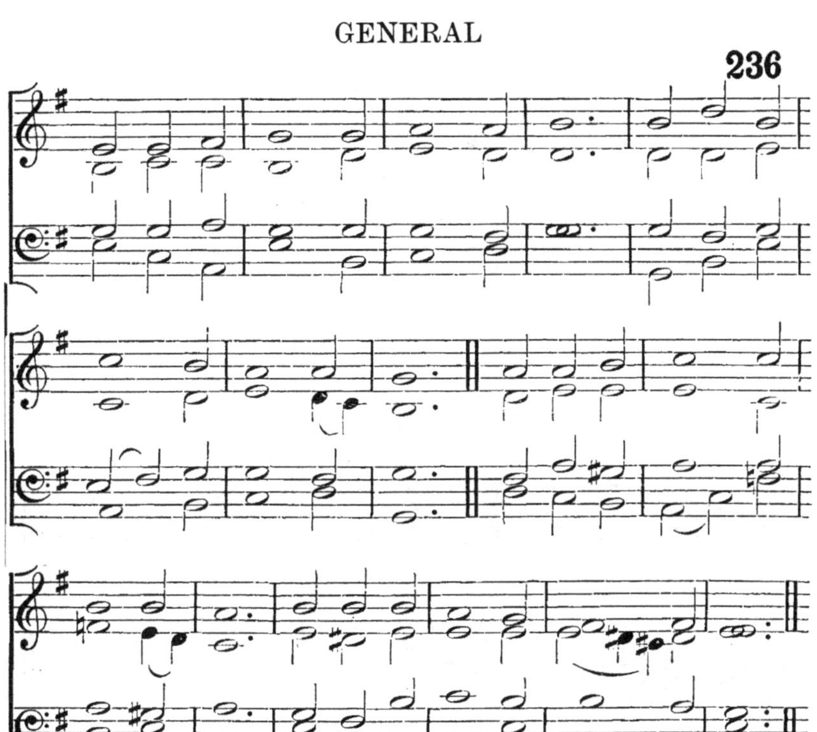

Jam sol recedit igneus.

SATURDAY VESPERS.

AS fades the glowing orb of day,
To Thee, great source of light, we pray;
Blest Three in One, to every heart
Thy beams of life and love impart.

At early dawn, at close of day,
To Thee our vows we humbly pay;
May we, 'mid joys that never end,
With Thy bright saints in homage bend.

[TR. T. J. POTTER]

GENERAL.

237

GENERAL.

AMIDST the City's golden towers
A throne of light doth stand:
And there the King, sun-crowned, doth bear
A splendour on each Hand
O Jesus, by Thy Sacred Wounds,
Be evermore our Friend,
Until we reach, through gates of pearl,
Our journey's blissful end.

Beside the altar and the throne
Doth rise a shining stream;
And life and joy and light for all
Are blended with its gleam.
O Jesus, by Thy Precious Blood,
Be with us evermore,
Until, with all our sins forgiven,
We pass the temple's door.

Within the temple's holiest shrine,
Where stands the mightiest choir,
With beatings of a deathless love
Doth throb a sea of fire.
O Jesus, by Thy Sacred Heart,
Through griefs and pains and fears,
Uplift us to Thy sheltering Home,
And wipe away all tears.

Thou dwellest where that Home of love
Is filled with light divine,
Whilst weary wanderers on the earth
In lingering darkness pine.
O Jesus, pitiful and kind,
With loving eyes look down,
That on our darkened way may fall
The brightness of Thy Crown.

GENERAL.

238

CHRISTMAS comes to bless the earth
With its wondrous heavenly birth;
Bright and high the dawning Light
Burneth through the gloom of night.

God hath come with men to dwell,
Christ is born in Israel;
Thrilling songs His Angels sing,
Worshipping their Infant King.

Easter with its flaming crown
Tramples all the darkness down;
Tyrant spectres of the gloom
Die before the open Tomb.

Christ hath risen from the grave,
Christ hath risen, strong to save;
Thrilling songs His Angels sing,
Worshipping their Victor King.

Thus He reigns beyond the sky
In the love that cannot die;
Yet with men doth ever dwell,
In the midst of Israel.

So before His Altar now
All His radiant Angels bow;
Thrilling songs they ever sing,
Worshipping their hidden King.

Comes the shadow of the tomb,
Comes the fearful day of doom;
Darkling clouds about us lower;
Jesus, save us in that hour.

By the Christmas frost and snow,
Easter's bright and burning glow,
Light around Thine Altar shed,
Save us in that hour of dread.

239

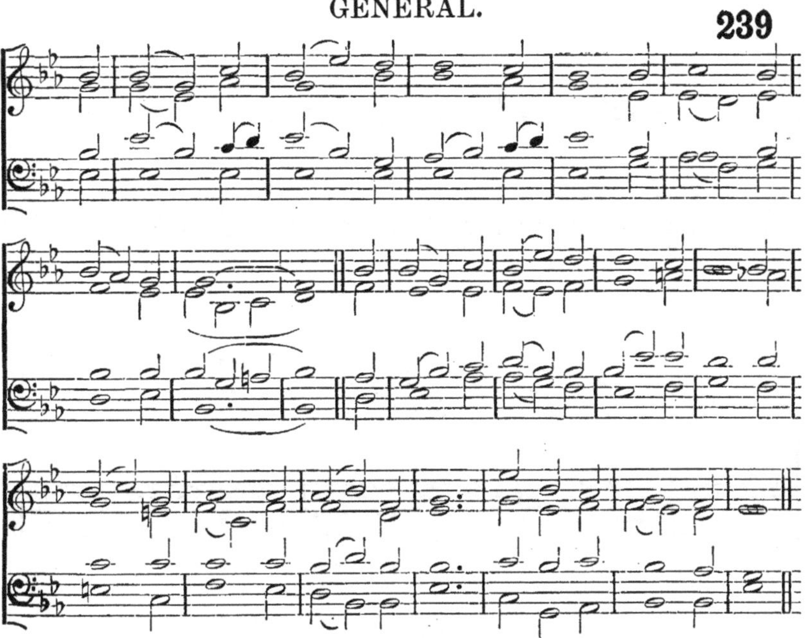

THERE is a land of peace and love,
Where troubled hearts find rest;
No gloom, nor storm, nor lonely night
Can ever dim th' eternal light
Of that bright home above.

Angels and sainted throngs are there
Circling the Throne of God;
Crowned with twelve stars, a Virgin Queen
In the pure light of God is seen
Immaculate and fair.

No sorrow e'er can reach that shore,
And there no tear shall fall:
Earth's glories all shall pass away,
Lost in the light of endless day,
And grief shall be no more.

And oh! when on our raptured gaze
Shall break the sight of God,
Then shall our harboured spirits rest
Wrapt in the vision of the bless'd
Mid songs of ceaseless praise.

How sweet for wearied souls to rest
Near to the Sacred Heart,
Sheltered within Love's sacred shrine,
Resting at Jesus' feet divine,
There to be ever blest.

Then shall life's fevered toil be o'er,
And restless hearts be calm;
Then shall these anxious yearnings cease,
And troubled spirits rest in peace
On Heaven's eternal shore.

Fear not, though still earth's darkening [gloom
O'ershadows life's lone path;
Jesus has shown the heavenward way
Which leads to realms of endless day,
To our dear Father's home.

[REV. FR. STANFIELD]

240

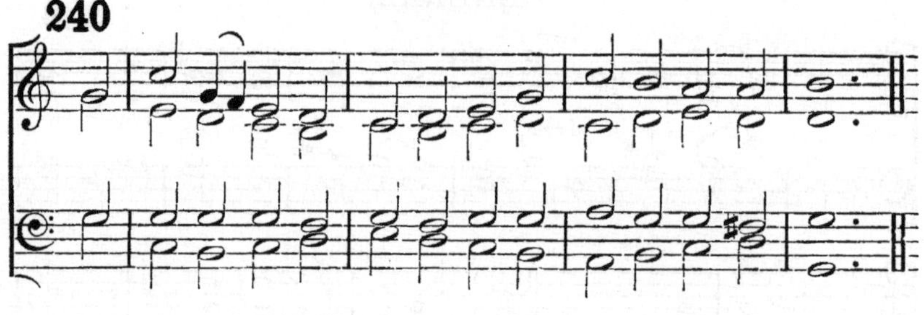

O Sol salutis intimis.

Lauds in Lent.

THE darkness fleets, and joyful earth
Welcomes the newborn day;
Jesu, true Sun of human souls!
Shed in our souls Thy ray.

Thou, who dost give the accepted time,
Give tears to purify,
Give flames of love to burn our hearts
As victims unto Thee.

That fountain, whence our sins have flow'd,
Shall soon in tears distil,
If but Thy penitential grace
Subdue the stubborn will.

The day is near when all re-blooms,
Thy own blest day, O Lord;
We too would joy, by Thy right hand
To life's true path restored.

All-glorious Trinity: to Thee
Let earth's vast fabric bend;
And evermore from souls renew'd
The Saints' new song ascend.

[TR. REV. E. CASWALL]

241

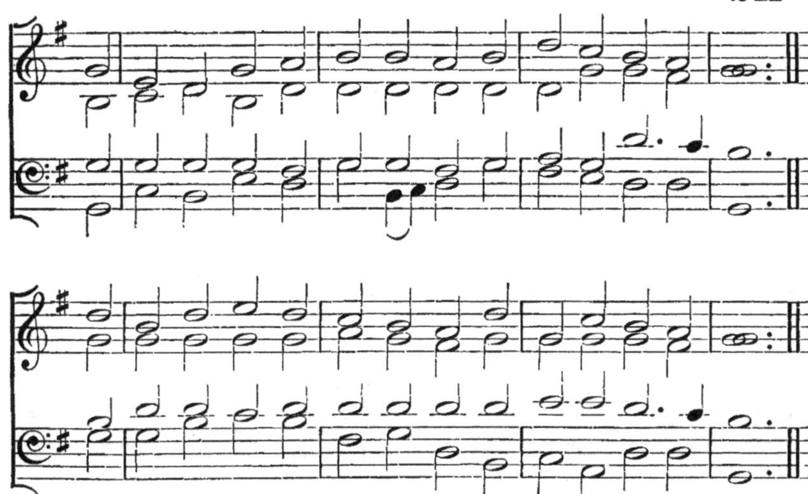

Jesu corona celsior.

LAUDS OF A CONFESSOR.

JESU! eternal Truth sublime!
Through endless years the same!
Thou crown of those who through all time
Confess Thy Holy Name:

Thy suppliant people, through the prayer
Of Thy blest Saint, forgive;
For his dear sake Thy wrath forbear,
And bid our spirits live.

Again returns the sacred day,
With heavenly glory bright,
Which saw him go upon his way
Into the realms of light.

All objects of our vain desire,
All earthly joys and gains,
To him were but as filthy mire;
And now with Thee he reigns.

Thee, Jesu, his all-gracious Lord,
Confessing to the last,
He trod beneath Him Satan's fraud,
And stood for ever fast.

In holy deeds of faith and love,
In fastings and in prayers,
His days were spent; and now above,
Thy heavenly Feast he shares.

Then, for his sake Thy wrath lay by,
And hear us while we pray;
And pardon us, O Thou most high,
On this his festal Day.

All glory to the Father be;
And sole Incarnate Son;
Praise, holy Paraclete, to Thee,
While endless ages run.

[TR. REV. E. CASWALL]

242

Lux alma Jesu mentium.

LAUDS OF TRANSFIGURATION.

LIGHT of the soul, O Saviour blest!
Soon as Thy presence fills the breast,
Darkness and guilt are put to flight,
And all is sweetness and delight.

Son of the Father! Lord most high!
How glad is he who feels Thee nigh!
How sweet in Heav'n Thy beam doth glow,
Denied to eye of flesh below!

O Light of Light celestial!
O Charity ineffable!
Come in Thy hidden majesty;
Fill us with love, fill us with Thee.

To Jesus, from the proud conceal'd,
But evermore to babes reveal'd,
All glory with the Father be,
And Holy Ghost, eternally.

[TR. REV. E. CASWALL]

243

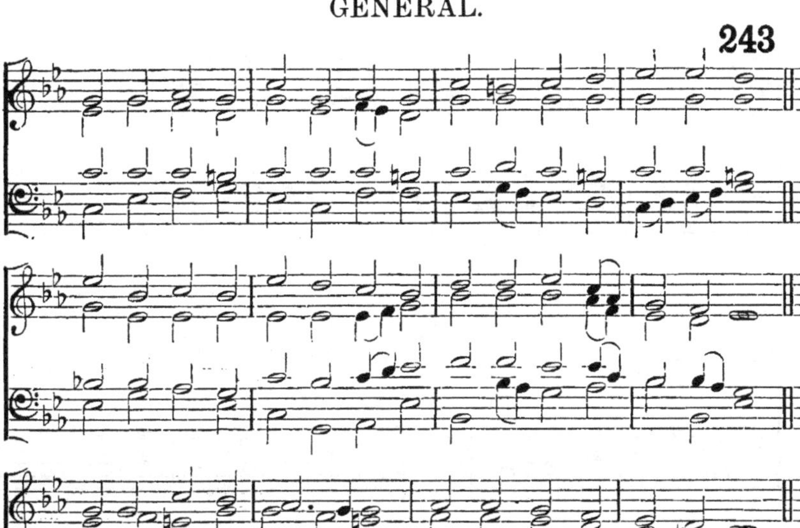

Nocte mox diem fugata.

SOON the fiery sun ascending
  Will have chased the midnight gloom:
Rise, O Thou High Priest eternal,
  Break the bondage of the tomb!
And above the vaulted sky
Bear Thy victim Flesh on high!

Once on earth for guilty mortals
  Sacrificed in torment sore,
There may It, on Heaven's high altar,
  Plead our cause for evermore;
And appease an injured God,
With the Lamb's atoning Blood.

Named of old High Priest for ever,
  By the Father's stedfast oath,
Rise, O Advocate Almighty!
  Rise, O Priest and Victim both!
Swiftly, swiftly, speed Thy way
Back to golden realms of day.

Lo, 'tis done! O'er death victorious
  Christ ascends His starry throne;
There from all His labours resting
  Still He travails for His own;
Still our fate His Heart employs
E'en amid eternal joys.

There He sits in tranquil glory;
  There He stands His aid to lend;
There He offers to His Father
  Every single prayer we send;
There Himself receives each sigh
As omniscient Deity.

[TR. REV. E. CASWALL]

244

GENERAL.

EASTER.

WITH one accord now let us sing (Alleluia !)
Glad praise to our victorious King.
Hymn His triumph !
Through Red Sea waters He hath brought us ; (Alleluia !)
And with His Precious Blood hath bought us.
Alleluia, Alleluia, Alleluia, Alleluia !

Lo, Christ our Victim, Christ our Priest, (Alleluia !)
Now bids us to His royal feast.
Come with gladness !
See, how in charity, for food (Alleluia !)
He gives us of His Flesh and Blood.
Alleluia, &c.

In olden time, by Egypt's shore, (Alleluia !)
Th' avenging angel passed each door
Blood-besprinkled.
The Red Sea wave o'erwhelms the foe, (Alleluia !)
And Israel's cohorts onward go.
Alleluia, &c.

So Satan, passing, harmeth not (Alleluia !)
Souls that from every stain and spot
Christ's Blood cleanseth.
Christ hath o'erwhelmed the powers of sin, (Alleluia !)
That we the gates of heaven may win.
Alleluia, &c.

Then let us sing, while we have breath, (Alleluia !)
Praise to the Victor over death.
Alleluia !
Dear risen Lord, all praise to Thee, (Alleluia !)
With Father and with Spirit be.
Alleluia, &c.

[R. R. T.]

GENERAL.

245

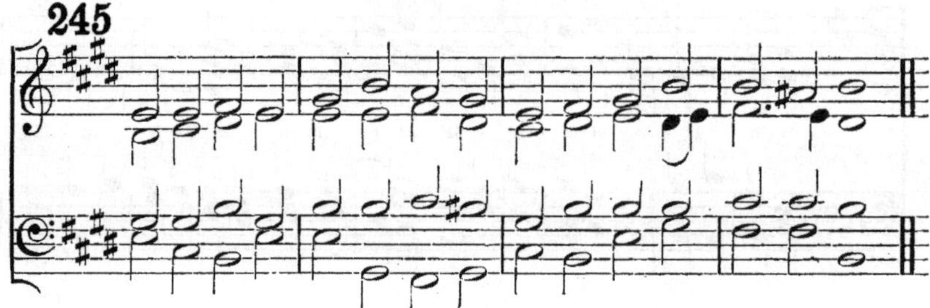

An Act of Faith.

FIRMLY I believe and truly
  God is Three, and God is One;
And I next acknowledge duly
  Manhood taken by the Son.

And I trust and hope most fully
  In that Manhood crucified;
And each thought and deed unruly
  Do to death, as He has died.

Simply to His grace and wholly
  Light and life and strength belong;
And I love supremely, solely,
  Him the Holy, Him the Strong.

And I hold in veneration,
  For the love of Him alone,
Holy Church, as His creation,
  And her teachings, as His own.

Adoration aye be given,
  With and through the angelic host,
To the God of earth and heaven,
  Father, Son, and Holy Ghost.

[CARDINAL NEWMAN]

246

THE CELESTIAL CITY.

PART I.

JERUSALEM! my happy home!
  When shall I come to thee?
When shall my sorrows have an end?
  Thy joys when shall I see?

O happy harbour of the Saints,
  O sweet and pleasant soil,
In thee no sorrow may be found,
  No grief, no care, no toil.

Thy walls are made of precious stones,
  Thy bulwarks diamonds square,
Thy gates are of right orient pearl,
  Exceeding rich and rare.

Thy houses are of ivory,
  Thy windows crystal clear,
Thy tiles are made of beaten gold;—
  O God, that I were there!

Quite through the streets with silver [sound,
  The flood of life doth flow;
Upon whose banks on every side,
  The wood of life doth grow.

Thy gardens and thy gallant walks
  Continually are green;
There grow such sweet and pleasant [flowers
  As nowhere else are seen.

There trees for evermore bear fruit,
  And evermore do spring;
There evermore the Angels sit
  And evermore do sing.

Jerusalem! my happy home!
  Would God I were in thee!
Would God my woes were at an end,
  Thy joys that I might see!

PART II.

JERUSALEM! my happy home!
  When shall I come to thee?
When shall my sorrows have an end?
  Thy joys when shall I see?

Thy Saints are crowned with glory great,
  They see God, face to face,
They triumph still, they still rejoice,
  Most happy is their case.

There David stands with harp in hand,
  As master of the Choir,
Ten thousand times that man were blest
  That might this music hear.

Our Lady sings Magnificat,
  With tune surpassing sweet,
And all the virgins bear their part,
  Sitting about her feet.

There Magdalen hath left her moan,
  And cheerfully doth sing,
With blessèd Saints whose harmony
  In every street doth ring.

Ah my sweet home Jerusalem!
  Would God I were in thee!
Would God my woes were at an end,
  Thy joys that I might see!

[FR. LAURENCE ANDERTON, *alias* JOHN BRERELY, S.J.]

247

Slowly.

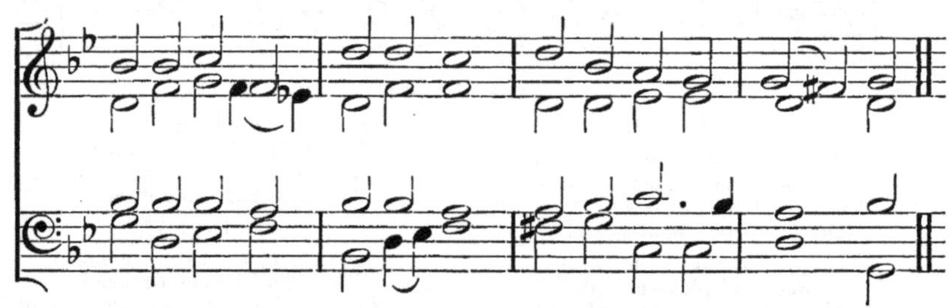

FOR THE FEAST OF THE SEVEN DOLOURS.

O MOTHER, dear,
As year by year
We keep thy Day of Sorrow,
Sorrowing to thee we come
Strength of thee to borrow.

O what a sea
Of agony
O'erflowed thy heart so tender!
Grant us in thy grief a share,
Love for love to render.

Thou saw'st thy Son,
Thine only One,
With stripes and bruises laden.
Who but would have pitying tears
Wept for thee, dear Maiden?

Thy Son so fair
Lies bleeding there;
Upon the Cross they slew Him
Pray for us that we may win
Life unending through Him.

[R. R. T.]

248

MARTYRS OF ENGLAND.

MARTYRS of England! still be near us;
Let not your torments and blood be vain.
Martyrs of England, hear, O hear us:
Bring the Faith to our land again.

Martyrs of England! rack and fetters
Could not drive you from English soil,
Can we forget that we are debtors
For Faith's dear light to your loving toil?

Martyrs of England! calm and smiling,
Drawn in shame through the crowded town,
Proud and glad under men's reviling,
To die for your King and a Heavenly crown.

Martyrs of England! nought could sever
Christ's dear name from your lips and heart;
Fire, and rope, and knife could never
The soldiers of Christ from their Captain part.

Martyrs of England! stay beside us,
Make us steadfast in hope and faith;
Martyrs of England! let nought divide us
From love of Jesu in life or death.

GENERAL.

249

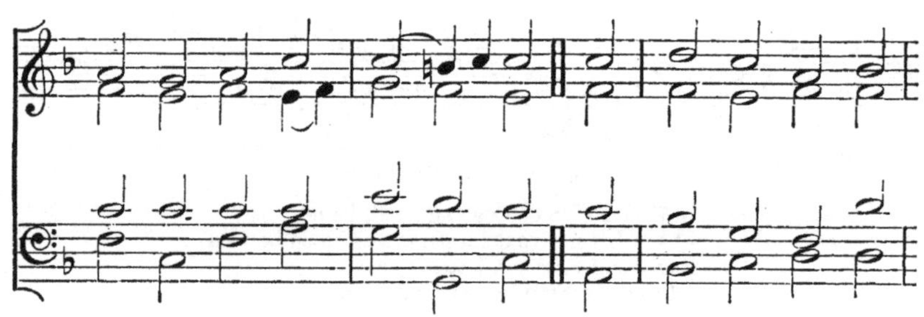

GENERAL.

To St. Bede.

LOVER of Christ's immortal Bride,
Whose triumphs here 'twas thine to tell,
Oft watching from thy narrow cell
The Tyne beyond thee seaward glide.

Thou toldest how from Rome a band
Of monks there came, what souls they won,
How kingdoms yielded, one by one,
Till Christ was king o'er all the land.

His empire stood a thousand years ;
For Peter is His chosen chief ;
And all were one in one belief,
Till faith was quenched in blood and tears.

Then from the Vine the branch was torn,
New teachers shaped the creed anew,
And new-made treasons thinned to few
The followers of a hope forlorn.

'Tis long since in the Galilee
Men wreaked their spite upon thy tomb ;
The night is o'er that laid its gloom
On hearts and homes, and we are free.

Now stand our altars unprofaned ;
Again our Victim lies thereon ;
Thence rises up that orison
By Gregory of old ordained.

But oh ! how much is yet undone !
What perils haunt our little flock !
How fierce will be the battle's shock,
Ere the great day be lost or won !

And who of all the heavenly throng
Will best bestead us in our need
But thou, the grave and gentle Bede,
Whose heart is still our hills among ?

Thy words are still a beacon clear,
A mighty cry, a piercing plea,
For them that have but eyes to see,
And hear with not unheeding ear.

Oh ! melt the mists of unbelief
Wherein so many stray to doom ;
Pity the souls that in the gloom
Founder upon the rocks and reef !

And we, thy children, may we hold
The written and the living Word,
Whose voice in God's own Church is heard,
Within the one true Shepherd's fold.

Make us in all seek Him alone,
And love the beauty of His face ;
So, when the darkness falls apace,
Our dying prayer may be thine own :

"O King of glory, Lord of might,
Who conquering didst to heav'n ascend,
Leave us not orphans ! on us send
Thy Spirit, source of truth and light !"

[RT. REV. AMBROSE BURTON, BISHOP OF CLIFTON]

GENERAL.

250 (First Tune.)

GENERAL.

HARK ! hark ! my soul ! angelic songs are swelling
O'er earth's green fields and ocean's wave-beat shore ;
How sweet the truth those blessèd strains are telling
Of that new life when sin shall be no more !
Angels of Jesus !
Angels of light !
Singing to welcome
The pilgrims of the night.

Darker than night life's shadows fall around us,
And, like benighted men, we miss our mark ;
God hides Himself, and grace hath scarcely found us,
Ere death finds out his victims in the dark.
Angels of Jesus, &c.

Onward we go, for still we hear them singing,
Come, weary souls ! for Jesus bids you come !
And through the dark, its echoes sweetly ringing,
The music of the Gospel leads us home.
Angels of Jesus, &c.

Far, far away, like bells at evening pealing,
The voice of Jesus sounds o'er land and sea,
And laden souls, by thousands meekly stealing,
Kind Shepherd ! turn their weary steps to Thee.
Angels of Jesus, &c.

Rest comes at length : though life be long and dreary,
The day must dawn, and darksome night be past ;
All journeys end in welcomes to the weary,
And heaven, the heart's true home, will come at last.
Angels of Jesus, &c.

Angels ! sing on, your faithful watches keeping,
Sing us sweet fragments of the songs above ;
While we toil on, and soothe ourselves with weeping,
Till life's long night shall break in endless love.
Angels of Jesus, &c.

[REV. F. W. FABER]

GENERAL.

250 (Second Tune.)

GENERAL.

HARK! hark! my soul! angelic songs are swelling
  O'er earth's green fields and ocean's wave-beat shore;
How sweet the truth those blessèd strains are telling
  Of that new life when sin shall be no more!
    Angels of Jesus!
      Angels of light!
    Singing to welcome
      The pilgrims of the night.

Darker than night life's shadows fall around us,
  And, like benighted men, we miss our mark;
God hides Himself, and grace hath scarcely found us,
  Ere death finds out his victims in the dark.
    Angels of Jesus, &c.

Onward we go, for still we hear them singing,
  Come, weary souls! for Jesus bids you come!
And through the dark, its echoes sweetly ringing,
  The music of the Gospel leads us home.
    Angels of Jesus, &c.

Far, far away, like bells at evening pealing,
  The voice of Jesus sounds o'er land and sea,
And laden souls, by thousands meekly stealing,
  Kind Shepherd! turn their weary steps to Thee.
    Angels of Jesus, &c.

Rest comes at length: though life be long and dreary,
  The day must dawn, and darksome night be past;
All journeys end in welcomes to the weary,
  And heaven, the heart's true home, will come at last.
    Angels of Jesus, &c.

Angels! sing on, your faithful watches keeping,
  Sing us sweet fragments of the songs above;
While we toil on, and soothe ourselves with weeping,
  Till life's long night shall break in endless love.
    Angels of Jesus, &c.

[REV. F. W. FABER]

LATIN HYMNS.

251

LATIN HYMNS.

CHRISTMAS.

ADESTE, fidéles,
Læti triumphántes ;
Veníte, venite in Béthlehem ;
Natum vidéte
Regem angelórum :
Venite adorémus,
Venite adorémus,
Venite adorémus Dóminum.

Deum de Deo,
Lumen de lúmine,
Gestant puéllæ víscera :
Deum verum,
Génitum, non factum :
Veníte adorémus Dóminum.

Cautet nunc Io !
Chorus angelórum :
Cantet nunc aula cœléstium,
Glória
In excélsis Deo !
Venite adorémus Dóminum.

Ergo qui natus
Die hodiérna,
Jesu tibi sit glória :
Patris ætérni
Verbum caro factum !
Venite adorémus Dóminum.

2 A

LATIN HYMNS.

252 (First Tune.)

Mode iv.

Sta-bat ma-ter do-lo-ró-sa Ju-xta cru-cem la-cry-mó-sa

Dum pen-dé-bat Fí-li-us. Cu-jus á-ni-mam ge-mén-tem

Con-tri-stá-tam et do-lén-tem, Per-trans-í-vit glá-di-us. A-men.

LATIN HYMNS.

Passiontide.

STABAT mater dolorósa
Juxta crucem lacrymósa
Dum pendébat Fílius.
Cujus ánimam geméntem
Contristátam et doléntem,
Pertransívit gládius.

O quam tristis, et afflícta,
Fuit illa benedicta
Mater Unigéniti!
Quæ mœrébat, et dolébat,
Pia Mater, dum vidébat
Nati pœnas ínclyti.

Quis est homo, qui non fleret,
Matrem Christi si vidéret
In tanto supplício?
Quis non posset contristári,
Christi matrem contemplári,
Doléntem cum Filio?

Pro peccátis suæ gentis,
Vidit Jesum in torméntis
Et flagéllis súbditum.
Vidit suum dulcem Natum
Moriéndo desolátum,
Dum emísit spíritum.

Eja, Mater, fons amóris,
Me sentíre vim dolóris
Fac, ut tecum lúgeam.
Fac, ut árdeat cor meum
In amándo Christum Deum,
Ut sibi compláceam.

Sancta Mater, istud agas
Crucifíxi fige plagas
Cordi meo válide.
Tui nati vulneráti,
Tam dignáti pro me pati,
Pœnas mecum divide.

Fac me tecum pie flere,
Crucifíxo condolére,
Donec ego víxero.
Juxta crucem tecum stare,
Et me tibi sociáre
In planctu desídero.

Virgo vírginum præclára,
Mihi jam non sis amára:
Fac me tecum plángere.
Fac ut portem Christi mortem,
Passiónis fac consórtem,
Et plagas recólere.

Fac me plagis vulnerári,
Fac me Cruce inebriári,
Et cruóre Fílii.
Flammis ne urar succénsus,
Per te, Virgo, sim defénsus,
In die judícii.

Christe, cum sit hinc exíre,
Da per Matrem me venire
Ad palmam victóriæ.
Quando corpus moriétur,
Fac ut ánimæ donétur
Paradisi glória. Amen.

LATIN HYMNS.

252 (Second Tune.)

LATIN HYMNS.

Passiontide.

STABAT mater dolorósa
Juxta crucem lacrymósa
Dum pendébat Fílius.
Cujus ánimam geméntem
Contristátam et doléntem,
Pertransívit gládius.

O quam tristis, et afflícta,
Fuit illa benedicta
Mater Unigéniti!
Quæ mœrébat, et dolébat,
Pia Mater, dum vidébat
Nati pœnas ínclyti.

Quis est homo, qui non fleret,
Matrem Christi si vidéret
In tanto supplício?
Quis non posset contristári,
Christi matrem contemplári,
Doléntem cum Fílio?

Pro peccátis suæ gentis,
Vidit Jesum in torméntis
Et flagéllis súbditum.
Vidit suum dulcem Natum
Moriéndo desolátum,
Dum emísit spíritum.

Eja, Mater, fons amóris,
Me sentíre vim dolóris
Fac, ut tecum lúgeam.
Fac, ut árdeat cor meum
In amándo Christum Deum,
Ut sibi compláceam.

Sancta Mater, istud agas
Crucifíxi fige plagas
Cordi meo válide.
Tui nati vulneráti,
Tam dignáti pro me pati,
Pœnas mecum dívide.

Fac me tecum pie flere,
Crucifíxo condolére,
Donec ego víxero.
Juxta crucem tecum stare,
Et me tibi sociáre
In planctu desidero.

Virgo vírginum præclára,
Mihi jam non sis amára;
Fac me tecum plángere.
Fac ut portem Christi mortem,
Passiónis fac consórtem,
Et plagas recólere.

Fac me plagis vulnerári,
Fac me Cruce inebriári,
Et cruóre Fílii.
Flammis ne urar succénsus,
Per te, Virgo, sim defénsus,
In die judicii.

Christe, cum sit hinc exíre,
Da per Matrem me veníre
Ad palmam victóriæ.
Quando corpus moriétur,
Fac ut ánimæ donétur
Paradisi glória. Amen.

LATIN HYMNS.

253 Mode i.

LATIN HYMNS.

VEXILLA Regis pródeunt :
Fulget Crucis mystérium,
Qua vita mortem pértulit,
Et morte vitam prótulit.

Quæ vulneráta lánceæ
Mucróne diro, críminum
Ut nos lávaret sórdibus,
Manávit unda et sánguine.

Impléta sunt, quæ cóncinit
David fidéli cármine,
Dicéndo natiónibus :
Regnávit a ligno Deus.

Arbor decóra, et fúlgida,
Ornáta Regis púrpura,
Elécta digno stípite
Tam sancta membra tángere.

Beáta cujus bráchiis
Prétium pepéndit sæculi,
Statéra facta córporis,
Tulítque prædam tártari.

O Crux, ave, spes única
Hoc Passiónis témpore *
Piis adáuge grátiam
Reísque dele crímina.

Te, fons salútis Trínitas,
Colláudet omnis spíritus :
Quibus crucis victóriam
Largíris, adde prǽmium. Amen.

* (May 3) Paschále quæ fers gaúdium. (Sept. 14) In hac triúmphi glória.

N.B.—If a modern tune is required for this hymn a selection may be made from those headed "Long Metre" in the metrical index.

LATIN HYMNS.

254 EASTERTIDE. Mode i.

LATIN HYMNS.

Re - gnat ví - vus. Dic nó - bis, Ma - rí - a, Quid vi - dí - sti in ví - a?
Se - púl-chrum Chrí-sti vi - vén - tis, Et gló - ri - am vi - di re - sur - gén - tis.
An - gé - li - cos té - stes, Su - dá - ri - um et vé - stes. Sur - ré - xit

Chri - stus spes mé - a; Præ - cé - det su - os in Ga - li - lǽ - am.
Scí - mus Chri - stum sur - re - xís - se A mór - tu - is vé - re: Tu nó - bis,
Vi - ctor Rex, mi - se - ré - re. A - men. Al - le - lu - ia.

Mode viii. **255**

PENTECOST.

VENI, Creátor Spiritus,
Mentes tuórum vísita,
Imple supérna grátia,
Quæ tu creásti, péctora.

Qui díceris Paráclitus,
Altíssimi donum Dei,
Fons vivus, ignis, cáritas,
Et spiritális únctio.

Tu septifórmis múnere,
Dígitus patérnæ déxteræ,
Tu rite promíssum Patris
Sermóne ditans gúttura.

Accénde lumen sénsibus,
Infúnde amórem córdibus,
Infirma nostri córporis
Virtúte firmans pérpeti.

Hostem repéllas lóngius,
Pacémque dones prótinus;
Ductóre sic te prævio,
Vitémus omne nóxium.

Per te sciámus da Patrem,
Noscámus atque Fílium,
Teque utriúsque Spíritum
Credámus omni témpore.

Deo Patri sit glória,
Et Fílio qui a mórtuis
Surréxit, ac Paráclito,
In sæculórum sǽcula. Amen.

N.B.—If a modern Tune is desired for this hymn a selection may be made from those headed "Long Metre" in the metrical index.

LATIN HYMNS.

256 (First Tune.) Verses 1 and 2.
Mode i.
Vé - ni, Sán-cte Spí - ri - tus, Et e - mít - te cœ́ - li - tus Lú - cis tú - æ rá - di-um.
Vé - ni pá - ter paú - pe-rum, Vé - ni dá - tor mú - ne-rum, Vé - ni lú-men cór - di-um.
Verses 3 and 4.
Con - so - lá - tor ó - pti - me, Dúl-cis hó - spes á - ni - mæ, Dúl-ce re - fri - gé - ri - um.
In la - bó - re ré - qui - es, In ǽ - stu tem - pé - ri - es, In flé-tu so - lá - ti - um.
Verses 5 and 6.
O lux be - a - tís - si - ma Ré - ple cór - dis ín - ti - ma Tu - ó - rum fi - dé - li - um.
Sí - ne tu - o nú - mi-ne, Ní - hil est in hó - mi - ne, Ní - hil est in - nó - xi - um.

Verses 7 and 8.
Lá - va quod est sór - di - dum, Ri - ga quod est á - ri - dum, Sá - na quod est saú - ci - um.
Flé - cte quod est rí - gi - dum, Fó - ve quod est frí - gi - dum, Ré - ge quod est dé - vi - um.
3
3
3
3
Verses 9 and 10.
Da tu - is fi - dé - li - bus, In te con - fi -
Da virt - ú - tis mé - ri - tum, Da sa - lú - tis
3
dént - i - bus, Sá - crum se - pte - ná - ri - um.
éx - i - tum, Da per - én - ne gaú - di - um. - men.

256 (Second Tune.)

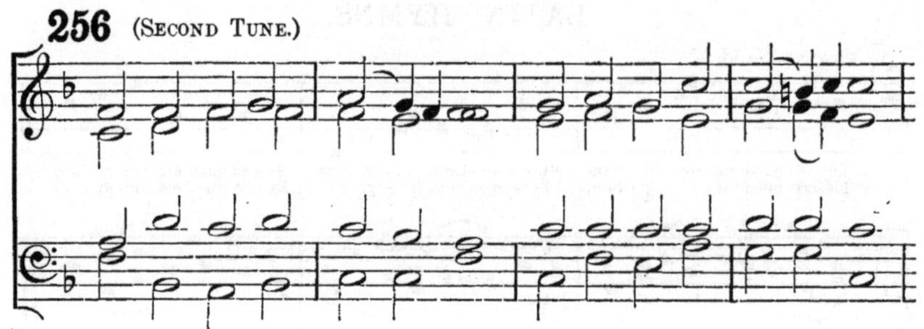

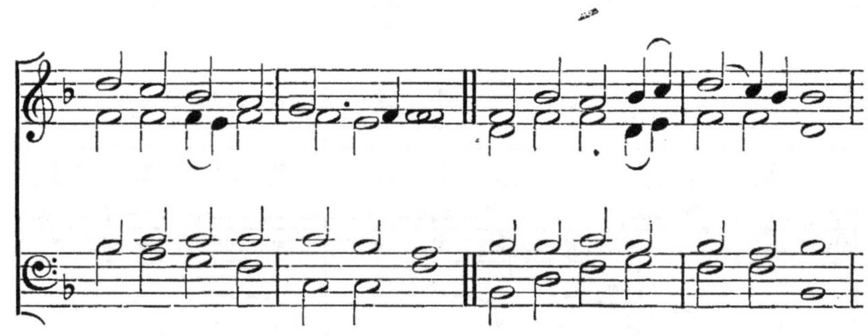

LATIN HYMNS.

VENI, Sáncte Spíritus,
Et emítte cœ́litus
Lúcis túæ rádium.
Véni páter paúperum,
Véni dátor múnerum,
Véni himen córdium.

Consolátor óptime,
Dúlcis hóspes ánimæ,
Dúlce refrigérium.
In labóre réquies,
In ǽstu tempéries,
In flétu solátium.

O lux beatíssima,
Réple córdis íntima,
Tuórum fidélium.
Síne tuo númine,
Níhil est in hómine,
Níhil est innóxium.

Láva quod est sórdidum,
Ríga quod est áridum,
Sána quod est saúcium.
Flécte quod est rígidum,
Fóve quod est frígidum,
Rége quod est dévium.

Da tuis fidélibus,
In te confidéntibus,
Sácrum septenárium.
Da virtútis méritum,
Da salútis éxitum,
Da perénne gaúdium.

LATIN HYMNS.

257

THE BLESSED SACRAMENT.

Mode vi.

sán - gui - ne,
E - sto nó - bis præ - gu - stá - tum
Mor - tis
in ex - á - mi - ne.
O clé - mens,
O
pí - e,
O dúl - cis Jé - su,
Fi - li Ma - rí - æ.

2 B

258 (First Tune.) Mode iii.

LATIN HYMNS.

PANGE lingua gloriósi,
  Córporis Mystérium,
Sanguinísque pretiósi
  Quem in mundi prétium,
Fructus ventris generósi
  Rex effúdit géntium.

Nobis datus, nobis natus
  Ex intácta Virgine ;
Et in mundo conversátus,
  Sparso verbi sémine,
Sui moras incolátus
  Miro clausit órdine.

In suprémæ nocte cœnæ
  Recúmbens cum frátribus,
Observáta lege plene
  Cibis in legálibus :
Cibum turbæ duodénæ
  Se dat suis mánibus.

Verbum caro, panem verum
  Verbo carnem éfficit :
Fitque sanguis Christi merum ;
  Et si sensus déficit,
Ad firmándum cor sincérum
  Sola fides súfficit.

Tantum ergo Sacraméntum
  Venerémur cérnul ;
Et antiquum documéntum
  Novo cedat rítui :
Præstet fides suppleméntum
  Sénsuum deféctui.

Genitóri, genitóque
  Laus, et jubilátio,
Salus, honor, virtus quoque
  Sit et benedíctio :
Procedénti ab utróque
  Compar sit laudátio. Amen.

258 (SECOND TUNE.)

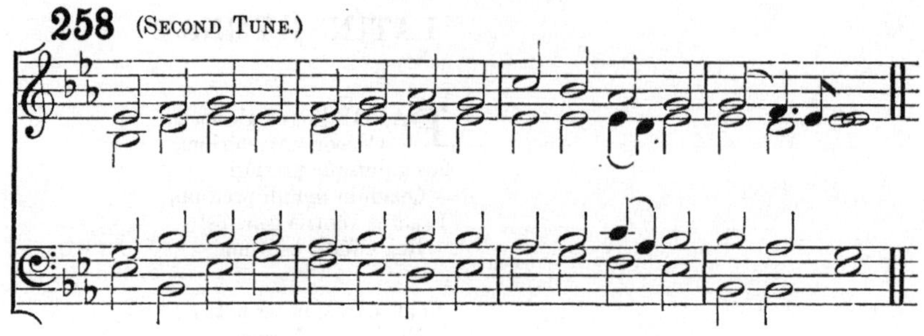

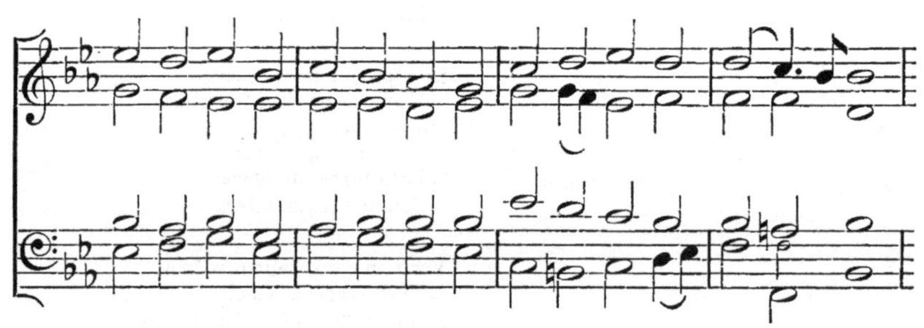

LATIN HYMNS.

PANGE lingua gloriósi,
  Córporis Mystérium,
Sanguinísque pretiósi
  Quem in mundi prétium,
Fructus ventris generósi
  Rex effúdit géntium.

Nobis datus, nobis natus
  Ex intácta Vírgine :
Et in mundo conversátus,
  Sparso verbi sémine,
Sui moras incolátus
  Miro clausit órdine.

In suprémæ nocte cœnæ
  Recúmbens cum frátribus,
Observáta lege plene
  Cibis in legálibus :
Cibum turbæ duodénæ
  Se dat suis mánibus.

Verbum caro, panem verum
  Verbo carnem éfficit :
Fitque sanguis Christi merum ;
  Et si sensus déficit,
Ad firmándum cor sincérum
  Sola fides súfficit.

Tantum ergo Sacraméntum
  Venerémur cérnui ;
Et antíquum documéntum
  Novo cedat rítui :
Præstet fides suppleméntum
  Sénsuum deféctui.

Genitóri, genitóque
  Laus, et jubilátio,
Salus, honor, virtus quoque
  Sit et benedíctio :
Procedénti ab utróque
  Compar sit laudátio. Amen.

LATIN HYMNS.

259

ADORO te devóte latens Déitas
  Quæ sub his figúris vere látitas :
Tibi se cor meum totum súbjicit,
Quia te contémplans totum déficit.

Visus, tactus, gustus in te fállitur,
Sed audítu solo tuto créditur :
Credo quidquid dixit Dei Fílius,
Nil hoc verbo Veritátis vérlus.

In cruce latébat sola Déitas,
At hic latet simul et humánitas ;
Ambo tamen credens, atque cónfitens
Peto quod petívit latro pœnitens.

Plagas, sicut Thomas non intúeor,
Deum tamen meum te confíteor,
Fac me tibi semper magis crédere,
In te spem habére, te dilígere.

O memoriále mortis Dómini,
Panis vivus, vitam præstans hómini :
Præsta meæ menti de te vívere,
Et te illi semper dulce sápere.

Pie pellicáne, Jesu Dómine,
Me immúndum munda tuo sánguine :
Cujus una stilla salvum fácere
Totum mundum quit ab omni scélere.

Jesu quem velátum nunc aspício,
Oro fiat illud, quod tam sítio,
Ut te reveláta cernens fácie,
Visu sim beátus tuæ glóriæ. Amen.

260

Modes vii and viii.
Verse 1.
Lau-da, Si - on, Sal-va - tó - rem, Lau-da du-cem et pa - stó - rem, In hymnis et cán-ti-cis:
Quantum pot - es, tan-tum au - de, Qui - a ma - jor om - ni lau - de, Nec laudá-re súf-fi-cis.
Verse 2.
Laudis thema spe-ci - á - lis, Panis vi-vus et vi - tá - lis Ho-di - e pro-pó-ni - tur:
Quem in sac-ræ men-sa cœ - næ, Tur-bæ fratrum du - o-de-næ Datum non am-bí-gi - tur.
Verse 3.
Sit laus ple-na, sit so - nó - ra, Sit ju-cún-da, sit de - có - ra, Mentis ju-bi-lá - ti - o:

LATIN HYMNS.

Di-es e - nim solémnis á - gi - tur, In qua mensæ prima re -có -li - tur Hu-jus in- sti- tú- ti - o.
VERSE 4.
In hac men-sa no - vi Re- gis, Novum Pascha no-væ le - gis, Phase ve- tus tér-mi - nat :
Ve - tu - stá- tem nó - vi - tas, Umbram fu - gat vé - ri - tas, ·Noctem lux e - li - mi - nat.

VERSE 5.
Quod in cœ-na Christus gess-it, Fa - ci- éndum hoc expréssit In su - i mem-ó - ri - am:
Do - cti sa-cris in - sti - tú - tis, Panem, vinum in sa - lú - tis Con-se - crá-mus hó - sti - am.
VERSE 6.
Dogma da-tur Christi- á - nis, Quod in carnem trans-it pan -is, Et vi-num in sánguinem:

Quod nou capis, quod non vides, A - ni - mó - sa fir - mat fi - des, Præ-ter re - rum ór - di-nem.
3
3
VERSE 7.
Sub di - vér - sis spe - ci - é - bus, Sig-nis tantum et non re - bus, Latent res ex - í - mi - æ :
Ca - ro ci - bus, sanguis po - tus ; Manet tamen Christus to-tus Sub u - trá-que spéci - e.

VERSE 8.
A su - mén - te non con - cí - sus, Non con-frá-ctus, nou dí - vi -sus, Ín-te-ger ac - cí - pi - tur:
Su - mit u - nus, sumunt mil - le : Quantum i - sti, tantum il - le : Nec sumptus con - sú - mi-tur.
VERSE 9.
Sumunt bo -ni, sumunt ma - li : Sort-e ta - men in - æ - quá-li, Vi-tæ, vel in-tér-i-tus:
Mors est ma-lis, vi - ta bo - nis: Vi- de pa - ris sum-pti - ó - nis Quam sit dis-par éx - i - tus.

VERSE 10.
Fra - cto de - mum Sa - cra - mén - to, Ne va - cil - les, sed me-mén - to,
Null - a re - i fit scis - sú - ra: Si - gni tan - tum fit fra - ctú - ra:
Tant - um es - se sub frag - mén - to Quan - tum to - to té - gi - tur:
Qua nec sta - tus nec sta - tú - ra Si - gná - ti mi - nú - i - tur.
3
3
VERSE 11.
Ec - ce pa - nis an - ge - ló - rum, Fa - ctus ci - bus vi - a - tó - rum:
In fi - gú - ris præ - si - gná - tur, Cum I - sá - ac im - mo - lá - tur:

LATIN HYMNS.

Ve - re pa - nis fi - li - ó - rum, Non mit - tén - dus cá - ni - bus.
A - gnus pa - schæ de - pu - tá - tur: Da - tur man - na pá - tri - bus.
3
3
3
3
VERSE 12.
Bo - ne Pa-stor, pa - nis ve - re, Je - su no - stri mi - se - ré - re: Tu nos pa - sce,
Tu qui cun-cta scis et va - les, Qui nos pa - scis hic mor - tá - les: Tu - os i - bi
3
3
nos tu - é - re: Tu nos bo - na fac vi - dé - re In ter - ra vi - vén - ti - um,
commensá - les Co - hæ - ré - des et so - dá - les Fac san - ctó - rum ci - vi - um. A - men.
3
3

THE BLESSED VIRGIN.

AVE maris stella,
Dei Mater alma,
Atque semper Virgo,
Felix cœli porta.

Sumens illud Ave
Gabriélis ore,
Funda nos in pace,
Mutans Hevæ nomen.

Solve vincla reis,
Profer lumen cæcis,
Mala nostra pelle,
Bona cuncta posce.

Monstra te esse matrem,
Sumat per te preces,
Qui pro nobis natus
Tulit esse tuus.

Virgo singuláris,
Inter omnes mitis,
Nos culpis solútos
Mites fac et castos.

Vitam præsta puram,
Iter para tutum,
Ut vidéntes Jesum,
Semper collætémur.

Sit laus Deo Patri,
Summo Christo decus,
Spirítui sancto,
Tribus honor unus. Amen.

(SECOND TUNE.) **261**

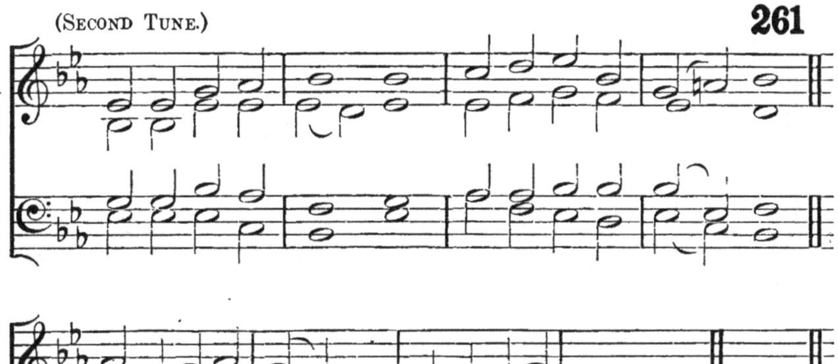

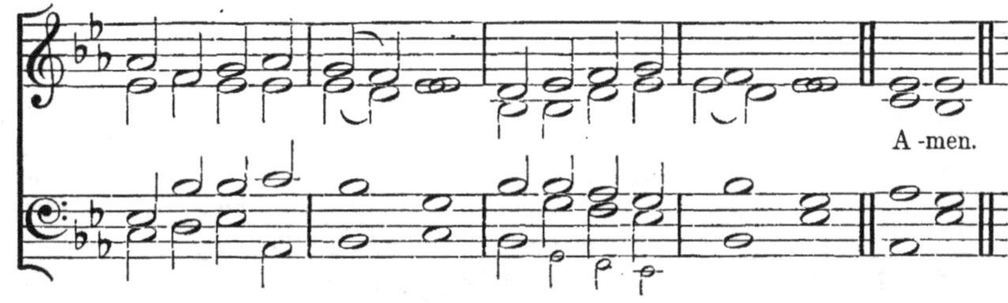

THE BLESSED VIRGIN.

AVE maris stella,
Dei Mater alma,
Atque semper Virgo,
Felix cœli porta.

Sumens illud Ave
Gabriélis ore,
Funda nos in pace,
Mutans Hevæ nomen.

Solve vincla reis,
Profer lumen cæcis,
Mala nostra pelle,
Bona cuncta posce.

Monstra te esse matrem,
Sumat per te preces,
Qui pro nobis natus
Tulit esse tuus.

Virgo singuláris,
Inter omnes mitis,
Nos culpis solútos
Mites fac et castos.

Vitam præsta puram,
Iter para tutum,
Ut vidéntes Jesum,
Semper collætémur.

Sit laus Deo Patri
Summo Christo decus,
Spirítui sancto,
Tribus honor unus. Amen.

261 (Third Tune.)

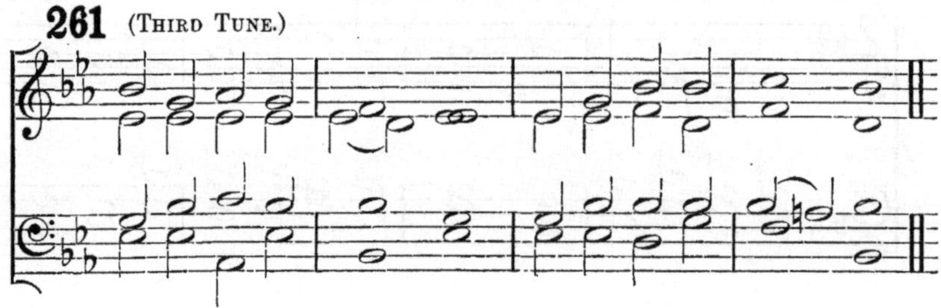

The Blessed Virgin.

Ave maris stella,
Dei Mater alma,
Atque semper Virgo,
Felix cœli porta.

Sumens illud Ave
Gabriélis ore,
Funda nos in pace,
Mutans Hevæ nomen.

Solve vincla reis,
Profer lumen cæcis,
Mala nostra pelle,
Bona cuncta posce.

Monstra te esse matrem,
Sumat per te preces,
Qui pro nobis natus
Tulit esse tuus.

Virgo singuláris,
Inter omnes mitis,
Nos culpis solútos
Mites fac et castos.

Vitam præsta puram,
Iter para tutum,
Ut vidéntes Jesum,
Semper collætémur.

Sit laus Deo Patri,
Summo Christo decus,
Spirítui sancto,
Tribus honor unus. Amen.

(FOURTH TUNE.) *Melody of previous Tune forms the Tenor.* **261**

N.B.—This Tune may be sung to alternate verses with the previous one; the congregation keeping to the original melody, and the choir singing the harmony.

THE BLESSED VIRGIN.

AVE maris stella,
Dei Mater alma,
Atque semper Virgo,
Felix cœli porta.

Sumens illud Ave
Gabriélis ore,
Funda nos in pace,
Mutans Hevæ nomen.

Solve vincla reis,
Profer lumen cæcis,
Mala nostra pelle,
Bona cuncta posce.

Monstra te esse matrem,
Sumat per te preces,
Qui pro nobis natus
Tulit esse tuus.

Virgo singuláris,
Inter omnes mitis,
Nos culpis solútos
Mites fac et castos.

Vitam præsta puram,
Iter para tutum,
Ut vidéntes Jesum,
Semper collætémur.

Sit laus Deo Patri,
Summo Christo decus,
Spirítui sancto,
Tribus honor unus. Amen.

LATIN HYMNS.

262
Verses 1, 2, 7, 8, 13, 14.
Modes i and ii.
Di - es i - ræ, di - es il - la Sol - vet sæ - clum in fav - il - la,
Tes - te Da - vid cum Si - býl - la.
Verses 3, 4, 9, 10, 15, 16.
Tu - ba mi - rum spar - gens so - num
Per se - púl - chra re - gi - ó - num, Co - get o - mnes an - te thrô - num.
Verses 5, 6, 11, 12, 17.
Li - ber scri - ptus

Dies Iræ.

DIES iræ, dies illa
Solvet sæclum in favílla,
Teste David cum Sibýlla.

Quantus tremor est futúrus,
Quando Judex est ventúrus,
Cuncta stricte discussúrus!

Tuba mirum spargens sonum
Per sepúlchra regiónum,
Coget omnes ante thrónum.

Mors stupébit et natúra,
Cum resúrget creatúra,
Judicánti responsúra.

Liber scriptus proferétur,
In quo totum continétur,
Unde mundus judicétur.

Judex ergo cum sedébit,
Quidquid latet apparébit:
Nil inúltum remanébit.

Quid sum miser tunc dictúrus?
Quem patrónum rogatúrus,
Cum vix justus sit secúrus?

Rex treméndæ majestátis,
Qui salvándos salvas gratis,
Salve me fons pietátis.

Recordáre, Jesu pie,
Quod sum causa tuæ viæ,
Ne me perdas illa die.

Quærens me sedísti lassus,
Redemísti crucem passus:
Tantus labor non sit cassus.

Juste Judex ultiónis,
Donum fac remissiónis
Ante diem rationis.

Ingemísco tanquam reus,
Culpa rubet vultus meus,
Supplicánti parce Deus.

Qui Maríam absolvísti,
Et latrónem exaudísti,
Mihi quoque spem dedísti.

Preces meæ non sunt dignæ:
Sed tu bonus fac benígne,
Ne perénni cremer igne.

Inter oves locum præsta,
Et ab hœdis me sequéstra,
Státuens in parte dextra.

Confutátis maledíctis,
Flammis ácribus addíctis,
Voca me cum benedíctis.

Oro supplex et acclínis,
Cor contrítum quasi cinis:
Gere curam mei finis.

Verse 18.
La - cry - mó - sa di - es il - la, Qua re - súr - get ex fa - víl - la
Ju - di - cán - dus ho - mo re - us.
Verse 19.
Hu - ic er - go par - - ce De - us;
Slower.
Pi - e Je - su Dó - mi - ne, Do - na e - is ré - qui - em. A - - men.

TE DEUM.

263

Tonus Simplex.
Modes iii. and iv.
Te De - um lau - - dá - mus: te Dó - mi - num con - fi - té - mur.
Te ae - tér - num Pa - trem o - mnis ter - ra ve - ne - ıá - tur.
Ti - bi o - mnes An - ge - li, ti - bi coe - li et u - ni - vér -

TE DEUM.

- sae Pot - e - stá - tes: Ti - bi Ché - rú - bim et Sé - ra - phim
in - ces - sá - bi - li vo - ce pro - clá - mant: San - - ctus:
San - - ctus: San - - ctus Dó - mi - nus De - us Sá - ba - oth.

TE DEUM.

Ple - ni sunt coe - li et ter - ra ma - je - stá - tis gló - ri - ae tu - ae.
Te glo - ri - ó - sus A - po - sto - ló - rum cho - rus; Te Pro - phe - tá - rum
lau - dá - bi - lis nú - me - rus; Te Már - ty - rum can - di - dá - tus

TE DEUM.

lau - dat ex - ér - ci - tus. Te per or - bem ter - rá - rum San - cta con - fi -
- té - tur Ec - clé - si - a: Pa - - trem im - mén - sae ma - je - stá - tis:
Ve - ne - rán - dum tu - um ve - rum, et ú - ni - cum Fí - li - um:

TE DEUM.

San - ctum quo - que Pa - rá - cli - tum Spí - ri - tum. Tu Rex gló - ri - ae, Chri - ste.
Tu Pa - tris sem - pi - tér - nus es Fí - li - us. Tu ad li - be - rán - dum su - sce -
- ptú - rus hó - mi - nem, non hor - ru - i - sti Vír - gi - nis ú - te - rum.

TE DEUM.

Tu de - ví - cto mor - tis a - - cú - - le - - o, a - pe - ru - í - sti cre -
- dén - ti - bus re - gna coe - ló - rum. Tu ad dé - xte - ram De - i se - des,
in gló - ri - a Pa - tris. Ju - dex cré - de - ris es - se ven - tú - rus.

TE DEUM.

Te er - go quaé - su - mus, tu - is fá - mu - lis súb - ve - ni,
quos pre - ti - ó - so sán - gui - ne red - e - mí - sti. Ae - tér - na faç
cum san - ctis tu - is in gló - ri - a nu - me - rá - - ri. Sal - vum

TE DEUM.

fac pé - pu - lum tu - um Dó - mi - ne, et bé - ne - dic hae - re - di -
3 3 3 3 3
- tá - ti tu - ae. Et re - ge e - os, et ex - tól - le
3 3 3 3
il - los us - que in ae - tér - num. Per sin - gu - los di - es, be - ne -
3 3

TE DEUM.

- dí - ci - mus te. Et lau - dá - mus no - men tu - um in saé - cu - lum, et in
saé - cu - lum saé - cu - li. Di - gná - re Dó - mi - ne di - e i - sto
si - ne pec - cá - to nos cu - sto - dí - re. Mi - se - ré - re no - stri Dó - mi - ne,

TE DEUM.

mi - se - ré - re no - stri. Fi - at mi - se - ri - cór - di - a tu - a Dó - mi - ne
su - per nos, quem - ád - mo - dum spe - rá - vi - mus in te. In te Dó - mi - ne
Slower.
spe - rá - - vi non con - fún - dar in ae - tér - num.
Molto rall.

BENEDICTION OF THE BLESSED SACRAMENT.

O Salutaris.

O salutaris Hostia,
Quæ cœli pandis ostium;
Bella premunt hostilia,
Da robur, fer auxilium.

Uni trinoque Domino
Sit sempiterna gloria,
Qui vitam sine termino
Nobis donet in patria. Amen.

O saving Victim, opening wide
The gate of heav'n to man below;
Our foes press on from every side;
Thine aid supply, Thy strength bestow.

To Thy great name be endless praise,
Immortal Godhead, one in three;
O grant us endless length of days
In our true native land with Thee. Amen.

Litany of the Blessed Virgin.

Ant. Sub tuum præsidium confugimus, sancta Dei Genitrix, nostras deprecationes ne despicias in necessitatibus nostris; sed a periculis cunctis libera nos semper, Virgo gloriosa et benedicta.

Kyrie eleison.
Kyrie eleison.
Christe eleison.
Christe eleison.
Kyrie eleison.
Kyrie eleison.
Christe audi nos.
Christe exaudi nos.
Pater de cœlis Deus,
Miserere nobis.
Fili Redemptor mundi Deus,
Spiritus Sancte Deus,
Sancta Trinitas, unus Deus,
Sancta Maria, *Ora pro nobis.*
Sancta Dei Genitrix,
Sancta Virgo Virginum,
Mater Christi,
Mater divinæ gratiæ,
Mater purissima,
Mater castissima,
Mater inviolata,
Mater intemerata,
Mater amabilis,
Mater admirabilis,
Mater boni consilii,
Mater Creatoris,
Mater Salvatoris,
Virgo prudentissima,

Ora pro nobis.

Ant. We fly to thy patronage, O holy Mother of God; despise not our petitions in our necessities; but deliver us always from all dangers, O glorious and blessèd Virgin.

Lord have mercy.
Lord have mercy.
Christ have mercy.
Christ have mercy.
Lord have mercy.
Lord have mercy.
Christ hear us.
Christ graciously hear us.
God the Father of heaven,
Have mercy on us.
God the Son, Redeemer of the world,
God the Holy Ghost,
Holy Trinity, one God,
Holy Mary, *Pray for us.*
Holy Mother of God,
Holy Virgin of virgins,
Mother of Christ,
Mother of divine grace,
Mother most pure,
Mother most chaste,
Mother inviolate,
Mother undefiled,
Mother most amiable,
Mother most admirable,
Mother of good counsel,
Mother of our Creator,
Mother of our Saviour,
Virgin most prudent,

Pray for us.

Ora pro nobis	*Pray for us*
Virgo veneranda,	Virgin most venerable,
Virgo prædicanda,	Virgin most renowned,
Virgo potens,	Virgin most powerful,
Virgo clemens,	Virgin most merciful,
Virgo fidelis,	Virgin most faithful,
Speculum justitiæ,	Mirror of justice,
Sedes sapientiæ,	Seat of wisdom,
Causa nostræ lætitiæ,	Cause of our joy,
Vas spirituale,	Spiritual vessel,
Vas honorabile,	Vessel of honour,
Vas insigne devotionis,	Vessel of singular devotion,
Rosa mystica,	Mystical rose,
Turris Davidica,	Tower of David,
Turris eburnea,	Tower of ivory,
Domus aurea,	House of gold,
Fœderis arca,	Ark of the covenant,
Janua cœli,	Gate of heaven,
Stella matutina,	Morning star,
Salus infirmorum,	Health of the sick,
Refugium peccatorum,	Refuge of sinners,
Consolatrix afflictorum,	Comfort of the afflicted,
Auxilium Christianorum,	Help of Christians,
Regina Angelorum,	Queen of Angels,
Regina Patriarcharum,	Queen of Patriarchs,
Regina Prophetarum,	Queen of Prophets,
Regina Apostolorum,	Queen of Apostles,
Regina Martyrum,	Queen of Martyrs,
Regina Confessorum,	Queen of Confessors,
Regina Virginum,	Queen of Virgins,
Regina Sanctorum omnium,	Queen of all Saints,
Regina sine labe originali concepta,	Queen conceived without original sin,
Regina Sacratissimi Rosarii,	Queen of the Most Holy Rosary,
Agnus Dei, qui tollis peccata mundi,	Lamb of God, who takest away the sins of the world,
Parce nobis Domine.	*Spare us, O Lord.*
Agnus Dei, qui tollis peccata mundi,	Lamb of God, who takest away the sins of the world,
Exaudi nos Domine.	*Graciously hear us, O Lord.*
Agnus Dei, qui tollis peccata mundi,	Lamb of God, who takest away the sins of the world,
Miserere nobis.	*Have mercy on us.*
Christe audi nos.	Christ hear us.
Christe exaudi nos.	*Christ graciously hear us.*
℣. Ora pro nobis, sancta Dei Genitrix.	℣. Pray for us, O holy Mother of God.
℟. Ut digni efficiamur promissionibus Christi.	℟. That we may be made worthy of the promises of Christ.

BENEDICTION OF THE BLESSED SACRAMENT.

TANTUM ERGO.

Tantum ergo Sacramentum
Veneremur cernui;
Et antiquum documentum
Novo cedat ritui;
Præstet fides supplementum
Sensuum defectui.

Genitori, Genitoque
Laus et jubilatio,
Salus, honor virtus quoque,
Sit et benedictio:
Procedenti ab utroque
Compar sit laudatio. Amen.

℣. Panem de cœlo præstitisti eis. [Alleluia.]

℟. Omne delectamentum in se habentem. [Alleluia.]

Deus, qui nobis sub Sacramento mirabili, passionis tuæ memoriam reliquisti: tribue, quæsumus, ita nos corporis et sanguinis tui sacra mysteria venerari, ut redemptionis tuæ fructum in nobis jugiter, sentiamus. Qui vivis, &c. Amen.

Lowly bending, deep adoring,
Lo! the Sacrament we hail;
Types and shadows have their ending
Newer rites of grace prevail;
Faith for all defects supplying
Where the feeble senses fail.

Glory, honour, might, dominion,
Be unto our God most high;
To the Father, Son, and Spirit,
Ever blessèd Trinity,
Praise be given, and power eternal,
Unto all eternity.

℣ Thou didst give them bread from heaven. [Alleluia.]

℟ Containing in itself all sweetness. [Alleluia.]

O God, who, under this wonderful Sacrament, hast left us a memorial of Thy passion; grant us, we beseech Thee, so to venerate the sacred mysteries of Thy body and blood, that we may ever feel within us the fruit of Thy redemption. Who livest, &c. Amen.

ADOREMUS IN ÆTERNUM.

Adoremus in æternum Sanctissimum Sacramentum.

Let us adore for ever the most Holy Sacrament.

Laudate.

Laudate Dominum omnes gentes; laudate eum omnes populi.

Quoniam confirmata est super nos misericordia ejus: et veritas Domini manet in æternum.

Gloria Patri, et Filio, et Spiritui Sancto.

Sicut erat in principio, et nunc, et semper, et in sæcula sæculorum. Amen.

Adoremus in æternum Sanctissimum Sacramentum.

Praise the Lord, all ye nations: praise Him, all ye people.

Because His mercy is confirmed upon us: and the truth of the Lord remaineth for ever.

Glory be to the Father, and to the Son, and to the Holy Ghost,

As it was in the beginning, is now, and ever shall be, world without end. Amen.

Let us adore for ever the most Holy Sacrament.

N.B.—To provide music for Benediction throughout the year is outside the scope of a hymnal. A selection of tunes for "O Salutaris" can be made from those headed "Long Metre" in the metrical index. "Tantum ergo" can be sung to any tune headed 8 7 8 7 8 7 *in the metrical index.*

BENEDICTION OF THE BLESSED SACRAMENT.

Tantum ergo.

INDEX.

INDEX.

First words of Hymn.	No.	Author or Source of Hymn.	Composer or Source of Tune.	Metre.
Forth comes the Standard of the King	30	*Tr.* Rev. E. Caswall	*Speier Gesangbuch*, 1599	L.M.
From where the rising sun ascends	13	*Tr.* Rev. Fr. Trappes	Thomas Tallis [1515 (?)-1585]	L.M.
Full in the panting heart of Rome	139	Cardinal Wiseman	i. Rev. C. A. Cox ii. *From* "*La Scala Santa*," 1681	8 8 8 8. 8 8.
Full of glory, full of wonders	55	Rev. F. W. Faber	R. R. Terry	Irreg.
Giver of life, eternal Lord	131	*Tr.* Rev. E. Caswall	*From* Dr. Christopher Tye	C.M.
Glory be to Jesus	95	*Tr.* Rev. E. Caswall	F. Filitz [1847]	6 5 6 5.
God of mercy and compassion	147	Rev. E. Vaughan, C.SS.R.	*Traditional*	8 7 8 7 D.
Great God, whatever through Thy	224	(?)	*From* Dr. Christopher Tye	D.C.M.
Great Saint Andrew, Friend of Jesus	193	Canon Oakeley	W. Birtchnell, Mus.B.	8 7 8 7 D.
Great Saint Joseph! Son of David	179	*Tr.* Bishop Casartelli	*Melody* ("*Heil'ger Joseph*,") by A. G. Stein, 1852	8 7 8 7 D.
Green are the leaves	118	Cardinal Newman	Anon.	C.M. (triple).
Guardian Angel	159	(?)	H. B. Collins, Mus.B.	Irreg.
Hail, full of grace and purity	227	Rev. P. Conway, O.P.	*Part i.* Laurence Ampleforth *Part ii.* Laurence Ampleforth *Part iii.* Thomas Tallis	C.M.
Hail, glorious Saint Patrick	201	"Sister Agnes"	*Old Irish Melody*	11 11 11 11.
Hail! holy Joseph, hail	173	Rev. F. W. Faber	"*Psalteriolum Harmonicum*," 1642	6 6 6 6.
Hail, holy mission, hail	141	Bishop Chadwick	i. Mgr. Crookall ii. *Limburg Gesangbuch*, 1838	6 6 6 6.
Hail, Jesus, hail! who for my sake	94	*Tr.* Rev. F. W. Faber	Vincent Novello	8 8 6. 8 8 6.
Hail Mary, Pearl of Grace	107	Rev. Bede Camm, O.S.B.	i. R. R. Terry ii. *Beuron Melody*	Irreg.
Hail, Queen of Heaven, the Ocean Star	101	Dr. Lingard	i. *Traditional* ii. R. R. Terry	8 8 8 8. 8 8.
Hail, thou resplendent star	109	(?)	R. R. Terry	6 6 6 6.
Hail, thou Star of ocean	110	*Tr.* Rev. E. Caswall	i. J. Richardson ii. R. R. Terry	6 6 6 6 D. 6 6 6 6.
Hail to Thee! true Body, sprung	70	*Tr.* Rev. E. Caswall	S. E. L. Spooner-Lillingston, Mus. B.	Irreg.
Hail, wounds! which through eternal	97	*Tr.* Rev. E. Caswall	*Andernach Gesangbuch*, 1608	C.M.
Happy we, who thus united	225	Rev. E. Vaughan, C.SS.R.	Geo. Herbert	8 7 8 7 D.
Hark! an awful voice is sounding	1	*Tr.* Rev. E. Caswall	*Korner's Gesangbuch*, 1631	8 7 8 7.
Hark, hark, my soul, angelic songs	250	Rev. F. W. Faber	i. H. B. Collins, Mus.B ii. Laurence Ampleforth	Irreg.
Have mercy on us, God Most High	53	Rev. F. W. Faber	*Old English*	C.M.
He who once, in righteous vengeance	35	*Tr.* Rev. E. Caswall	Vincent Novello [1781-1861]	8 7 8 7. 7 7.
Hear Thy children, gentle Jesus	150	Rev. F. Stanfield	S. P. Waddington	8 7 8 7.
Hear thy children, gentlest Mother	151	Rev. F. Stanfield	Sir Edward Elgar, O.M., Mus.D.	8 7 8 7.
Heart of Jesus! golden chalice	92	Bishop Casartelli	W. Schultes	8 7 8 7. 8 7.
Help, Lord, the souls which Thou hast made	132	Cardinal Newman	*Spanish Melody*	C.M.
Holy Queen! we bend before thee	104	S. Casimir. *Tr.* Rev. E. Vaughan, C.SS.R.	"*Sicilian Mariner's Hymn*"	8 7 8 7.
Holy Spirit, Lord of Light	48 i	*Tr.* Rev. E. Caswall	Samuel Webbe [1740-1816]	7 7 7. 7 7 7.
I come to Thee, once more, my God	79	Rev. F. W. Faber	Dr. Arne (1710-1798)	C.M.
I dwell a captive in His Heart	90	S. Alphonsus. *Tr.* Rev. E. Vaughan, C.SS.R.	Vincent Novello	C.M.
I love those precious Christmas words	153	Anon ("*Hymns for the Year*," 1867)	*Old English Carol*	D.C.M.
I met the Good Shepherd	63	Rev. E. Caswall	R. R. Terry	6 5 6 5 D.
I need Thee, precious Jesus	68	Anon ("*Hymns for the Year*," 1867)	Laurence Ampleforth	Irreg.
I see my Jesus crucified	36	(?)	P. Kevin Buckley	L.M.
I'll sing a hymn to Mary	112	Rev. Fr. Wyse	i. *Traditional* ii. R. R. Terry	7 6 7 6 D.
In caves of the lone wilderness	180	*Tr.* Rev. E. Caswall	Laurence Ampleforth	10 10 10 6.

INDEX.

INDEX.

INDEX.

INDEX.

INDEX.

LATIN HYMNS.

First words of Hymn.	No.	Author or Source of Hymn.	Composer or Source of Tune.	Metre.
Adeste, fidéles	251	*First mentioned in a Stonyhurst MS.* 1751 . . .	*Traditional* (18*th Century*) . .	Irreg.
Adoro te devóte latens Déitas . . .	259	S. Thomas Aquinas . .	*Plainsong* (17*th or* 18*th Century*)	11.11.11.11.
Ave maris stella	261	*Author uncertain* . . .	i. *Proper Plainsong Melody* . ii. *Leisentritt's Gesangbuch*, 1567 (*abridged*) . . . . iii. C. Ett . . . . iv. R. R. Terry (*Melody of Ett in Tenor*).	6 6 6 6.
Ave vérum Córpus nátum	257	*Attributed in a Richenau MS. of* 14*th Century to* Pope Innocent . . .	*Plainsong* (15*th or* 16*th Century*)	Irreg.
Dies iræ, dies illa	262	*Probably by* Thomas of Celano (*about* 1250) . .	*Plainsong* (*founded on Verse of Respond* " *Libera* ") . .	8 8 7.8 8 7.
Lauda, Sion, Salvatórem	260	S. Thomas Aquinas (*about* 1260)	*Plainsong* (*originally* "*Laudes crucis*," 1260)	Irreg.
Pange lingua gloriósi	258	S. Thomas Aquinas . . .	*Plainsong* (*attributed to* Venantius Fortunatus) . . .	8 7 8 7.8 7.
Stabat mater dolorósa	252	*Probably by* Jacopone de Todi (13*th Century*) . .	*French*. *Possibly* 17*th Century*	8 8 7.8 8 7.
Te Deum Laudamus	263	. . . .	*Plainsong*	Irreg.
Veni Creátor Spíritus	255	*Doubtful. Possibly* Rhabanus Maurus (776-856) .	*Plainsong* (4*th Century*) . .	L.M.
Vení Sáncte Spíritus	256	*Probably* Pope Innocent III. (1215)	*Plainsong* (11*th Century*) Samuel Webbe	7 7 7.7 7 7.
Vexilla Regis pródeunt	253	Venantius Fortunatus (569)	*Plainsong* (4*th Century*) . .	L.M.
Victimæ Pascháli laúdes	254	*Uncertain*.	*Plainsong*	Irreg.

METRICAL INDEX.

LONDON:
WM. CLOWES AND SONS, LTD., TYPE MUSIC AND GENERAL PRINTERS
DUKE STREET, STAMFORD STREET, S.E.

SD - #0050 - 150124 - C0 - 229/152/23 - PB - 9781330441596 - Gloss Lamination